Linda Hoyt and
Lynnette Brent

Mastering *the* Mechanics

Ready-to-Use Lessons for Modeled, Guided, and Independent Editing

SCHOLASTIC

NEW YORK • TORONTO • LONDON • AUCKLAND • SYDNEY
MEXICO CITY • NEW DELHI • HONG KONG • BUENOS AIRES

Photocredits: iStockphoto (pages 152 and 174)

Cover design by Jay Namerow
Interior design by Maria Lilja
Interior photos by Linda Hoyt, Lynnette Brent, Rolf Sandvold, Teresa Therriault, and Patrick Burke
Acquiring Editor: Lois Bridges
Production/Copy Editor: Danny Miller

ISBN 13: 978-0-545-22300-3

Printed in the U. S. A.
2 3 4 5 6 7 8 9 10 40 19 18 17 16 15 14

Linda dedicates this book to teachers who understand and utilize the power of modeling—of showing, rather than simply assigning.

Lynnette dedicates this book with gratitude to three teachers and mentors who understood so well how to show rather than tell—Morris Bruns, Bonnie Kepplinger, and R. Baird Shumann.

ACKNOWLEDGMENTS

We want to acknowledge the very special role of Teresa Therriault, whose heart is in this book. Through her partnership with Linda as Title 1 teacher, staff developer, and trusted friend and colleague, Teresa helped to lay the groundwork for this volume of *Mastering the Mechanics* by investing an amazing amount of time, energy, and expertise into the research behind the skills continuum

After lending her thinking to the resources for the earlier grades, Lynnette is thrilled to be part of the author team for the middle school volume. We also wish to thank the many dedicated teachers, administrators, and consultants who paved the way for *Mastering the Mechanics,* and especially the middle school volume, by providing valuable confirmation of the validity of the lesson cycles. Our sincere thanks go to Teri Anderson, Heather Delabre, Penny Dowdy, Allison Eitzen, Catherine Johansen, Joan Knowlton, Kerry Proczko, Nancy Schatzman, Ann Stewart, and Evan Voboril. A special thank you to Kerry Proczko and Haley Deicken, who opened their classrooms so that we could capture images of their fantastic writers at work! We are also grateful for all the student writers whose work graces this book, especially Brittany, Hayley, Robert Brent, Anne Johansen, and René Zerfas.

We appreciate the support and patience of Lois Bridges, our amazing editor and trusted friend, who always smoothes the way with careful suggestions, time-saving support, and unflagging optimism.

TABLE OF CONTENTS

PART I

Anatomy of a Lesson Cycle: How to Use This Book

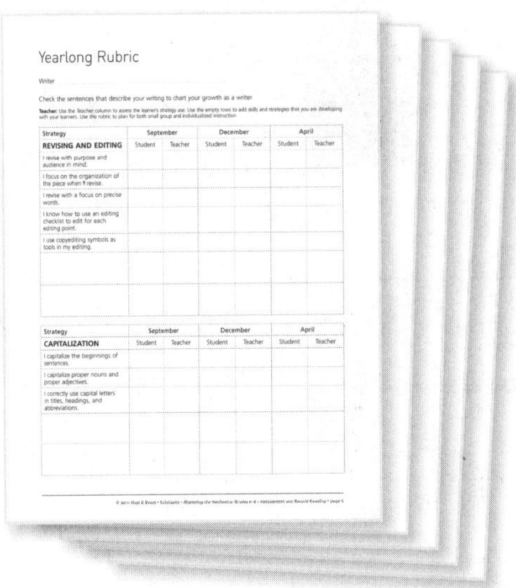

Yearlong Rubric

Writer

Check the sentences that describe your writing to chart your growth as a writer.

Teacher: Use the Teacher column to assess the learner's strategy use. Use the empty rows to add skills and strategies that you are developing with your learners. Use the rubric to plan for both small group and individualized instruction.

Strategy	September		December		April	
REVISING AND EDITING	Student	Teacher	Student	Teacher	Student	Teacher
I revise with purpose and audience in mind.						
I focus on the organization of the piece when I revise.						
I revise with a focus on precise words.						
I know how to use an editing checklist to edit for each editing point.						
I use copyediting symbols as tools in my editing.						

Strategy	September		December		April	
CAPITALIZATION	Student	Teacher	Student	Teacher	Student	Teacher
I capitalize the beginnings of sentences.						
I capitalize proper nouns and proper adjectives.						
I correctly use capital letters in titles, headings, and abbreviations.						

Yearlong Planner

Consider: Are there any lessons that should appear multiple times?

	September	October	November	December	January	February	March	April	May	June
WEEK 1										
WEEK 2										
WEEK 3										
WEEK 4										

- **Examine the lesson gatefold and consider the needs of your students as you plan your lesson cycles.** The blank yearlong planner is a tool you can use to customize the lessons. Throughout the lesson cycles, you'll want to continually observe, assess, and gauge students' needs to adjust your instruction.

- **Focus on each lesson cycle for three days.** Choose one cycle per week to supplement your instruction. Weave lesson cycles into content area classes as well to show students that the new skills they are using apply to all the writing they do.

- **Follow up each lesson cycle with a Pulling It All Together lesson** (pages 160–194). Use the Pulling It All Together lessons as they are in this resource, or adapt the rigorous writing forms to the lesson cycles that you've chosen. The cycles covered are flexible!

- **As time allows, dip into a short Power Burst Lesson** (pages 195–203). You can use these lessons multiple times, making powerful use of instructional time by reinforcing and extending skills and strategies learned in lesson cycles.

Day 1

Use or adapt the sample read aloud to crack open your thinking and show the processes writers use before, during, and after drafting.

A modeled writing sample is provided to allow you to focus on meeting your students' needs as you share your thinking about the skill.

[1] A Turn and Talk moment allows students time to process what they've learned as you listen carefully to clear up mistakes and misconceptions. [2]Sum up the day's learning.

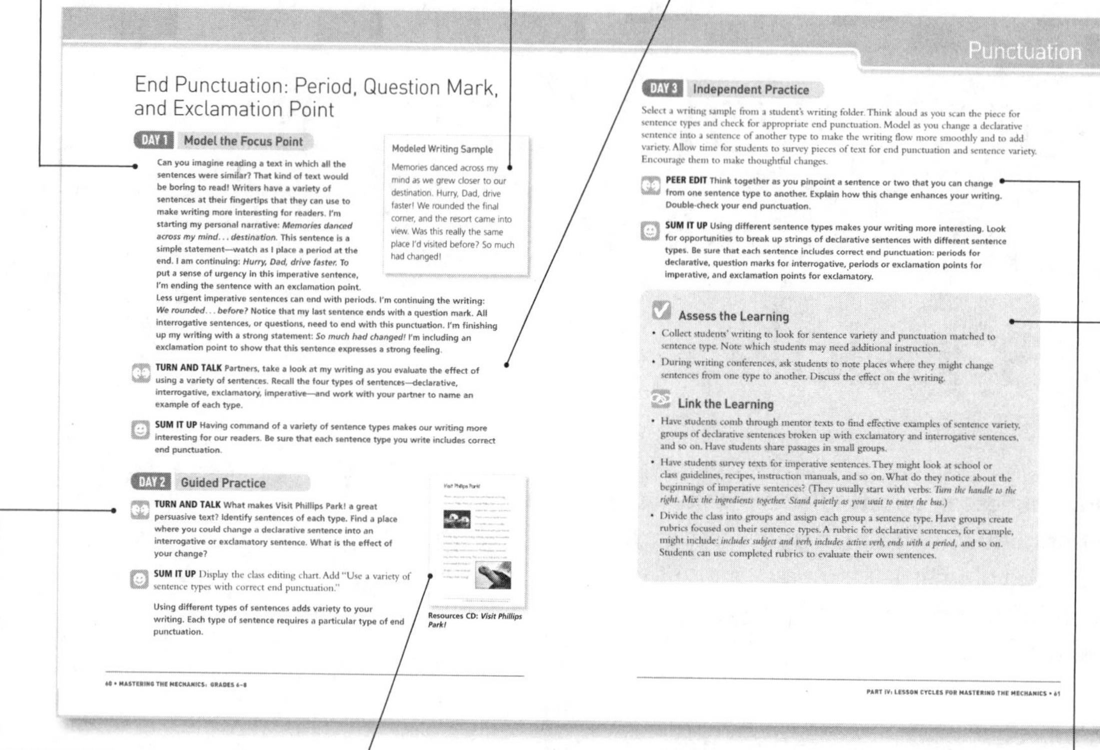

Punctuation

End Punctuation: Period, Question Mark, and Exclamation Point

DAY 1 Model the Focus Point

Can you imagine reading a text in which all the sentences were similar? That kind of text would be boring to read! Writers have a variety of sentences at their fingertips that they can use to make writing more interesting for readers. I'm starting my personal narrative: *Memories danced across my mind... destination.* This sentence is a simple statement—watch as I place a period at the end. I am continuing: *Hurry, Dad, drive faster.* To put a sense of urgency in this imperative sentence, I'm ending the sentence with an exclamation point. Less urgent imperative sentences can end with periods. I'm continuing the writing: *We rounded... before?* Notice that my last sentence ends with a question mark. All interrogative sentences, or questions, need to end with this punctuation. I'm finishing up my writing with a strong statement: *So much had changed!* I'm including an exclamation point to show that this sentence expresses a strong feeling.

Modeled Writing Sample

Memories danced across my mind as we grew closer to our destination. Hurry, Dad, drive faster! We rounded the final corner, and the resort came into view. Was this really the same place I'd visited before? So much had changed!

TURN AND TALK Partners, take a look at my writing as you evaluate the effect of using a variety of sentences. Recall the four types of sentences—declarative, interrogative, exclamatory, imperative—and work with your partner to name an example of each type.

SUM IT UP Having command of a variety of sentence types makes our writing more interesting for our readers. Be sure that each sentence type you write includes correct end punctuation.

DAY 2 Guided Practice

TURN AND TALK What makes Visit Phillips Park! a great persuasive text? Identify sentences of each type. Find a place where you could change a declarative sentence into an interrogative or exclamatory sentence. What is the effect of your change?

SUM IT UP Display the class editing chart. Add "Use a variety of sentence types with correct end punctuation."

Using different types of sentences adds variety to your writing. Each type of sentence requires a particular type of end punctuation.

Resources CD: *Visit Phillips Park!*

60 • MASTERING THE MECHANICS: GRADES 6–8

DAY 3 Independent Practice

Select a writing sample from a student's writing folder. Think aloud as you scan the piece for sentence types and check for appropriate end punctuation. Model as you change a declarative sentence into a sentence of another type to make the writing flow more smoothly and to add variety. Allow time for students to survey pieces of text for end punctuation and sentence variety. Encourage them to make thoughtful changes.

PEER EDIT Think together as you pinpoint a sentence or two that you can change from one sentence type to another. Explain how this change enhances your writing. Double-check your end punctuation.

SUM IT UP Using different sentence types makes your writing more interesting. Look for opportunities to break up strings of declarative sentences with different sentence types. Be sure that each sentence includes correct end punctuation: periods for declarative, question marks for interrogative, periods or exclamation points for imperative, and exclamation points for exclamatory.

Assess the Learning

- Collect students' writing to look for sentence variety and punctuation matched to sentence type. Note which students may need additional instruction.
- During writing conferences, ask students to note places where they might change sentences from one type to another. Discuss the effect on the writing.

Link the Learning

- Have students comb through mentor texts to find effective examples of sentence variety, groups of declarative sentences broken up with exclamatory and interrogative sentences, and so on. Have students share passages in small groups.
- Have students survey texts for imperative sentences. They might look at school or class guidelines, recipes, instruction manuals, and so on. What do they notice about the beginnings of imperative sentences? (They usually start with verbs: *Turn the handle to the right. Mix the ingredients together. Stand quietly as you wait to enter the bus.*)
- Divide the class into groups and assign each group a sentence type. Have groups create rubrics focused on their sentence types. A rubric for declarative sentences, for example, might include: *includes subject and verb, includes active verb, ends with a period*, and so on. Students can use completed rubrics to evaluate their own sentences.

PART IV: LESSON CYCLES FOR MASTERING THE MECHANICS • 61

Day 2

Use a sample from one of your own students or an authentic sample provided in this resource as the basis of guided practice.

Discuss the content of the piece, before linking to the learning from Day 1.

A Turn and Talk moment allows writers to think together as they are still learning this strategy.

Sum up the day's learning as you add a reminder to the class editing chart to use the skill to edit and revise.

Day 3

Model your thinking as you edit a piece of writing from a student writing folder that works with the current lesson cycle. This deliberate return to previous work shows that writing is an ongoing process and that writers grow and can return to previous pieces for more fine-tuning.

Instructions for peer editing allow for gradual release—students have watched you model and worked with you in guided editing. Now is the time for students to look carefully at their own writing with partners and apply what they've learned.

Sum It Up allows for one last powerful statement about the skill and shows students how that skill is important to their writing.

Assess the Learning with authentic and ongoing assessment ideas that allow you to plan for future instruction and meet individual needs in your classroom.

Link the Learning with these targeted ideas that allow for deeper exploration of the strategy or application of the strategy to other contexts.

PART II

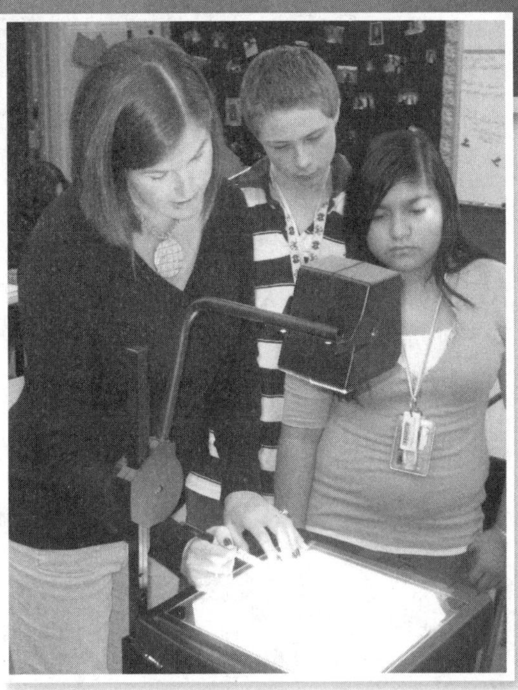

Introduction: Mastering the Mechanics

Putting Editing in Perspective

> "Just as the baker who creates a cake from scratch takes pride in adding buttercream roses atop chocolate swirls, students must learn to delight in knowing how to add the important touches of correct spelling, grammar, and punctuation."
>
> —*Shelley Harwayne*

Conventions
spacing, handwriting, spelling, and grammar

Mechanics
periods, capital letters, and so on

We care about the conventions of written language—and we are not alone. The parents of the students we serve, the community, and the public all care about and expect students to show growing expertise in the conventions of written language—writing that is legible and includes correct spelling, grammar, punctuation, and capitalization.

Our middle-level students are looking ahead toward the rigors of writing in high school, college, and the workplace. As we work with our writers to become more proficient and capable, they become flexible enough to move from one writing context to another. As we prepare middle school students for the more complex writing requirements they will encounter, one of our paramount goals is to help them feel confident and capable as they craft messages for a variety of reasons—to write a report, to express an opinion, to make a request, to learn about content. Because writing is a tool for deepening content knowledge (Keys, 2000; Shanahan, 2004; Sperling & Freedman, 2001), you will see content area examples used as mentor texts and examples throughout this resource. It is our sincere hope that all teachers at the middle level will embrace the modeling and practice of content area reading and writing using their subject matters as a backdrop, with writing as a tool for gaining understanding. The study of writing throughout the content areas should include the same emphasis on conventions and mechanics as the writing that students do in "writing class." Infusing short bursts of writing throughout the curriculum—with an emphasis on the mechanics and conventions that make messages clear—will go a long way toward creating confident, capable, and flexible writers!

As we focus students on mechanics and conventions, we want to be very clear about our goals:

1. To nurture writers who understand that rich, well-crafted messages are their first and most important focus.
2. To help developing writers understand that a study of mechanics and conventions is about *adding tools* that enhance our messages, not about correctness and being "right."

It is important to state that we are not in favor of prepackaged programs that cast editing and conventions as "mistakes," or exercises in correction. These programs have very little embedded instruction and consistently overwhelm students with sentences that are so laden with errors that meaning is easily lost, leaving a writer with few connections to his or her own work.

> **"It matters little if my text is perfectly edited and spelled, if what I have to say is trivial, boring, and a waste of the reader's time."**
> ***—Regie Routman***

Above all, as we cast attention upon mechanics and conventions, we must be sure that creative thinking flourishes during drafting and revision. If mechanics and editing are overemphasized, they can have the negative effect of reducing writing volume, paralyzing students, who may limit their writing to words they are able to spell correctly or to overly simplistic sentence structures.

Recast Mechanics and Conventions as Tools to Lift Writing Quality

Writers must understand that mechanics are not tedious obligations. They are tools that add clarity and interest to our writing and help us connect with readers. Carefully crafted modeled writing lessons improve craft, mechanics, grammar, and spelling. Our goal is to develop the understanding that writers integrate conventions into craft rather than seeing them simply as elements of "correctness." Modeled writing with a think-aloud recasting mechanics as craft might sound like this:

> I want to write about how quiet it was when I was walking in the woods. I could say: "I went walking in the woods. It was quiet." That is okay, but if I think about how punctuation can help me write in more interesting ways, I think I can make it even better.
>
> What do you think of: "Shhh! Listen... As my feet crunch softly on the gravel path, the sound seems huge. It is so quiet in the forest that my footsteps sound loud!" Look how I used exclamation points and an ellipsis. These punctuation marks helped make my opening and my ending more interesting. And do you see the comma I used? The comma told my reader to take a little breath so the ending of my sentence is more dramatic. Using punctuation makes my writing better! It sets the scene, captures a mood, and makes my description more exciting and interesting for my readers.

It is our sincere hope that this resource will help educators and students alike see conventions and mechanics through new eyes. We believe conventions and mechanics are naturally woven into the writing process at two major points:

1. During drafting: Conventions and mechanics support our messages and enhance communication. Carefully chosen punctuation can clarify our messages, control writing volume and flow, and make our ideas sparkle!
2. During editing: Conventions and mechanics provide readers with access to our thinking. Correct spelling, grammar, spacing, and punctuation make our work accessible to readers.

Steep Conventions in Meaning

We believe that we must keep the focus on meaning while steeping learners in conventions and mechanics. With this emphasis, it would be perfectly natural to have a modeled writing that looks and sounds something like this:

> I love hockey! With speed, focus, and strength, the players send the puck flying at amazing speeds across the ice. I want to capture the excitement of waiting to see if the puck crosses into the net for a goal. Watch to see how I use exclamation marks to make my meaning more precise. I add the exclamation marks (!) so that my reader can hear the thwack of the stick hitting the puck and feel the swoosh of the air as the puck flies. My exclamation marks help my readers feel the excitement and drama of a game, giving the writing a "you are there" feeling.

Thwack! Zoom! I sat on the edge of my seat, waiting to see if the puck would land in the net.

By recasting punctuation as a tool that can make our writing sparkle and give our writing a real voice, we have maintained a clear focus on meaning. This kind of work on mechanics and conventions enriches communication and elevates writing quality.

Tiptoe Lightly With "Correctness"

We must avoid situations in which the fear of being incorrect freezes writers and forces them into a narrow zone of "correctness." In this kind of setting, writers can sometimes place too much emphasis on spelling, for example, and begin to limit their writing to words they know they can spell correctly. This dangerously limits the writing to the confines of spelling rather than letting it flourish through the writer's sense of language and imagination. While empowering writers with conventions, we must also take seriously our mission to keep meaning as the primary objective. Our goal: Students lift and elaborate their language with mechanics as a subset of the process.

Conventions and mechanics should support meaning, not limit it.

> "Unfortunately, many teachers and students believe that writing must be perfect. If this is so, where is the play and rehearsal? How many hours do baseball players spend practicing (and often getting it wrong) before they can make that wonderful ninth-inning walk-off home run?"
>
> —*Janet Angelillo*

But Have High Expectations

While we tiptoe lightly with correctness, we do believe it is appropriate to set high expectations and to make it clear to students that after completing a cycle, they have new tools we expect them to use correctly. After a lesson that focuses on rereading for strong organization, for example, we expect writers to create paragraphs that are cohesive units of meaning. After a lesson on sentence combining, we expect students to correctly use conjunctions with commas in compound sentences. Although our emphasis is on message rather than on correctness, we can—and should—still have high expectations for our students' development and growth.

Rereading: A Strategic Tool for Meaning, Mechanics, and Conventions

- Rereading during *drafting* helps our ideas flow and helps us maintain—or regain—momentum with the messages we are crafting.
- Rereading during *revision* helps us wonder about craft elements such as word choice, interesting leads, voice, volume, and focus of information. It is also a time when we can wonder if our punctuation is used in ways that help the reader, add clarity to our thinking, and make the writing more engaging.

Rereading when we edit for an audience takes on an entirely different dimension. This is the time when we slow down and think about our work from another perspective, making adjustments that are considerate of our readers' understanding of the entire message.

> "Rereading is the glue that connects the stages of writing. Writers continually reread what they've written, and this rereading changes at each stage of the craft cycle."
>
> —*Ralph Fletcher*

Rereading: Focused Edits

When students reread to edit for conventions and mechanics, we believe it is most effective if you have them engage in focused edits. In a focused edit, the writer reads multiple times, each time honing in on a single purpose. The writer, for example, might reread once to check for end punctuation, reread a second time to check for sentence fragments, and reread a third time to check for apostrophes used correctly in possessives and contractions. Each editing point gets its own rereading.

Facilitate the focused editing by having students use highlighter pens as they edit for particular conventions or mechanics. If students are reading to check for the correct use of apostrophes, for example, have them highlight well-placed apostrophes already in their writing as well as apostrophes that they added during the focused edit. Allow time for students to share and celebrate their masterful work. Show students that focused edits are about the care and concern they take with their own writing. A focused edit doesn't always showcase "mistakes"! A focused edit can also reveal understanding of concepts, helping writers gain confidence in their own strategy use.

When writers reread for all editing elements at the same time, they can be overwhelmed and overlook areas in which they are capable of using the convention correctly.

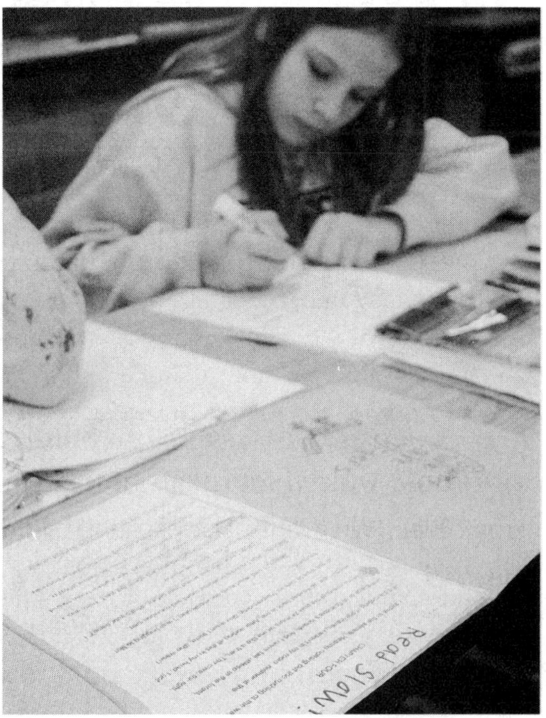

First focused edit: Reread for capital letters. Second focused edit: Reread through a new lens for end punctuation.

Rereading Power

- What do I see?
- Is the writing legible? Is writing that I created electronically arranged on the page so that it makes sense and is pleasing to the eye?
- Does my paragraphing make sense? Do other text features help my readers navigate through the text to understand my message?
- Does my punctuation add to the message?
- How is my spelling?
- What words might be overused or imprecise? With what words could I replace them?
- Have I used what I know about strong openers to capture my readers' attention?
- Sentence fluency: Have I used a variety of sentence types? Does this sound smooth when I read it aloud?

"Writers take their reading very seriously. When they read, they discover topics for their own writing. They become interested in new genre and formats. They study authors' techniques to learn how to improve their own writing."

—Shelley Harwayne

Focus on Reading and Writing as Reciprocal Processes

Reading and writing are reciprocal language processes. As writers create text, they are constantly rereading their work and applying all they know about how print works. When writers read, they are seeing models of language, spacing, conventional spelling, and punctuation that will inform their work as writers (Calkins & Louis, 2003).

Reading and writing are powerful partners, each extending and transforming the network of literacy understandings being constructed within our students. Research suggests that in classrooms where children write about their reading, embrace mentor texts as writing tutors, and consider writing a natural link to reading, academic achievement is lifted (Taylor, Pearson, Peterson & Rodriguez, 2002; Graves, 1994).

Research also suggests, however, that by the time learners reach adolescence, many are gaining proficiency as readers while lagging behind in their writing (Fitzgerald & Shanahan, 2000). While reading and writing often require the same kind of background knowledge, it is important that reading and writing have their own dedicated instruction in middle school. Within the confines of the middle school schedule, it's a wonderful idea to use reading mentors as links to writing and to help students write about literature. Be sure that both reading and writing have their time to take center stage!

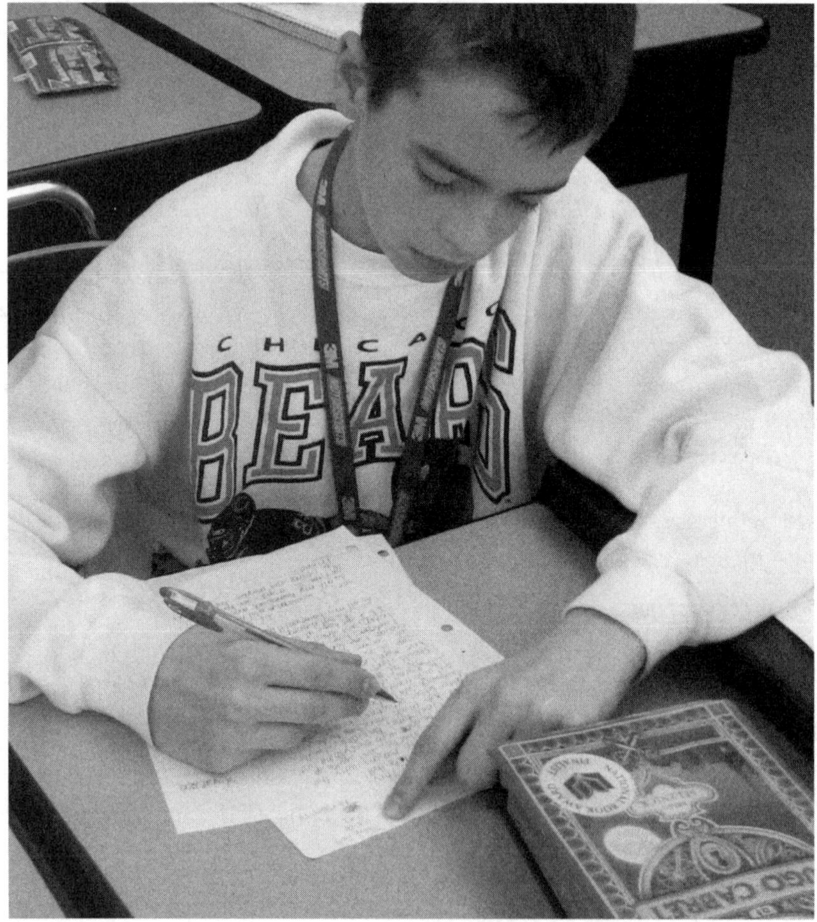

When students turn to trusted mentor books as guides to sentence structure, punctuation, and audience, their writing is elevated!

Highlight Mechanics and Conventions in Mentor Texts

We've turned to wonderful mentor texts to provide exposure to literary language, form, and craft. Literature is one of our most powerful tools for celebrating and noticing the interesting ways in which writers use punctuation, capitalization, and grammar.

Encouraging students to reread and look closely at a familiar text helps them attend to the fine points, noticing end punctuation marks, paragraph organization, sentence fluency, purposes for capital letters, and so on. Presenting mechanics within literature provides the opportunity to explore mechanics while helping students understand that all writers think about conventions as they draft and revise.

> **"Students need to stare at and relish some well-written snippets of effective mentor texts. Every day we look at some writing to aspire to or imitate—texts that teach with their artistic punctuation or their jaw-dropping grammar."**
>
> ***—Jeff Anderson***

Modeling: The Heart of Our Work

We believe it is critical to do a great deal of modeled writing as students observe and listen to us think out loud about conventions and mechanics and how they are woven into our messages. We *show* writers how we use punctuation and grammar to make our thinking accessible to a reader. We *show* how to turn to a mentor text for stimulating ideas about how to use commas. We show how to engage in multiple rereads for editing. Students should have the chance, every day, to observe the creation of quality writing that sets a model that they can attempt to emulate. Just as read-alouds model beautiful language and reading fluency, modeled writing sets a standard for the creation of beautifully constructed writing. The essence lies in *showing* writers what to do instead of *telling* them what to do.

Crack open the writing process by creating text in front of students.

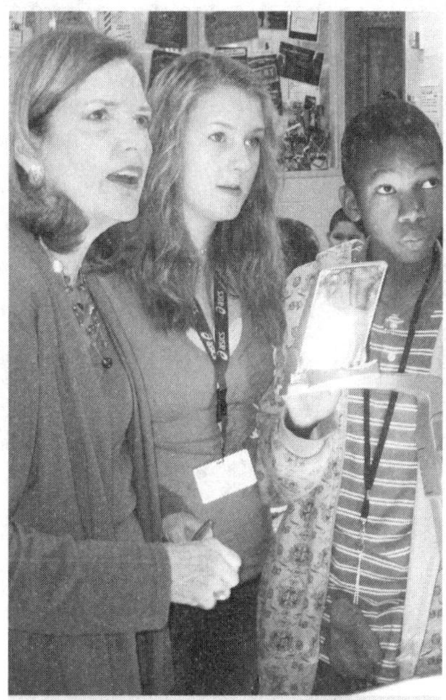

Think out loud; let students hear you consider options and make choices.

Show how conventions and mechanics fit into our thinking to support meaning.

These explicit demonstrations of writing are central to the work we do as writing coaches. We show great intentionality as we model interesting openings, such as insertion of an adverb phrase followed by a comma. We carefully plan and then demonstrate how to create descriptive phrases in a list, how to insert an appositive into a sentence, or how to be reflective about the grammar we use in our written work.

Modeled writing, like the picture on the front of a jigsaw puzzle box, sets the stage and helps writers establish a vision of possibility for their work as writers. It is a forum for sharing a broad range of genres, interesting sentence formations, sizzling interjections, and phrasing that can change the mood or voice of a piece. It is the springboard from which quality student writing evolves. Like read-alouds, modeled writing should be crafted by you as an expert, showing the best of what writing can be. This is when we show rather than tell what great writing looks like and sounds like. This is *not* a time to write like a middle school student, but rather a time to open the door into the world of wonderful possibility that awaits as writers gain control over their craft. Write at the top of your own game. Pull out all the stops with word choice, phrasing, and interesting punctuation. You will be amazed at how quickly elements of your quality work will begin to appear in your students' writing.

Important Note: Save your modeled writings! Students like to refer back to them, and you can use them for think-alouds on editing and revising.

Think Out Loud During Modeled Writing

The think-alouds we provide during modeled writing make the inner workings of the writing process transparent. If we allow our talk to flow around the creation of printed text, students can listen in as we make decisions about word choice, spelling, punctuation, and grammar. Let them accompany you on your writing journey as you construct and deconstruct your thinking. Talk about what you hope to say, make choices so that students can see your thinking process, and celebrate in front of your students when you make a great choice that powers up your writing. There is no more potent lesson for your students than watching you think out loud about phrasing or word choice, pausing midstream to reread and see how everything is coming together, and then return to drafting after rereading.

During a modeled write, the focus is on cracking open the writing process so the internal thinking of an experienced writer becomes transparent to the students.

Think-alouds during modeled writing open the door to the wonders that occur as we think, write, reread, and then write some more. Think-alouds show learners how we craft powerful messages, selecting the words and the conventions that make our ideas come alive on paper.

Model Rereading and Marking Up a Text

As we model drafting, revising, and editing, we need to help students understand that these essential processes can be messy work. Our students need to observe us changing our minds and crossing out words or even entire lines. They need to see how we might read a line, stand back, and say something like:

> I just wrote, "The dog barked." The words make a sentence. Who is the sentence about? The dog. What did the dog do? Barked. Even with both of the parts that are needed for a sentence, the sentence isn't very interesting. I am going to scratch that out and write this sentence another way. This is a good time to use what I know about sentence openers and commas to make the sentence sparkle. I'm going to use those elements to help my readers picture the dog and hear the bark: "With a low rumble from deep in its chest, the dog's bark erupted until the baying pierced the quiet night."

A complete rewrite isn't nearly as tidy as inserting a caret to show that you are adding a single carefully chosen word. But this "untidy revision" should be the essence of what you do as an active, thinking writer. Show your students how to wrestle with the creation of clear, sparkling messages that are empowered by punctuation and strong visual images. Show them how to scratch out and get a bit messy as they draft. Help them understand that this is what writers do during drafting, revising, and again during editing. Their focus is to draw readers into moments with great messages, but then continue fine-tuning their writing with spelling, spacing, punctuation, and so on. A heavily marked-up page reflects the work of a deeply thinking writer or editor!

The Joys of Fluent Writing

Writing in middle school is exciting. At this age, students have a sense of fluency and purpose as they pick up their writing tools. They have control over a range of text forms such as personal narrative, procedural texts, descriptive reports, and personal letters. At this stage of writing development, we expect that most writers will show variations in sentence beginnings and have a stronger sense of purpose and organization as they craft their work. What we must focus on now is lifting sentence structure, combining ideas in new and meaningful ways, incorporating precise words, and using mechanics and conventions to craft writing that sizzles with possibility.

Middle school writers are ready to launch into higher levels of craft, using punctuation as a deliberate tool in elevating sentence complexity and clarity. They are ready to shift text forms to suit their audiences and purposes. They are ready to push themselves to more sophisticated vocabulary use, sentence structures, and paragraphing. These writers are ready to master the mechanics at a high level of proficiency that will infuse conventions into their thinking during drafting, editing, and revising.

Heightening Spelling Consciousness

While many middle school students have an arsenal of sound-symbol relationships and know many sight words that facilitate their work as writers, one hallmark of the writing of even college-age and adult writers is spelling errors. As you work with your middle school writers, strive to help them develop a sense of spelling consciousness, an awareness that a word doesn't quite "look right." Work with students to stay focused on meaning and rich word choices while they craft their ideas. When they are aware of their spelling, they can mark questionable words and return to them later.

As students draft, they should use strategies to help them approximate spelling as best they can. They can ask themselves: *Does this word look right? Did I use this word correctly in the context of the sentence? Did I use spelling patterns that I know? Did I think about the root and about the parts of the word and what I know about spelling them?*

As you look over students' drafts, you should notice that students make rule-based decisions about their spelling and that they consciously integrate their knowledge about root words and units of meaning. Work with your students, though, to help them hone their spelling consciousness so that they will know which words they should revisit once they have crafted their messages with a focus on meaning. It may be far more useful to "keep on going," using spelling approximations, than to break the train of thought to ask for spelling help or reach for a dictionary. Model strategies for approximating spelling—and strategies for checking that approximations are correct (see box below). These kinds of demonstrations are incredibly useful for students' development as writers.

Consider including demonstrations of these strategies for approximating and checking spelling:

- Explicitly model spelling consciousness, or the awareness that a word doesn't quite "look right." As you think aloud, underline a word and put a small "sp" over it to remind you to return to check it later, after you've drafted your ideas.
- Apply multiple strategies: I tried ___, but I'm still not sure. Next, I'll try ___.
- Use the margin or a separate sheet of paper to model trying out several spellings of a word you're not sure of. Use spelling consciousness and what you know about spelling patterns to choose which spelling is correct.
- When spelling an unknown word, think about words you already know how to spell.
- Break words into syllables. Check the spellings of the syllables before putting them together into complete words. Think about double letters, endings, and so on as you put the syllables together.
- Model using what you know about letter patterns, such as double letters, silent letters, final e, and so on.
- Use the context to figure out the correct spelling of a homophone or homograph or to choose the correct word from a group of easily confused words, like *affect* and *effect*.
- After drafting, turn to tools for correcting spellings, such as checklists, word lists, portable word walls, dictionaries and thesauruses, electronic spell check, and so on.

Thinking About Audience

As students move into more sophisticated forms of writing, including content area writing, they will be sharing their work with wider audiences. Writers need to keep their audiences in mind as they draft, revise, and edit. As they reread their work, encourage students to think from the perspective of their readers. Will their readers be engaged by their ideas or will they get bogged down trying to understand the writing and not be able to focus on the content? Writers need to intentionally shift their thought process from writing for an audience of self to writing with readers in mind. With an authentic audience in mind, writers have a much stronger and more viable purpose for looking closely at their work and expecting more out of the messages they craft.

To build a sense of audience, we believe it's vitally important to provide authentic reasons for students to share their writing. Partner sharing, group work, and classroom publishing all help, but we can go further than that. The teacher as audience has limited appeal—editing work just to please the teacher becomes tedious and boring. Provide wider audiences for student work (see below), and you'll see that mechanics and conventions will become important for your writers in a personal way. Authentic audiences and authentic purposes provide both motivation and rationale for the importance of conventions and mechanics. Having an audience for our work makes us reread for correctness and lift all the aspects of our message to the highest level possible.

Ideas for Creating Authentic Audience

- Suggest students write notes to one another and to teachers. Have them write notes to share learning with parents.
- Involve students in drafting and editing a class or team newsletter that goes home to parents in print or is published on the school or district website.
- Have students work independently or in groups to make posters about writing.
- Post writing on the wall that exemplifies specific craft elements, such as: *Interesting Leads, Great Use of Interjections, Two-Word Sentences Mixed with Longer Sentences, Powerful Sentence Variety*, and so on.
- Ask students to write announcements for the school public address system.
- Create blogs or journals for sharing ideas on a content-based website community.
- Have students write a letter to ask an expert, such as asking for information for a report.
- Engineer writing projects to share with younger students.
- Collaborate on a script for a content-based skit or Readers Theater piece that can be performed for another class.
- Have students write thank-you letters to the school's parent organization after a parent-sponsored event. Students could also write thank-you notes after an assembly, guest speaker, career-day program, field trip, and so on.

Create the Right Environment

What kind of environment do middle school students need to write? A rich classroom environment needs areas set aside for modeled writing and teacher think-alouds as well as guided practice at an overhead or with a document camera or interactive whiteboard. Mentor books displayed in inviting arrangements, invite adolescent writers to apprentice themselves to the experts. You might label individual titles or group them by conventions and mechanics that are particularly evident in each selection.

Model the Use of Classroom Tools

When classroom walls reflect a rich tapestry of writing forms, tools, and supports, we send a strong message to students, parents, and colleagues that this is a classroom in which we celebrate writing in all its forms. It is important to remember, however, that rich visuals provide invitations, but real use will occur only with explicit and careful modeling of the tools in action.

Visuals are only helpful if students actively use them.

We believe that we must model the use of word walls, charts, and environmental print so our students understand that as writers, we select our tools carefully. Like a carpenter, we must select the tools that match our purposes, and we must know when to use each one.

During prewriting, we may turn to a mentor text for guidance on using commas in interesting ways or examine eye-catching punctuation in opening sentences. Our mentor texts may include modeled writing done by the teacher, the work of a peer, or a favorite book that is worth emulating.

During drafting, we generally minimize the use of tools. We might use a portable word wall if we are sure we can find a word so quickly that it won't interrupt the creation of the message. Otherwise, we keep tools set aside until we are revising.

As we *edit for an audience,* we shift our stance and emphasize the tools that will help us reach higher in our use of conventions and mechanics. Now, the editing checklists, word walls, and other resources empower our thinking and help our writing match its intent. As we edit, we encourage students to view classmates as powerful resources and enter into editing partnerships with them.

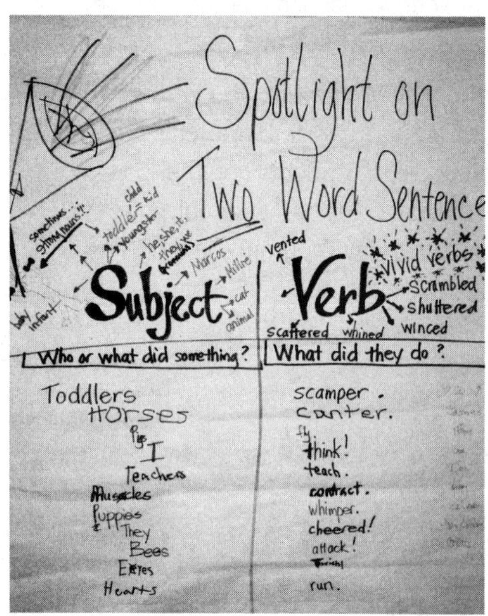

Make your walls real teaching tools. Cover your walls not only with charts that show the "rules," but also with great examples of those rules in action. Teach students to "read the walls" to find information and revisit their mechanics and conventions during revising and editing.

When you take time to demonstrate and think aloud about your options for using tools while you are modeling writing for your students, they develop a deeper understanding of how tools empower and lift writing. Talk to writers about why you are or are not electing to turn to a resource or use a tool. Let them hear you be deliberate as you consider whether a tool will help you . . . or distract you from your message. Let students hear you consider the use of a tool such as a portable word wall, then decide to wait until editing. Let them see you walk to a tool such as a homophone chart while editing, then use the tool to consider a word choice. Tools are helpful resources if writers take an active stance in their use.

Class Lists of Conventions and Mechanics

Class editing lists that grow with each cycle in this resource provide a cumulative record of your cycles. This cumulative record of lessons is a powerful visual reminder to writers of their evolving control over print and keeps writers focused on what they have learned. With each cycle, you will notice that you are reminded to pause, review the class chart, and then add a new understanding. Display the list in a clearly visible place so that writers can use it as a tool to assist their planning before drafting, as a reference while writing, or to support their thinking while editing.

Personal Tools to Support Editors

Writers and editors need well-organized writing folders in which they store their work and keep personal tools readily at hand. These personal tools might include topic lists, writers' notebooks, portable word walls, editing checklists, small dictionaries, and lists of skills that writers will be accountable for using in their completed pieces.

Skills I Can Use

In designing folders, we believe it is very helpful to keep a sheet of paper titled "Skills I Can Use" attached to one side of the folder. When we confer with a writer and observe that the student has correctly applied a convention or mechanic, we write the skill on the Skills I Can Use page and date it. Alternatively, students can use the chart to track their own progress, marking the skills they know how to use and rating their proficiency as they progress as writers.

This list can then become an ongoing, personal reminder to the writer, the writer's editing partner, and the teacher of skills that each writer has mastered. Once students learn a skill, they become accountable for applying that skill in their writing. You can also call on a student to assist another writer with a skill that has been mastered.

Editing Checklists

The goal of editing checklists is to teach students to take responsibility to reread their own writing and be their own first editors. The checklist, in combination with Skills I Can Use pages and the class editing poster, scaffolds learners for success. Checklists are tools that support use of known skills. They do not provide instruction.

It is important to remember that editing checklists do not "teach." They simply remind students to use the processes that you have modeled.

Remember Focused Edits:

Simultaneous rereading for every element on a checklist can be too great of a challenge and result in less effective editing. Each item on an editing checklist should get its own focused edit. If there are four items on the checklist, writers will reread at least four times.

We like to encourage the following steps:

1. The author reads his or her piece to a partner or partners.
2. The partners offer a compliment to the author.
3. The partners and the author together begin a series of focused edits using an editing checklist.
4. The team then decides whether to invite in another editor for a last round of edits or if the piece is ready for a teacher conference.

Just as we differentiate in other areas of the curriculum, personal editing checklists can be modified to scaffold and support learners across the range of writing abilities in your classroom. We encourage you to explore the checklists in the Assessment and Record Keeping section of this resource (pages 214–220). While these examples may offer matches to some of your students, consider creating your own checklists that match up precisely with the *Mastering the Mechanics* cycles you have selected for instruction.

Checklists for Partner Editing

Once writers review their work on their own, they are ready to engage in partner edits. During partner editing, writers collaboratively use editing checklists and their shared sense of language and convention to lift a piece to a level that an individual writer may not have reached alone.

Creating Checklists With Your Students

When students are involved in creating editing checklists, they must reflect on what they know about conventions and mechanics and then design tools that will help them be accountable for what they know. We believe in having students work with us in whole-class and small-group settings to design editing checklists that match phases of development or are specific to a certain kind of writing. Writers gain a profound sense of ownership and empowerment when they develop their own editing checklists.

The Teaching/Assessing Loop

Assessment is our essential guide to quality instruction. As we observe writers during drafting, meet with them in small groups, or confer with individuals, we are constantly assessing to determine what they do and do not know. Our assessments are the best possible guides to instruction. The data we gather through thoughtful, sensitive assessment helps us choose the next skills our students need and also helps us determine whether our students are fully grasping the material we're teaching.

Selecting Editing Skills for Instruction

To determine which conventions and mechanics are expected at your grade level, look first at your state standards. We suggest that you consider highlighting these standards on a photocopy of the Skills Continuum located on pages 28–29. If you are working with a mandated language arts resource, you might identify the skills for spelling, punctuation, grammar, and so on in the program and then highlight those on the grid as well. (We like to add program-driven goals in a second color so we can see where they deviate from state standards.) Now, as you look at the skills grid, you have a unified picture that shows state standards and program requirements in a single, easy-to-follow format that will round out your editing work with your writers. Before determining which cycles in this resource to use, you'll need to assess the skills your students are already implementing in their writing.

Assess the Skills Your Students Can Use

We feel that it is critical to collect unedited writing samples and use the Class Record-Keeping Grid provided in the assessment section (page 219). It takes only a few minutes to list student names in the first column and jot target conventions and mechanics across the top of the other columns. With a stack of writing samples in hand, you are ready to place check marks for writers whose work demonstrates punctuation in dialogue, subject-verb agreement, and so on.

Once you have a profile of your students and their needs, you are ready to select a cycle and "master the mechanics"!

In the "How an Octopus..." example below, our assessment review shows this writer is using some transition words to link ideas *(first, then)*. The sentences are complete. One sentence, "When an animal tries to attack her,..." uses a strong opening with a comma to draw in the reader. In terms of need, this writer/editor would benefit from some work on paragraphs and headings, which are conventions of organization that make informational text more manageable for a reader. To fill out the chart, we could place a tally or date observed under transition words, openers with a comma, and complete sentences. Since this is only one example, we would make a point to collect more evidence of these skills before assuming that the writer has truly mastered the learning.

Careful assessment of writing samples informs instruction and shapes think alouds.

With the support of the grid, we quickly expose patterns of strength as well as needs for individuals, small groups, or the class as a

How An Octopus Protects Herself

An octopus has many ways to protect herself. First, She can take her eight legs and wrap them around other animals. She can use the suction cups on her legs to grip things. When an animal tries to attack her, she can make her body squish together so she can hide out in little places. That was a surprise to me! An octopus can squirt ink into the water and blind the attacker for a little bit of time. Then she swims off. Pretty cool. ~~ways to protect herself~~

by Stephanie J.

whole. The grid allows us to identify groups of writers who share similar needs and easily gather small groups for explicit instruction.

Notice Oral Language Patterns

Grammar in student writing is tightly linked to oral language. With this in mind, we challenge ourselves to *listen* carefully and try to notice which students need support with noun-verb agreement, verb tenses, or the use of pronouns in oral speech. You may hear your students using oral patterns such as "My mom, she went to the store," "Me and Bobby raced on our skateboards," and "I seen a dog trying to get in the school." Record your observations and compare the patterns you notice in oral language with those in the written materials produced by your students. This provides a balanced assessment of oral and written language use that can help you make critical decisions about which cycles to select. If you have only a small group of students for whom grammatical structures are an issue, you may elect to differentiate by engaging the group in a cycle directly targeted to their needs. If a larger number of learners have the same need, the grammar cycles on this topic may be the perfect choice for the entire class. Again, assessment leads the way to quality instruction.

Supporting and Respecting

We must always respect home languages and community culture, yet we have a responsibility to help learners understand and apply the more formal registers of English that are seen in published books and expected of proficient writers. While we would never show disrespect to language patterns that are native to our students, we may explain to them that language shifts to match the audience. For example, we speak to the principal or a police officer differently than the way we speak to our friends on the playground. There are certain formal registers of language that we are expected to use as writers that aren't always expected when we talk to our friends or relax in our homes.

To support conventional grammar use, we can highlight conventional grammar in our favorite books, think aloud about grammar while crafting sentences for modeled writing, or respond with elaborated language when students use non-standard structures. The trick to elaborating and extending language use is to mirror the learner's message using correct form in your response. There is no reprimand for incorrect usage; you simply mirror what the student has said by restating it in conventional English.

If a student says:	You might reply:
I seen a movie with my brother.	You *saw* a movie? Tell me about it!
Me and my dad went fishing.	*My dad and I* used to go fishing, too. Did you have a wonderful time?
My sister, she fell and broke her arm.	*Your sister fell* and broke her arm! How awful. How is she doing?
I don't got no pencils.	You don't *have any* pencils? Can you borrow one from a neighbor?

Editing Conferences

Assuming that you have already held a revision conference with a writer, an editing conference is at least the second time when you and the writer can think together about a piece of writing. The first time, the emphasis was on meaning, which may have included the use of interesting punctuation to lift the writing. This time the focus of the conference is on editing.

During this editing conference, select one or two skills to address with the student. Never teach more than one or two things at a time. Writers are not likely to be able to retain that much information. We like to keep sticky notes on hand during editing conferences. We believe that when writers make their own corrections and retain control of the pencil, they are more likely to remember and reuse what they have learned. By jotting suggested edits on sticky notes, writers retain control of the pen and understand that they have responsibility for editing their own work. During an editing conference, the writer has responsibility for his or her actions. This is not about teacher corrections. It is about guiding writers as they move forward in their use of conventions and mechanics.

With this in mind, an editing conference might sound something like the following:

> Alexa, you must be so pleased you have decided to publish your piece on skateboarding. As a reader, I could totally visualize the tension of entering a half-pipe and the enormous energy you expend as you try to get air for a spin. Your verbs are very powerful, and they make a big difference in my ability to visualize the action.
>
> As we begin editing, please tell me what you and your editing partner have already discovered and worked on in your writing. Be sure to point out any changes or additions you and your editing partner have already made.
>
> Let's take a look at what you prepared for our conference. You underlined and marked words that you want to check for spelling, you jotted a grammar question about the last sentence on a sticky note, and you brought the skateboarding book to use as a reference. These are terrific strategies that are important to top-notch editing. I have some sticky notes we can use to record suggestions for editing. Then you can return to your desk and enter any changes you would like to make in the piece.

Steps for Editors When Writing for an Audience

We teach writers these final steps in preparing their work for an audience.

1. Use the editing checklist to do a focused edit for each item on the list.
2. Work with an editing partner. Read the work together, thinking about how to make it the best it can be.
3. Sign up for an editing conference with the teacher.

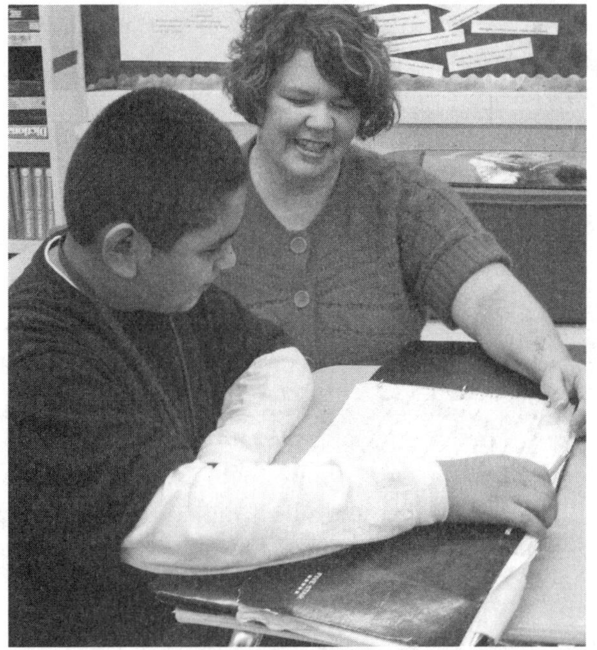

A Note About the Yearlong Planner

The Yearlong Planner featured on the gatefold (the inside front cover) of this book is a tool to help you map your curriculum for mechanics and conventions for the year. As you can see, this planner provides week-by-week suggestions for three content cycles followed by a Pulling It All Together cycle to solidify the learning with authentic, interactive purpose. During a Pulling It All Together cycle, no new skills are added. This is a time for learners to apply their learning from the previous cycles in authentic contexts. With this plan as your guide, students will have four weeks of instruction along with opportunities to transfer skills to their long-term memories.

Please note that there is a blank version of the Yearlong Planner in the Tools file on the Resources CD. With this planner, you can use your own assessments along with your state standards to build a personalized curriculum map.

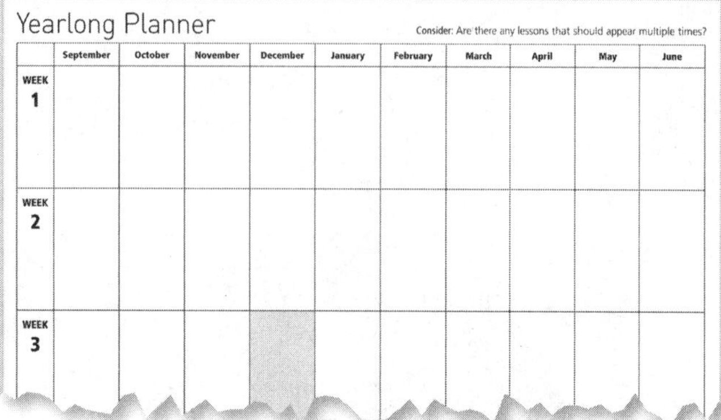
Yearlong Planner

Consider: Are there any lessons that should appear multiple times?

	September	October	November	December	January	February	March	April	May	June
WEEK 1										
WEEK 2										
WEEK 3										

Important Note: This sample planner does not contain all of the lessons in this book. We built a range of lessons to support your responses to the needs of your students. There are many paths through this resource. You may elect to use all of the planner or portions of it. You can select lessons based entirely upon the needs of your learners. You can adapt Pulling It All Together lessons to focus on different skills. The choices and the path you select are up to you. You should base your choices on your assessments of your writers' needs.

On Your Way!

The lesson cycles that are the centerpiece of this resource are meant to celebrate writers and their ever-growing control over craft and form. As you enter these cycles, we challenge you to recast conventions and mechanics as tools for enhancing meaning and to have a joyous journey as you "master the mechanics."

PART III

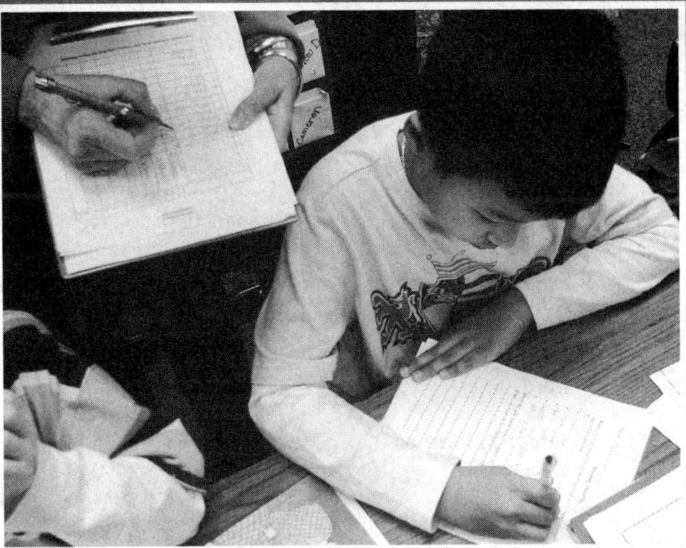

Skills Continuum

The Skills Continuum profiles a broad spectrum of development in mechanics and conventions to empower your thinking as you differentiate for the range of learners you serve. For less experienced writers, you may need to reach into the continuum to access skills and understandings normally addressed in younger grades. For advanced writers, you may want to stretch your writers by introducing skills listed above your target grade level.

Skills:
- Editing and Revising
- Spacing
- Capitalization
- Punctuation
- Spelling
- Grammar and Sentence Structure
- Text Features

Each convention listed on the continuum is supported by an explanation that often includes an example for clarity. To the right of each listed convention is a designation of grade level(s) at which writers should control the convention. When a convention is support by a lesson in this resource, the page number on which the lesson appears is also listed. If there isn't a lesson for the convention you want to target, just follow the normal three-day cycle and model a piece of writing with the convention that you want to address.

Many teachers find it helpful to photocopy the continuum and keep a copy on a clipboard. (To make this easier, you'll find a complete version of the Skills Continuum in the Assessment and Record Keeping file on the Resources CD.) This copy serves as:

- a quick reference when planning your own mini-lessons or cycles of support for conventions
- a source of support when conferring with students during writing conferences
- a place to highlight and date when you provide mini-lessons on a convention

PAGE NUMBER	CONVENTIONS & MECHANICS	EXPLANATION AND EXAMPLES	K	1	2	3	4	5	6	7	8
		EDITING AND REVISING									
	Put your name on the paper	Writers should habitualize writing their names on papers prior to creating text or drawings.	•	•							
	Count the words in a message	Before writing, young writers count the words in their messages to match speech to print.	•	•	•						
	Reread and touch each word	Writers touch each word to check for omissions.	•	•	•						
50	**Reread to focus on message**	Meaning should always be the first emphasis when creating text. Writers must reread to confirm or revise for meaning before focusing on surface conventions.	•	•	•	•	•	•	•	•	•
46	**Reread to focus on purpose and audience**	Writers need to carefully consider the purpose for which the writing was intended (summarizing, narrating, persuading, and so on) and edit to ensure that the writing matches its intended purpose.					•	•	•	•	•
	Reread to focus on support	Writers need to be sure they have included adequate support for their ideas, including facts and quotations.							•	•	•
40	**Reread to edit for conventions**	Once meaning is clear, writers reread to check for surface structures and grammar that give their writing uniformity.	•	•	•	•	•	•	•	•	•
40	**Focused edit: reread for each editing point**	Rereading helps writers check for surface structures and grammar. Writers should focus on one editing point at a time.	•	•	•	•	•	•	•	•	•
50	**Reread to focus on precise words**	Reread to check for precise nouns, verbs, adverbs, and adjectives; reread to eliminate redundancy.							•	•	•
	Reread to focus on sentences	Sentence combining is of utmost importance in working with adolescent writers. Students edit their work looking toward constructing sophisticated sentences. They also focus on sentence variety and consider sentence length as they edit.							•	•	•
48	**Reread to focus on organization**	Writing should have a coherent organizational strategy, such as sequence of events, cause-effect, compare-contrast, and so on. Writers plan for an appropriate organizational strategy and edit to be sure their writing follows that organization. They make sure to narrow their topic before writing and continue to check the focus and organization while rereading.							•	•	•
40	**Use an editing checklist**	Checklists matched to developmental levels of writers are used to guide personal and partner edits.	•	•	•	•	•	•	•	•	•

PAGE NUMBER	CONVENTIONS & MECHANICS	EXPLANATION AND EXAMPLES	K	1	2	3	4	5	6	7	8
42	**Use copyediting symbols to support editing**	Authors and editing partners use standardized copyediting symbols to identify areas for improvement and to support their editorial work.	•	•	•	•	•	•	•	•	•
	Edit with a partner	When partners work together to proofread and revise, they elevate each other's thinking about text.	•	•	•	•	•	•	•	•	•
	Edit for accuracy and fair use of information; cite sources	Students need to consider the accuracy of sources they use, make sure they properly credit sources, and know how to paraphrase information without plagiarizing.							•	•	•
	Celebrate and self-reflect	To advance, writers must take time to reflect on their own growth as communicators of meaning.	•	•	•	•	•	•	•	•	•
		SPACING									
	Word boundaries: Keep letters in a word close together	Letters in a word need to be clustered so word boundaries are apparent.	•	•							
	Use entire page	Writers should write from top to bottom, left to right, using return sweep.	•	•							
	Use multiple pages	Writers need to expand their thinking beyond single-page writing experiences.	•	•	•	•	•	•	•	•	•
	Use appropriate margins	Allow appropriate margins, headers, and footer spaces.	•	•	•	•	•	•	•	•	•
	Use pagination in a multiple-page piece	Page breaks are governed by arrangement around visuals and available space on a page. Each page of the text should have a page number.	•	•	•	•	•	•	•	•	•
	Consider spacing of visuals in nonfiction	Visuals carry important messages in nonfiction and can appear in many positions on a page. Writers must consider not only the position of visuals, but also which types of visuals are most appropriate to convey meaning in nonfiction.	•	•	•	•	•	•	•	•	•
	Consider placement of nonfiction features	Nonfiction features such as tables of contents, captions, headings, indices, and glossaries have their own conventions for spacing.	•	•	•	•	•	•	•	•	•
	Paragraphs and paragraph breaks	Paragraphs should be arranged on a page so they are clearly set apart from one another. Each paragraph should focus on one idea or topic. Each paragraph should have unity, coherence, and adequate development.			•	•	•	•	•	•	•
	Line breaks and spacing	Poems should be written with careful consideration of line breaks, spacing, and capitalization to enhance a poem's message and/or imagery.				•	•	•	•	•	•

PAGE NUMBER	CONVENTIONS & MECHANICS	EXPLANATION AND EXAMPLES	K	1	2	3	4	5	6	7	8
	Use spacing in a letter	Spacing for friendly and business letters follows a uniform format for date, greeting, closing, and signature.		•	•	•	•	•	•	•	•
	Use spacing on an envelope	Envelopes have clearly defined spaces for addressee and return addresses.			•	•	•	•	•	•	•
		CAPITALIZATION									
	Capitalize the pronoun *I*	I am going to Anna's house.	•	•	•	•	•	•	•	•	•
	Use mostly lowercase letters	Capital letters need to be used for specific purposes.	•	•							
	Capitalize the beginning of sentences	Capitalize the first word in each sentence	•	•	•	•	•	•	•		
54	**Capitalize proper nouns: names and places**	My sister, **Anna**, is taking dance lessons in **Seattle**. She hopes to perform at the **Keller Auditorium**.	•	•	•	•	•	•	•	•	•
	Capitalize a title before a name	**Mrs.** Jones works in the office of **Judge** Jacobs.	•	•	•	•	•	•	•		
54	**Capitalize proper adjectives**	Proper adjectives are formed from a proper noun used as an adjective: **American** figure skaters; **French** bread.				•	•	•	•	•	•
54	**Capitalize proper nouns: days of the week and holidays**	Monday, Thanksgiving				•	•	•			
56	**Capitalize the main words in the title of a book, the heading of a section, or the title of a piece of student writing**	*Where the Wild Things Are* "My Swimming Party" "Types of Cloud Formations"	•	•	•	•	•	•	•	•	•
	Capitalize for emphasis	HOORAY!		•	•	•	•	•	•		
	Capitalize AM and PM	Abbreviations for morning and afternoon need to be capitalized when they are written without a period.				•	•	•	•	•	•
	Capitalize abbreviations for state names (OR, CA, NY)	Names of states are abbreviated with two capital letters.				•	•	•	•	•	•
54	**Understand the difference between common nouns and proper nouns with people's names**	A common noun, used as a name of a person, is capitalized when there is no possessive or article preceding it: **Grandma** and **Mom** went shopping. *My grandma and my mom went shopping.*				•	•	•	•	•	•

PAGE NUMBER	CONVENTIONS & MECHANICS	EXPLANATION AND EXAMPLES	K	1	2	3	4	5	6	7	8
		PUNCTUATION									
60	**Period: end of sentence**	A declarative sentence needs a period at the end.	•	•	•	•	•	•	•	•	•
	Period with abbreviation	Mr. Jones, a.m. or p.m.				•	•	•	•	•	•
60	**Exclamation point: exclamatory sentence and interjection**	An exclamation point is used for emphasis. Drip! Drop! I can't believe it is still raining!	•	•	•	•	•	•	•	•	•
60	**Question mark: interrogative sentences**	Question marks are placed at the end of sentences that inquire.	•	•	•	•	•	•	•	•	•
70	**Comma: in a series**	I need to buy shoes, socks, an umbrella, and a jacket.		•	•	•	•	•	•	•	•
70	**Comma: to separate adjectives in a list**	The lost, lonely puppy looked up the dark, deserted street.			•	•	•	•	•	•	•
	Comma: to separate day of the month and the year	December 28, 2008		•	•	•	•	•	•	•	•
	Comma: to separate city and state	Portland, Oregon		•	•	•	•	•	•	•	•
72	**Comma: to follow a transition word at the beginning of a sentence**	Finally, our long-awaited order arrived.		•	•	•	•	•	•	•	•
76	**Comma: precedes connecting word (coordinating conjunction) in a compound sentence**	Anna has my library book, and Devon has my lunch. (Coordinating conjunctions include *so, or, but, and.*)			•	•	•	•	•	•	•
	Comma: in direct address	Renee, grab your coat!			•	•	•	•	•	•	•
	Comma: in a letter	Place commas after the greeting and after the closing in friendly letters.		•	•	•	•	•	•	•	•
78	**Comma: surrounding an appositive**	Jean, the amazing runner, won the medal.				•	•	•	•	•	•
72	**Comma: after introductory phrase or clause**	When they heard the final bell, the students headed for the bus.			•	•	•	•	•	•	•
74	**Comma: to set off closer**	The waves crashed, pounding relentlessly against the fragile seashore.					•	•	•	•	•
82	**Semicolon: to join two sentences without a conjunction; to join two sentences with a conjunction when one or more commas appear in one of the sentences**	I am tired; I am going home now. When we are finished, he'll clear the table; and we can have dessert!								•	•

PAGE NUMBER	CONVENTIONS & MECHANICS	EXPLANATION AND EXAMPLES	K	1	2	3	4	5	6	7	8
82	**Semicolon: to separate items in a series when one or more of the items contains a comma**	We have students visiting our school from Chicago, Illinois; St. Louis, Missouri; and Dubuque, Iowa.							•	•	•
62	**Punctuation: in dialogue**	"Hurry up," cried Eliot. "We'll be late!" "Can you help me find my keys?" her mother replied.		•	•	•	•	•	•	•	•
64	**Apostrophe: in contractions**	Can't, won't, shouldn't	•	•	•	•	•	•	•	•	•
66, 68	**Apostrophe: in possessives**	Lynnette's bike is bright pink. The boys' bikes are black.	•	•	•	•	•	•	•	•	•
	Colon: in reporting the time	10:30 a.m.			•	•	•	•	•		
82	**Colon: at the beginning of a list**	They had a long list of errands: the grocery store, the post office, and the health food store.			•	•	•	•	•	•	•
	Hyphen: to join compound descriptors	Heavy-handed, hunter-like, lightning-fast				•	•	•	•	•	•
	Hyphen: to separate syllables	At the end of a line, if there isn't room for the entire word, syllables are separated with a hyphen.				•	•	•	•	•	•
84	**Underline or italicize a book title**	When a book title or play is handwritten, it should be underlined.				•	•	•	•	•	•
84	**Follow additional rules for underlining**	The following should be underlined (in handwriting) or italicized: titles of long poems, magazine titles, movie titles, titles of television series, titles of musical CDs, titles of paintings and sculptures, titles of long works of music, and names of air, sea, and space crafts.							•	•	•
84	**Quotation marks**	Use quotation marks to indicate titles of short stories, chapter titles, and titles of magazine articles.					•	•	•	•	•
	Ellipses	Use to indicate a pause in thought, omitted words or sentences: Sweet. . . Incredibly sweet.				•	•	•	•	•	•
	Parentheses and brackets	Use to indicate omissions and interruptions or incomplete statements.							•	•	•
80	**Dashes**	Use a dash to emphasize a point, to indicate the beginning and end of a series separated by commas, to indicate a break in thought, or to replace *namely*, *in other words*, or *that is* before an explanation. *The car—the one with two flat tires—was left at the side of the road.* *Our teacher wouldn't change our test date—even with the big science fair coming up!*							•	•	•

PAGE NUMBER	CONVENTIONS & MECHANICS	EXPLANATION AND EXAMPLES	K	1	2	3	4	5	6	7	8
		SPELLING									
136	**Spelling consciousness**	Students should have a high level of awareness that spelling is important and be able to recognize when a word doesn't "look right" on the page.	•	•	•	•	•	•	•	•	•
	Stretch words	Writers say words slowly to pull them apart auditorily.	•	•	•	•	•	•			
	Reread: to add more letters	Rereading allows writers opportunities to modify spelling.	•	•	•						
	Big words have more letters than small words	Writers need to expect to use more letters in longer words as they develop spelling consciousness.	•	•							
	Spelling reference: picture alphabet card	Alphabet cards with picture cues help writers identify sound-symbol relationships.	•	•							
	Spelling reference: portable word wall	Writers need a collection of alphabetized high-frequency words at their fingertips. Writers keep lists of words they want to remember how to spell. Content word walls support spelling of content-specific words.	•	•	•	•	•	•	•	•	•
	Spelling reference: electronic resources	Writers need to know how to use electronic resources, such as spell-check, while realizing that these sources may provide incorrect information, such as a different word with the same spelling.					•	•	•	•	•
140	**Use known words and root words to spell other words**	Spelling by analogy allows students to use known words and word parts to spell other words. Students can use words parts, such as root words and morphemes, to spell words of which they are unsure.	•	•	•	•	•	•	•	•	•
	Notice syllables: each syllable needs a vowel	Writers need to expect to place at least one vowel in every syllable.	•	•	•	•	•	•	•		
138	**Try different spellings for words**	When faced with an uncertain spelling, writers benefit from trying various spellings in the margin or on a separate sheet of paper.		•	•	•	•	•	•	•	•
144	**Choose the correct homophone**	Homophones are words that sound the same but have different spellings and meanings (*their, there, they're*; *no, know*).		•	•	•	•	•	•	•	•
144	**Choose the correct word from easily confused words**	Students need to know how to spell and when to use words in pairs of easily confused words, such as *affect/effect*, *farther/further*, *access/excess*.					•	•	•	•	•

PAGE NUMBER	CONVENTIONS & MECHANICS	EXPLANATION AND EXAMPLES	K	1	2	3	4	5	6	7	8
	GRAMMAR AND SENTENCE STRUCTURE										
88	**Write complete sentences vs. fragments**	Writers avoid unintentional sentence fragments. They need to acquire a strong foundation in writing complete, interesting sentences.	•	•	•	•	•	•	•	•	•
	Sentence parts: simple subject and simple verb	Writers understand the essential components of a sentence, the who or what does something (subject) and what the subject does (verb). *Toddlers scamper. Brian cheered.*	•	•	•	•	•	•	•		
	Sentence parts: complete subject and complete predicate	Writers understand that a subject may contain multiple nouns and their modifiers. A predicate may contain multiple verbs and their modifiers.				•	•	•	•	•	•
90, 98	**Control sentence length vs. run-on sentences**	Writers use simple, compound, or complex sentences to enrich writing, while avoiding run-ons. Non-standard: *The fuzzy puppy snuggled in my arms and then it ate fast and played and barked and then it.... Standard: The fuzzy puppy, while snuggling in my arms, fell quickly asleep. Then, it...*			•	•	•	•	•	•	•
	Phrases	A phrase is a group of words that takes the place of a specific part of speech. *The house at the end of the street* is a phrase that acts like a noun. The phrase *at the end of the street* is a prepositional phrase that acts like an adjective.				•	•	•	•	•	•
	Clauses	A clause is a word or group of words ordinarily consisting of a subject and a predicate. A clause usually contains a verb and may or may not be a sentence in its own right. (Example: *I didn't know that the cat ran up the tree. That the cat ran up the tree* is a clause. The clause includes the phrase *up the tree*.)				•	•	•	•	•	•
	Use transition words	We use transition words to organize ideas in writing and alert readers to changes in the text. *Finally, our long-awaited order arrived.*	•	•	•	•	•	•	•	•	•
	Use transitions: between paragraphs and within paragraphs	Students should use a variety of sentence structures and words to link ideas in and between paragraphs.					•	•	•	•	•
	Use singular and plural nouns	Writers understand the difference between singular and plural nouns and can form both regular and irregular plurals.	•	•	•	•	•	•	•		
	Single vs. double subject	Writers avoid the nonstandard double subject (*My mom, she prefers...*) and select single subjects for sentences (*My mom prefers...*).	•	•	•	•	•	•	•	•	•
112	**Subject-verb agreement: singular subject**	Singular nouns and pronouns (subjects) agree with their verbs in number, case, and person. (*Mary giggles.*)	•	•	•	•	•	•	•	•	•

PAGE NUMBER	CONVENTIONS & MECHANICS	EXPLANATION AND EXAMPLES	K	1	2	3	4	5	6	7	8
114	**Subject-verb agreement: plural subject**	Plural nouns and pronouns (subjects) agree with their verbs in number, case, and person. (*The girls giggle.*)	•	•	•	•	•	•	•	•	•
104	**Verb tenses: present and past**	Writers differentiate present- and past-tense verbs in writing (with both regular and irregular verbs) to show when an action takes place. (*I* ***sit*** *on the edge of my bed. I* ***sat*** *on the edge of my bed.*)	•	•	•	•	•	•	•		
104	**Verb tense: future**	Writers expand their use of verbs to show a future action or state of being. (*Mario will be a stellar teacher.*)	•	•	•	•	•	•	•	•	•
	Verb mood: subjunctive	A verb is in the subjunctive mood when it expresses a condition that is doubtful. Often, the clause begins with *if*: *If I were you, I would run.* These verbs are often followed by subjunctive mood: ask, demand, determine, insist, prefer, recommend, regret, request, suggest, wish.									•
	Verb types: action	The most common verb is an action verb, which tells what the subject is doing. (*Mario swam across the lake.*)	•	•	•	•	•	•	•	•	•
108	**Verb types: linking**	Writers use linking verbs (non-action verbs) to connect the subject with nouns, pronouns, or adjectives that describe or identify the subject. The following forms of *to be* are linking verbs: is, am, are, were, was, being, and been. (*Margarita is my maternal aunt.*) The following state-of-being verbs can also function as linking verbs: feel, taste, look, smell, appear, grow, remain, stay, turn, seem, sound, become, prove. (*The snow feels cold. In the face of a crisis, our mother remains calm.*)	•	•	•	•	•	•	•	•	•
	Verb types: main	When a verb is composed of two or more words, the verb at the end of the verb phrase is the main (principal) verb. (*Anna is* ***dancing*** *down the hall.*)			•	•	•	•	•	•	•
108	**Verb types: auxiliary**	Writers use helping (auxiliary) verbs to create verb phrases that consist of a helping verb and the main (principal) verb. (*Anna* ***is*** *dancing down the hall.*)			•	•	•	•	•	•	•
106	**Verb forms: regular**	Most verbs are regular. Writers add *-ed* to show a past action. Writers use a helping verb (has, had, have) to indicate the perfect tenses: past perfect (*We had helped Mom with dinner*) and future perfect (*We will have helped Mom finish dinner before the guests arrive*).			•	•	•	•	•	•	•
106	**Verb forms: irregular**	Some verbs are irregular. Their past-tense form is not made by adding *-ed*. Past tense is expressed with a new word. (*run, ran*)			•	•	•	•	•	•	•

PAGE NUMBER	CONVENTIONS & MECHANICS	EXPLANATION AND EXAMPLES	K	1	2	3	4	5	6	7	8
110	**Verbs: active and passive voices**	Writers understand the difference between active and passive voices, know how to use them both, and work toward writing sentences with active rather than passive verbs. Active voice: *Ms. Hansen delivered our mail.* Passive voice: *Our mail was delivered by Ms. Hansen.*							•	•	•
	Pronoun order: person's name followed by pronoun	Standard form: *My mom and I went to the door. I saw Sally and him at the grocery store.* Nonstandard form: *I and my mom went to the door. I saw him and Sally at the grocery store.*	•	•	•	•	•	•	•	•	•
116	**Pronouns and their antecedents**	Writers identify the nouns to which pronouns refer. Standard: *Niva is an exceptional cook. She whipped up dinner last night. Nonstandard: She is an exceptional cook. She whipped up dinner last night.*			•	•	•	•	•	•	•
118	**Possessive pronouns**	Possessive pronouns take the place of a noun and show ownership. Most possessive pronouns are written without an apostrophe (mine, ours, theirs).	•	•	•	•	•	•	•	•	•
122	**Pronouns and nouns: subjective and objective cases**	Nouns remain the same for both subjective and objective cases, while pronouns require differentiation between the subjective (I, he, she, we, they) and objective (me, him, her, it, us, them) cases.				•	•	•	•	•	•
120	**Indefinite pronouns**	Writers make sure that indefinite pronouns (e.g., all, both, nothing, anything) agree with verbs and with any antecedents.								•	•
	Double negatives	Only one word should be used to express a negative idea. Frequent errors occur when writers use *not* with *never, no, hardly*, and so on. Standard: *We don't have any paper towels.* Nonstandard: *We don't have no paper towels.*				•	•	•	•	•	•
128	**Adjectives: to lift descriptions**	Writers include adjectives, words that describe nouns and pronouns, to strengthen text. (*The brilliant butterfly zipped past the decrepit barn.*) Writers choose adjectives with precision.				•	•	•	•	•	•
128	**Adjectives: comparative and superlative forms**	Adjectives can be used to compare two or more people, places, things, or ideas: bigger, biggest; more/less helpful, most/least helpful.			•	•	•	•	•	•	•
	Articles	Articles are adjectives. *The* indicates a specific (definite) article. (*Bring me the striped sweater.*) *A* and *an* refer to no particular thing. *A* is used before a consonant sound (*Bring me a sweater.*); and *an* is used before a vowel sound. (*Bring me an apple.*)		•	•	•	•	•	•	•	•

PAGE NUMBER	CONVENTIONS & MECHANICS	EXPLANATION AND EXAMPLES	K	1	2	3	4	5	6	7	8
130	**Adverbs and adverb phrases**	Adverbs modify verbs, adjectives, or other adverbs. Most adverbs tell when, where, how, and to what extent/degree. (*Marcos* ***quickly*** *zipped over the goal line.*)				•	•	•	•	•	•
130	**Adverbs: comparative and superlative forms**	Adverbs can be used to compare two or more people, places, things, or ideas: faster, fastest; more/less carefully, most/least carefully.				•	•	•	•	•	•
	Interjections	Interjections are words and phrases that are used to express a strong emotion and are separated from the rest of the sentence by a comma or an exclamation point. (*Wow! This is cool! Wow, this is cool!*)	•	•	•	•	•	•	•	•	•
132	**Prepositions and prepositional phrases**	Prepositions are not modifiers; their function is to relate a noun or pronoun to another word in the sentence. A prepositional phrase includes a preposition, the object of the preposition, and any modifiers. (*The cat snoozed* ***under*** *the lawn chair.*)			•	•	•	•	•	•	•
90	**Conjunctions: coordinating**	Conjunctions connect words or groups of words. Coordinating conjunctions connect equal parts: words, phrases, or independent clauses (sentences). Examples: for, and, nor, but, or, yet, so				•	•	•	•	•	•
90	**Conjunctions: subordinating**	Conjunctions connect words or groups of words. Subordinating conjunctions connect two clauses to make complex sentences. Examples: after, because, before, until, when, while				•	•	•	•	•	•
124	**Gerunds**	Gerunds are verbals that end in *–ing* and function as nouns: *One of my favorite activities is drawing. Building with blocks can be fun, too!*						•	•	•	•
126	**Infinitives**	Infinitives are verbals that consist of *to* plus a verb in its simplest form. An infinitive can function as a: Noun—*All the hungry campers wanted* **to eat**. Adjective—*We had the right* **to refuse**. Adverb—*I rode by bike* **to get** *more exercise.*								•	•
	Participles	A participle is a verb that ends in *–ing* or *–ed* and functions as an adjective: *The smiling clown entertained the children. Heartbroken after losing, I vowed to try again!*									•

PAGE NUMBER	CONVENTIONS & MECHANICS	EXPLANATION AND EXAMPLES	K	1	2	3	4	5	6	7	8
102	**Parallel structure**	Parallelism is a balance of two or more similar words, phrases, or clauses. Examples: Not parallel—*In spring, summer, or in winter* Parallel—*In spring, summer, or winter* Not parallel—*Cameron has wit, charm, and he is extremely smart.* Parallel—*Cameron has wit, charm, and intelligence.* Not parallel—*I enjoy mixing the batter, kneading the dough, and to taste the bread fresh out of the oven.* Parallel—*I enjoy mixing the batter, kneading the dough, and tasting the bread fresh out of the oven.* Not parallel—*The class has space for bookshelves but not a media center.* Parallel—*The class has space for bookshelves but not for a media center.*									•
		TEXT FEATURES									
148	**Title, headings, and subheadings**	Writers use titles to prepare readers for the message of the text. Headings and subheadings provide logical organization and allow readers to preview the piece for main ideas.		•	•	•	•	•	•	•	•
158	**Bulleted lists**	A bulleted list allows writers to organize ideas that appear in list form but do not need to be in sequential order. Bullet points can be nouns, noun phrases, or clauses—but they must be parallel.			•	•	•	•	•	•	•
152	**Captions**	Captions are complete sentences that explain what is shown in a photograph or other visual.			•	•	•	•	•	•	•
156	**Text boxes**	A text box is set apart from main text to show information that is interesting or important.			•	•	•	•	•	•	•
150	**Table of contents**	A table of contents is a listing of chapter titles or headings listed in the order in which they appear in a text. Listings are accompanied by page numbers.	•	•	•	•	•	•	•	•	•
	Index	An index is a list of topics in a text that appears at the end of the text. The topics are in alphabetical order, listed with page numbers for reference.			•	•	•	•	•	•	•
	Glossary	A glossary is a list of words in a text that appears at the end of the text. The words are listed in alphabetical order and accompanied by definitions. Glossary entries may also include pronunciations.			•	•	•	•	•	•	•
154	**Bolded words and font changes**	Bolded words and other font changes allow writers to emphasize important words in the text.		•	•	•	•	•	•	•	•

PART IV

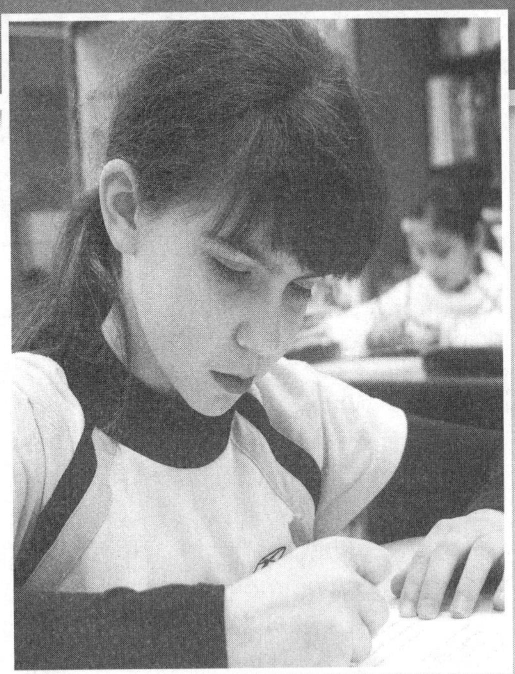

Lesson Cycles for Mastering the Mechanics

Cycles for Understanding the Editing Process

Writers need to consider mechanics and conventions as tools to lift their messages, clarify meaning, and focus their editing as they prepare their writing for an audience.

Rereading is a tool that engages writers in processing print while supporting them at every phase of the drafting, revising, and editing processes. It is, unquestionably, our greatest tool for supporting the editing process.

- Writers need to reread constantly. They reread to confirm their messages, to maintain or regain momentum, and to consider what they will write next. They reread to think about organization and how their writing sounds. They reread to edit for spelling, punctuation, capitalization, and so on.
- Editing checklists guide writers in rereading for specific points of conventions and mechanics. They do not teach. Rather, they remind writers of what they already know.
- Focused edits engage writers in a process of rereading once through for each editing point. Have students edit with highlighters in hand, highlighting in their writing instances of where they show evidence of mastering the skill as well as places where they revised to include correct use of the skill in their writing.

Use an Editing Checklist

DAY 1 Model the Focus Point

Note: You will need (1) an enlarged copy of one of the editing checklists from the Assessment and Record Keeping file (on the Resources CD), either on a chart or projected for students; and (2) a piece of writing created in a previous modeled writing session.

> **Modeled Writing Sample**
>
> Its a tiny organ and some doctors aren't sure what it's purpose is. What is it. It's the appendix. Some docters believe this body part was once useful. They think people long ago needed the appendix to digest tough leaves and bark. Which were parts of their diet.

When we edit, we go back to the great writing we've done and make sure it's polished for our readers. A checklist keeps my editing on track! I focus on one point of the checklist at a time, rereading for each point. Notice that the first point of my editing checklist is to focus on end punctuation. Watch as I reread the piece, looking only at end punctuation. I am noticing that the second sentence is a question, so I am replacing the period with a question mark. The rest of the end punctuation looks fine. On my next rereading, I'm focusing on complete sentences. Watch as I check each sentence to be sure it has both a subject and a verb. This last group of words does not have a subject. That makes this group of words a fragment. Watch as I use a comma to combine it with the sentence that comes before: *They think people long ago needed the appendix to digest tough leaves and bark, which were parts of their diet.*

Continue with additional editing points, sharing your thinking as you add a comma to the compound sentence *It's a tiny organ, and....* Model using a resource to find the correct spelling of *doctors.* Edit for correct use of homophones.

TURN AND TALK **Recall the steps in using an editing checklist. Evaluate how using an editing checklist helped guide my work. Why is it helpful to focus on just one editing point at a time rather than reading for all the editing points at once?**

SUM IT UP **After writing, use a checklist to proofread and edit for one item at a time to find and fix errors.**

DAY 2 Guided Practice

TURN AND TALK **Use your editing checklist to proofread for one item at a time in Tubas. Check off each item after you address it. Think together. Based on your edit, what suggestions will you offer to the writer?**

SUM IT UP Display the class editing chart. Add "Use editing checklists to edit for one editing point at a time."

Remember, when you use an editing checklist, check for one item at a time.

Tubas

The sound of a tuba, a large brass instrument, is a warm deep rich sound that is my most favorite sound in this world. The moment I send air through it and I can make it in tune I feel safer than before. I feel loved and like no one can touch me. I know I become invincible when I can play a song like Gustav Holst's First Suite in E-flat for Military Band. The low brasses, the most important instruments in a band, are the foundation for the sound. Being a tuba player I have much control of the volume of the entire band. It is a great feeling. I also get to play the sousaphone which is another version of the tuba that gives you the opportunity to march comfortably. I love running around with it in. You can do so many creative and interesting moves with it that really awes people. Which makes me really happy.

Resources CD: Tubas

DAY 3 Independent Practice

Model selecting a piece of writing from a student's writing folder (always with permission) to edit with a checklist. Remind students how to use the checklist to proofread and edit for one targeted point at a time. Turn the process over to student editors.

PEER EDIT Share with your partner changes that you made based on the editing checklist. Then think together. How did using the checklist help you focus your work as an editor?

SUM IT UP Editing helps you polish your writing for an audience. Use an editing checklist to focus on one aspect of writing at a time.

Assess the Learning

- Have students create guidelines for using editing checklists to edit for one point at a time. Assess their guidelines for understanding.
- As you confer with writers in conferences, have them explain how they used an editing checklist and show you the changes they made based on their editing. Provide additional instruction to small groups as necessary.

Link the Learning

- Work with students to create editing checklists based on current cycles of study. Encourage students to consider the editing points they might add based on genre and purpose of writing.
- Post examples of editing checklists as well as "before and after" pieces of writing to showcase the positive effects of using editing checklists.
- Have students identify resources that can help them in their editing, such as dictionaries, lists of easily confused or often misspelled words, and so on. Discuss with them how each resource supports their work as writers. Be sure you gather all the resources in an "editor's corner" for easy access.

Use Copyediting Symbols

DAY 1 Model the Focus Point

Note: Prepare the writing in advance and have an enlarged copy of the Copy Editor's Symbols from the Tools file (on the Resources CD) for students to view.

It takes effort to make our work free of errors, but it's worth the work so our readers understand our messages! I'm rereading a piece of text with a closer eye as I think like a copy editor. When we all use the same symbols to copyedit, it creates a common language for revising. Reading the first sentence, I notice the word *stood* is misspelled. Watch as I place the letters *sp* above the word as a signal to correct spelling. Now I am focusing on the next sentence. Who or what is this sentence about? I think the writer may have left out the subject. Watch as I insert this mark, called a caret, and write words that will complete the sentence: *I had.* Reading on, I am focusing on the word *stomach*. A stomach is a body part, but it's not a proper noun. I am drawing a slash through the letter *s* and writing the letters *lc*. This shows the writer that *stomach* begins with a lowercase *s*. This last sentence has a series of verb phrases: *gulped one... moved my*. The verb phrases need to be separated by commas to keep readers from becoming confused. Notice that I indicate commas by drawing these marks. If I am unsure of the copy editor's symbol to use, I can check the chart.

Modeled Writing Sample

(sp)
I stoode on the end of the diving board. Looking down, [^ I had] an empty feeling in the pit of my (lc) Stomach. I was higher than I'd ever been. I gulped one last breath[^,] moved my toes toward the end of the board[^,] and jumped toward the refreshing waters below.

TURN AND TALK Think together as you clarify how copyediting symbols help us make our writing better. Describe how you might use copyediting symbols to assist writing partners.

SUM IT UP Copyediting symbols give us a common language to focus on errors in our writing. Published pieces need to be error-free so that readers can understand our messages. As we copyedit, we make strong writing even stronger.

DAY 2 Guided Practice

TURN AND TALK Think like copy editors. What copyediting symbols will benefit the writer of the Letter to the Editor? Where should they be placed in the work?

SUM IT UP To the editing chart, add "Use copyediting symbols to edit."

Copyediting symbols signal errors to fix that make writing stronger—and error-free.

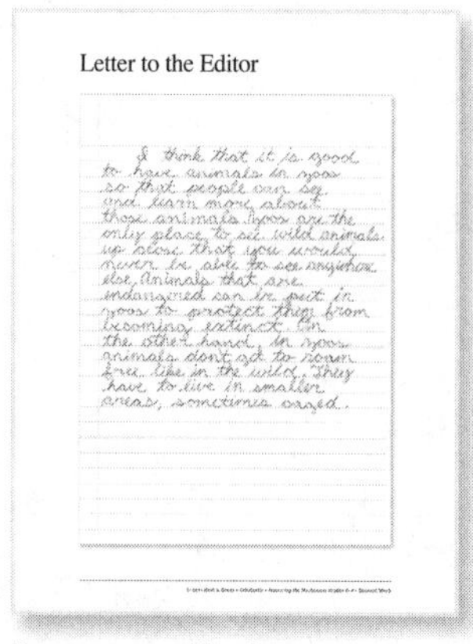
Letter to the Editor

I think that it is good to have animals in zoos so that people can see and learn more about those animals. zoos are the only place to see wild animals up close that you would never be able to see anywhere else. Animals that are endangered can be put in zoos to protect them from becoming extinct. On the other hand, in zoos animals don't get to roam free like in the wild. They have to live in smaller areas, sometimes caged.

Resources CD: Letter to the Editor

DAY 3 Independent Practice

Make multiple copies of a piece of student writing, either from your class or from a sample in this resource, and distribute to partners along with the Copy Editor's Symbols.

PEER EDIT Partners, work together as copy editors to apply what you learned to prepare this piece of writing for a final, error-free version. Insert copyediting symbols into the text. Be ready to share this work with another set of partners and explain your thinking.

SUM IT UP Copyediting symbols tell writers where they have made mistakes and how they should correct them. They lead to error-free final copies, a must for any published piece.

Assess the Learning

- Observe students' use of copyediting symbols to mark up their writing, making sure they use symbols correctly and identify true errors. Note which students may need additional instruction.
- Confer individually with writers and ask them to demonstrate their use of a copyediting symbol chart. Assess writers' understanding.

Link the Learning

- Have students create posters to show copyediting symbols. They can add sentence strips with examples of copyediting symbols in action.
- Students might enjoy creating an electronic slide show about copyediting. Each student (or pair of students) can create a slide about a symbol and describe how it's used. Put the slides together to make a show that you can view and then present to another class.
- Discuss with students when they might not use copyediting symbols (personal writing, learning logs, and so on), and when they should (for any piece of writing shared with an audience). Have them use copyediting symbols to prepare pieces for publishing, such as newsletter articles, letters to businesses, and so on.

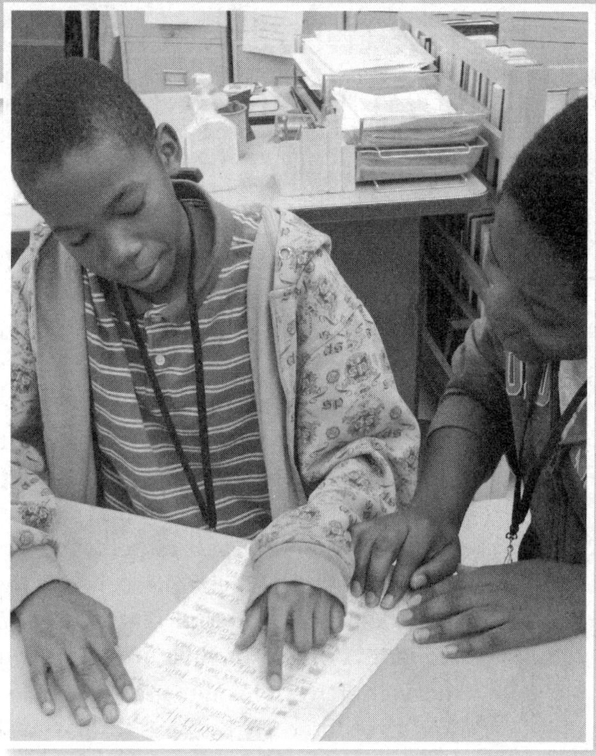

Cycles for Revising

Revision is a time when writers challenge themselves to reach deeper and put themselves in the role of a reader. This is a time when they wonder about the clarity of the message and reach for precise word choices, richly constructed sentences, and powerful leads.

Model revising for your students. Share your thinking as you answer such questions as: *Does my beginning catch readers' attention? Does my writing have a logical ending? What about my word choice—is there a way to say this with more precision? Can I improve the verbs, adjectives, and nouns? Are the sentences in the correct order?*

Cycles for Revising

Reread to Focus on Purpose and Audience

DAY 1 Model the Focus Point

Rereading is one of my most important jobs as a writer. I read and reread to be sure that I notice things that don't sound right and fix them. As I reread this letter, I am focusing both on the purpose—to persuade—and my audience, the principal. Watch as I begin: *Hey, Dr. Meares! You know what? My kids have done a great job with their book reports*. Stepping back from this, I'm thinking that this might be a bit informal. My purpose is to persuade, and I want the principal to grant my request. Take a look as I revise into the form of a friendly letter: *Dear Dr. Meares, My students... books of their own*. This tone will be a lot more effective for communicating with the principal. And I've stated my purpose for persuasion. Now to continue: *Next Thursday works for me. Does it work for you? Let me know*. Hmmm... I think that I might talk with a friend this way, but not with the principal! He won't be persuaded. So watch as I revise: *The last day of the... sales*. Now I've used more respectful language and included a great reason to go on Thursday. I'll end my letter with a closing and my signature: *Thank you so much! Ms. Thompson*.

Modeled Writing Sample

Dear Dr. Meares,

My students have done a fantastic job with their book reports! I am so impressed with their work that I'd like to take them on a special outing to a book fair, where they can choose books of their own.

The last day of the Book Fair is Thursday. If you'd allow me to take the students on that day, they can take advantage of last-minute sales.

Thank you so much!

Ms. Thompson

TURN AND TALK Now it's your turn to evaluate my writing. Do you think this letter fits its purpose—to persuade? What about its audience—the principal? What changes would you suggest?

SUM IT UP Rereading helps us make good decisions about our writing. The purpose of my letter was pretty clear, but it was too informal for its intended audience. It's important to focus on purpose and audience as we reread.

DAY 2 Guided Practice

TURN AND TALK Identify the purpose of Advice for 5th Graders. Analyze whether the writer met his or her purpose. What suggestions do you have for this writer? Then focus on the audience. Evaluate whether the writing will work for the audience. Why do you think so?

Advice for 5th Graders

Dear incoming students,

I am sure you have heard rumors about middle school, like the teachers were mean, and that the eighth graders will pick on 6th graders. None of that is true. The teachers are not mean but they expected you to get your homework in. So if I will have one tip. Keep your locker clean and organized!! There is nothing worse than getting an assignment in 1st period then by the end of day not knowing were it is in your locker. I know this from experience. You can organize your locker with just a few simple supplies: folders, plastic bins, and an extra set of shelves. Don't worry about 8th graders; keep your locker clean and organized.

Your 7th grade friend,

Robert

Resources CD: *Advice for 5th Graders*

SUM IT UP Add "Reread to focus on purpose and audience" to the class editing chart.

It's important to reread to make sure that your purpose is clear and your writing is appropriate for your readers.

DAY 3 Independent Practice

Look through a student's writing folder and select a piece to read with a focus on purpose and audience. Start by identifying the purpose and audience. Model rereading, considering whether the writing "works" and making any necessary revisions. Then turn responsibility over to students to revise, focusing on audience and purpose.

PEER EDIT Did you make any changes when you considered the purpose of the piece of writing? How about when you read it again with a focus on the audience? Explain why focusing on the audience and purpose is so important.

SUM IT UP Strategic writers reread their pieces multiple times, each time focused on a different point. Rereading to consider audience and purpose makes your writing more accessible to readers and helps you get your message across!

Assess the Learning

- As you meet with writers, ask them to identify their target purpose and audience. Then ask them to point out examples in their work that show their consideration of audience and purpose.
- Share a writing sample with students. Ask them if they can identify purpose and audience. What clues help them figure it out?

Link the Learning

- Ask students to write about the same topic with two different purposes. For example, they could write a summary of a nonfiction text (or part of one) and then write a review of the same text. How does the writing differ with each purpose?
- Help students identify purposes for writing, such as to persuade, inform, instruct, respond, and so on. Use the Word Bank resource (in the Tools file on the Resources CD) and work with groups to list words that they might use for each writing purpose.
- Have students work in pairs or small groups to create a two-column chart to complete as they focus on audience. Over one column, they should write *audience.* Over the other, *characteristics.* They can list possible audiences and the characteristics of writing appropriate for the audience.

Reread to Focus on Organization

DAY 1 Model the Focus Point

If you've ever tried to follow directions that are out of order, you know that organization is important in your writing! Rereading during and after writing can help you focus on organization. As I write today, my focus is on cause and effect—that's just one way to organize writing. Watch as I begin: *A zig zag... in the sky?* Notice that I use the word *cause*—that word signals that the writing will be organized in a cause-and-effect pattern. Now I am writing about the causes of lightning: *During a thunderstorm... build up in clouds.* I want to start the next sentence with a phrase that signals that I am going to take about the effect, lightning: *As a result, the charges... lightning!*

Write the last sentence of the model, sharing your thinking as you use the phrase *because of* to signal another cause-and-effect relationship.

Modeled Writing Sample

Flash in the Sky!

A zig zag of light streaks from a cloud straight to the earth. Lightning! But what causes these flashes in the sky? During a thunderstorm, liquid and ice particles collide high up in the sky. The movement causes electrical charges to build up in clouds. As a result, the charges build until they make sparks. Those sparks are lightning! Because of drafts in the air, lightning can move from cloud to cloud, cloud to air, or cloud to ground.

TURN AND TALK **Think together as you reread the model. What words signal cause and effect? Rereading the whole piece, identify another place you might insert organizational words.**

SUM IT UP **Cause and effect is just one way to organize a piece of writing. Rereading to focus on organization allows you to be sure that your message is clear to your readers.**

DAY 2 Guided Practice

TURN AND TALK **Partners, reread Tsunamis to discover the pattern of organization. Identify the words and phrases that helped you figure it out. What other words would you add? Reread with your additions to see if the text makes more sense.**

Students may identify elements of both cause and effect and sequence in the writing.

SUM IT UP Display the class editing chart. Add "Reread to focus on organization."

Remember to think about your organization before and as you write. When you revise, check to be sure that you've followed the same organization and that you've used words and phrases that help your organizational strategy.

Tsunamis

A tsunami is a large ocean wave that is caused by sudden motion on the ocean floor. This sudden motion could be anything from an earthquake, a powerful volcanic eruption, an underwater landslide, or even the impact of a large meteorite. Most tsunamis are caused by earthquakes. What happens is that there are two plates that have a lot of friction between them. They then become "stuck." As the stuck plate continues to descend into the mantle, there becomes a large buildup of energy. It can be stored for long periods of time – decades or even centuries. Energy keeps building until it exceeds the amount the plate can hold. When there is too much energy, the stuck plate snaps back into a position where it is not stuck. This sudden release of energy is the beginning of the tsunami. The moving wave then starts to travel to where the earthquake occurred. The shoreline has lowered from the tsunami, so the waves rush toward land to flood the shore. The waves will travel swiftly through open waters. When it hits it is like a "wave train" because the multiple waves will follow the large wave. After the tsunami hits, it can cause a substantial amount of damage. Only one tsunami can destroy an entire coastal village and remove all the sand from the beach that took hundreds of years to create. Tsunamis can also destroy islands of all its natural habitats and can cause death to surrounding areas. Overall, tsunamis are very dangerous and its good to know how they occur.

Resources CD: Tsunamis

DAY 3 Independent Practice

Thumb through a student's writing folder and choose a piece with a definite organizational pattern (or a piece that would benefit from additional organization). Model rereading the piece to identify the organizational pattern. Model another rereading to insert words and phrases that help make the organization clear. Then have students follow your lead to revise a piece, considering organization.

PEER EDIT Partners, reread to identify the organizational patterns of your writing pieces. What would you do to make the organization even stronger? Think together—how did rereading help you focus more on organization?

SUM IT UP Focusing on organization is one reason to reread. As you reread, look for places to add words or phrases or to move sentences and paragraphs to make the organization stronger.

Assess the Learning

- As you confer with writers, ask them to identify the organizational pattern they used and to point out revisions they made during a rereading focused on organization.
- Use the Class Record-Keeping Grid (in the Assessment and Record Keeping file on the Resources CD) to keep track as you observe your editors at work. Note which students are making changes to strengthen organization based on their rereading. Plan additional instruction for those who are not.

Link the Learning

- Provide mentor texts with different organizational patterns, such as cause-effect, compare-contrast, sequence of events, and so on. Have partners work together to read and reread the pieces to identify the organization of each one. Encourage them to use sticky notes to add words, phrases, or sentences that might make the organization even stronger.
- Have students use the Word Bank form (in the Tools file on the Resources CD) to create lists of words and phrases that they might add to pieces of writing to make organization stronger.
- Begin a chart with the title "Reasons to Reread." As you work through the lessons in this section, continue to add reasons. Students may have other reasons for rereading as well—be sure to honor their thinking and add those ideas to the list.

Reread to Focus on Precise Words

DAY 1 Model the Focus Point

> **Modeled Writing Sample**
>
> My breath emerged, forming small clouds of condensation that hung in the air. Icicles clung to the branches, sharp tips pointing toward the crunchy snow.

Precise nouns, verbs, and adjectives paint vivid pictures in our readers' minds and help us engage with our audience. As I describe my impressions of a wintry walk in the woods, I'm focusing on precise words. Watch as I begin: *My breath came out.* Hmmm. I'm thinking that I want to convey more strongly what it's like to breathe in this environment. It's almost hard to push air out of your lungs! Watch as I revise: *My breath emerged.* To give this more precision, I'm adding a closer that should help my readers create pictures in their minds: *forming. . . air.* Now I continue: *Icicles were on the branches.* The verb *were* works here, but I can be more precise. Watch as I revise for a more precise verb: *Icicles clung to the branches, pointing toward the snow.* Wow! *Clung* gives such a strong visual! I am going to revise one more time to add some adjectives: *Icicles clung to the branches, sharp tips pointing toward the crunchy snow.*

TURN AND TALK **Partners, think together about the precise words that I added. How did these words affect your experience as a reader? Identify some precise nouns, adjectives, and verbs you might use if you were adding a new sentence.**

SUM IT UP **When we reread tuned in to precise words, we add language that engages our readers and appeals to their senses.**

DAY 2 Guided Practice

No Power!

One perfectly normal Wednesday night, I went over to my neighbors' house to have dinner with their family. The grayish green clouds and the rumbling thunder signaled an approaching storm. My neighbor's mom had just finished cooking tacos and nachos. We were all eating and then all of a sudden the power went out. It was still pretty light outside so we could see but it went out! We all assumed it would go back on shortly because it normally does. So we finished eating and waited. One of my neighbors had to go to basketball practice and she went. By then, it was pouring outside. Rain pounded the street. The gutters were already full of swiftly moving mini-rivers. I ran across the street to my house to see if our power was on and it wasn't.

A couple of hours passed, we were all very hot and the power wasn't on yet! It was getting dark, so we lit a bunch of candles. It had finally stopped raining. So, my neighbors' dad drove us around to see how the damage was. Trees were split in half at the trunk! There was debris all over the road! It was worse then we all thought. When we got back, my mom had called our power company, and they said it would be on my 7:45 that night. Then it turned 8. Later on, I took a shower in the dark and went to bed. The power was then supposed to come on at 7:45 in the morning. I woke up and... nothing. Still no power!

My friends walked over a little later and we went to the park and hung out. We came home and ate the little things that we could without the oven or the microwave. Then they went home. Before I knew it, it was 6 at night. The power was supposed to come on at 7:45 again but nope. We were waiting around and it had been over 24 hours without power. My phone was about to die and all our food in the fridge spoiled. Trees were still toppled over. I took a shower and read until it got too dark and the candles didn't really help. Then finally at 9 pm... POWER!!! It was so exciting! I turned on lights, I went on my computer, I charged my phone, and I set all the clocks in the house. Finally! And we've had power ever since. That was the first time the power had ever gone out for more then 20 minutes in my lifetime.

Resources CD: No Power!

TURN AND TALK **Think together about a compliment you'd offer the writer of this personal narrative. Then reread this text, focusing on precise words. Identify vivid verbs, exact nouns, and specific adjectives. Identify places in the writing that would benefit from more precise words.**

SUM IT UP To the class editing chart, add "Reread to focus on precise words."

Precise words add sparkle to our writing. One focus for a rereading is to locate precise words and to identify places in the writing that would benefit from them.

DAY 3 Independent Practice

Select a piece of writing from a student writing folder that might benefit from adding or replacing words to create more precision. Share your thinking as you celebrate precise words and deliberately replace or add words to make the writing more engaging. Then turn responsibility for revising for precise words over to students.

PEER EDIT Read together to identify precise words in your writing. Apply what you've learned to replace a tired verb, add a more specific noun, or insert a vivid description.

SUM IT UP Reread with a fresh eye on precise words. Look for words and phrases that create great images and excite our readers—and change or add information to create even more precision and excitement.

Assess the Learning

- Ask writers to point out instances in which they used precise words. On a focused rereading, ask them to identify places where they could be more precise. Note which students may need additional instruction.
- On a classroom grid, create column entries for nouns, verbs, adjectives, adverbs, and prepositional phrases. Note patterns in student work. In what areas do they need the most assistance to add precision?

Link the Learning

- On separate pieces of chart paper, write verbs such as *went, said, walk,* and *put.* Give each piece of paper to a group, challenging the group to list more precise words that could replace the verbs. Display the charts and encourage students to add examples from mentor texts.
- Share mentor texts with precise words. Discuss the impact of these words on the author's overall message. Choose texts such as Robert Burleigh's *Black Whiteness,* articles from engaging magazines such as National Geographic's *Extreme Explorer,* any title by Seymour Simon, Jerry Spinelli's *Maniac Magee,* Patricia Reilly Giff's *Pictures of Hollis Woods,* and Karen Hesse's *Out of the Dust.*
- Have students summarize an event from history, their learning in a science text, and so on, focusing on using precise words.
- Students might use the Word Bank (in the Tools file on the Resources CD) to collect amazing verbs, nouns, and adjectives they have found in mentor texts or used in their writing. Encourage them to use the list for inspiration.

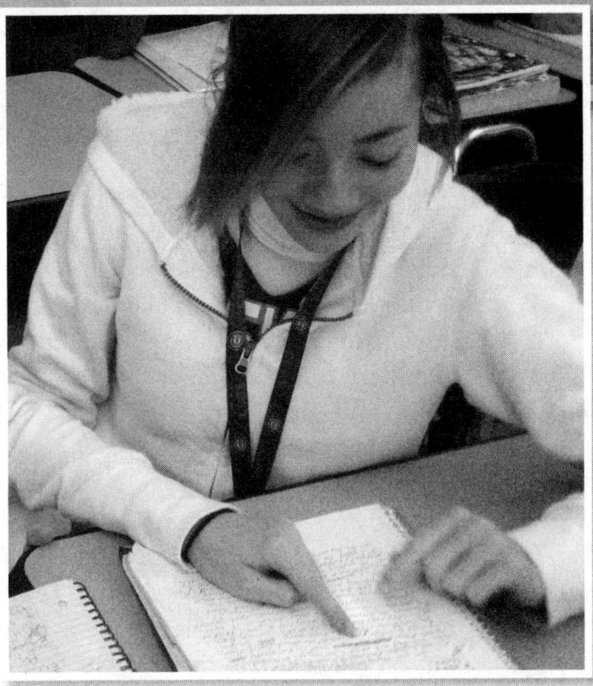

Cycles for Success With Capitalization

Capitalization alerts readers and writers when words carry significance, when new sentences are beginning, or when a word is a proper noun or proper adjective. Writers in the intermediate grades and middle school have often gained control over using capital letter at the beginnings of sentences and of proper nouns. They are ready to branch out and explore a wide range of purposes for capitalization and to consider the ways in which capitalized words are integrated into both their reading and their writing.

You might feature capitalization on your editing checklists and have students highlight places where they used capitalization for proper nouns, proper adjectives, titles, and so on. Encourage students to look for use of capital letters in mentor texts. They might copy sentences that include capital letters used in many ways, highlight the capital letters, and display the sentences for reference. Include masterful student writing as well! Have writers note on their Skills I Can Use charts (see the Assessment and Record Keeping file on the Resources CD) the various uses of capital letters that they have mastered in their own writing.

Cycles for Success With Capitalization

Capitalize Proper Nouns and Adjectives

DAY 1 Model the Focus Point

When I write, I use words that are as specific as possible. That's why proper nouns and proper adjectives have such an important place in my writing. Common nouns like *boy, store,* and *city* name people, places, and things, but they are not specific. Proper nouns like *Ted, Marion's Toy Store,* and *Batavia* are exact. Watch as I write an explanation of origami: *People debate... folding. Because ancient chinese inventors created paper, many believe that origami began in china.* I am noticing that I may need to capitalize some of these letters. China is a certain country, so I am revising to add capital letters to the name of the country, *China,* and to the adjective that describes the inventors—*Chinese.* Watch as I write my next sentence: *Paper was... flourished.* Did you notice another capital letter? I capitalized another specific country, Japan. I'll continue: *Most Historians recognize that... designs*! Now I may have capitalized a common noun. I don't know which historians have talked about Japanese origami artists, so that's a common noun—it describes a whole group of unspecific people! So I need to revise to use a lowercase letter: *historians.*

Modeled Writing Sample

People debate the origin of origami—the art of decorative and intricate paper folding. Because ancient Chinese inventors created paper, many believe that origami began in China. Paper was later introduced to Japan, where origami flourished. Most historians recognize that, whether or not they invented origami, Japanese artists made paper folding an amazing art form. Today, people all over the world love folding paper into interesting designs!

TURN AND TALK Take a look back at the model. Identify common and proper nouns and adjectives. Generalize—how do you form proper adjectives?

SUM IT UP The names of specific people, places, things, or ideas are proper nouns. They start with capital letters. Proper adjectives are made from proper nouns.

DAY 2 Guided Practice

TURN AND TALK What advice would you give the writer of I'd Like to Visit Australia about proper nouns? Identify a place in the writing where you could insert a proper adjective.

SUM IT UP Add "Capitalize proper nouns and adjectives" to the class editing chart.

We can't always use a proper noun or proper adjective to make our writing more specific. But when we do, we need to start the words with capital letters.

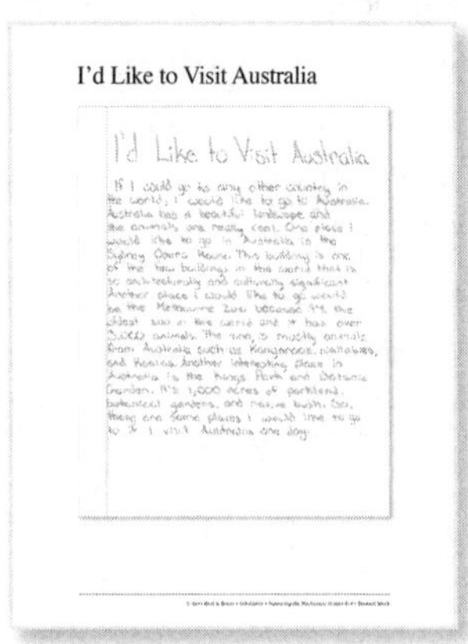
I'd Like to Visit Australia

I'd Like to Visit Australia

Resources CD: I'd Like to Visit Australia

DAY 3 Independent Practice

As you thumb through a student's writing folder, select a sample that includes proper nouns and adjectives. Model proofreading to be sure that proper nouns and adjectives begin with capital letters—and that common ones do not. Then have students select writing to edit with a close eye on proper nouns and proper adjectives.

PEER EDIT Share examples of common and proper nouns and adjectives in your writing. Evaluate them. Do they add specificity? Do they start with capital letters? How might you include more proper nouns and proper adjectives?

SUM IT UP Proper nouns and adjectives begin with capital letters. Proper adjectives are often created from proper nouns, such as *England/English*.

Assess the Learning

- Review students' writing for use of common and proper nouns and adjectives. Note those who may need extra support in capitalizing specific words and in changing common nouns and adjectives to proper ones.
- Have students point out proper nouns and adjectives in their writing. Ask them to explain how to form a proper adjective from a proper noun.

Link the Learning

To extend the lesson, share some additional rules for capitalization:

- Capitalize important words in titles and headings.
- Capitalize words such as *Grandma, Mom,* and *Uncle* when they are used as names. When possessives or articles precede these words, they are common nouns. (*I went with Uncle Joe to the store. My uncle and I picked out ingredients.)*
- Capitalize the names of specific geographical locations, but do not capitalize compass directions unless they are used as names. *(We are leaving the Northwest. We'll drive south on Highway 101.*)
- Capitalize names of months, days of the week, and holidays, but do not capitalize the names of seasons. *(When is the first day of spring? The warmer season finally begins on Tuesday!)*
- Give students categories of common nouns, such as fictional characters, famous battles, songs, national landmarks, artists, newspapers, composers, museums, and so on. Challenge students to work in groups to name as many proper nouns as they can for the categories. Challenge them further to create proper adjectives from the nouns.

Capitalize Titles, Headings, and Some Abbreviations

DAY 1 Model the Focus Point

Writers of informational writing use text features to help us navigate the content. Have you ever noticed features like titles and headings? I am writing a report about mountains, and I know my readers will appreciate the way I organize with headings. Watch as I write the title. I capitalize the first and last words of every title I write. But what other words in the title need to be capitalized? I need to figure out which words are important. I'm capitalizing *Mountains, United States*, and *Tallest*. *Mountains* and *United States* are nouns, so they are important. *Tallest* is an adjective, so it's another important word. The words *in* and *the* do not need capital letters. My first heading is about Mount McKinley. I'm using the abbreviation for *Mount* (*Mt.*) and for *Alaska* (*AK*). When we abbreviate state names, we capitalize both letters.

> Modeled Writing Sample
>
> The Tallest Mountains in the United States
>
> Mt. McKinley, AK: Home of Glacier-Feeding Snowfields
>
> Located in the Alaska Range, Mt. McKinley is the highest point in North America.

TURN AND TALK Take a closer look at the heading. **Explain why I capitalized all the words except *of*. What can you generalize about words that are not capitalized in titles and subheadings?**

SUM IT UP **The first and last words of titles and headings are always capitalized. So are important words—nouns, pronouns, verbs, adverbs, adjectives, and conjunctions and prepositions that have four letters or more. When we abbreviate state names, we capitalize both letters.**

DAY 2 Guided Practice

TURN AND TALK **What do you notice about capitalization in The Grassy Savanna? Do you see any letters that should be capitalized—and capitalized letters that should not be? Describe the rules you applied to help you figure out which words need capital letters.**

SUM IT UP Display the class editing chart. Add "Capitalize the first and last words and other important words in titles and headings."

Remember, titles and headings need capital letters—but not for every word, only the first, last, and important words. State abbreviations are capitalized, too.

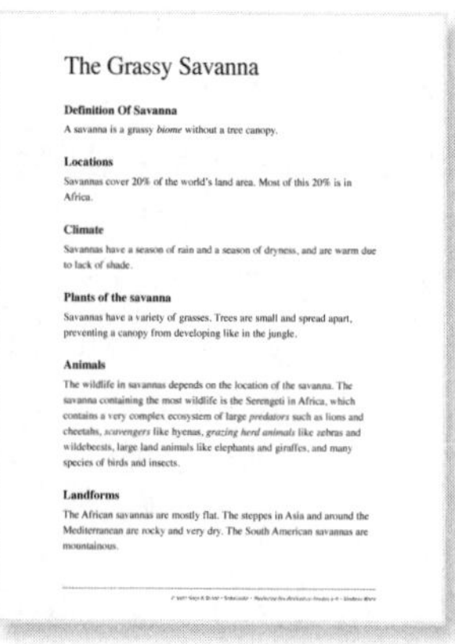

The Grassy Savanna

Definition Of Savanna

A savanna is a grassy *biome* without a tree canopy.

Locations

Savannas cover 20% of the world's land area. Most of this 20% is in Africa.

Climate

Savannas have a season of rain and a season of dryness, and are warm due to lack of shade.

Plants of the savanna

Savannas have a variety of grasses. Trees are small and spread apart, preventing a canopy from developing like in the jungle.

Animals

The wildlife in savannas depends on the location of the savanna. The savanna containing the most wildlife is the Serengeti in Africa, which contains a very complex ecosystem of large *predators* such as lions and cheetahs, *scavengers* like hyenas, *grazing herd animals* like zebras and wildebeests, large land animals like elephants and giraffes, and many species of birds and insects.

Landforms

The African savannas are mostly flat. The steppes in Asia and around the Mediterranean are rocky and very dry. The South American savannas are mountainous.

Resources CD: The Grassy Savanna

DAY 3 Independent Practice

Look through a student's writing folder to choose a piece that has a title and headings, or a piece that could benefit from more organization. Model your thinking as you add a heading to the piece, paying attention to capitalization rules. Then invite students to choose from their own folders writing pieces with titles and headings or pieces of writing that would benefit from inserting them.

PEER EDIT If your writing already includes a title and headings, apply what you've learned to be sure they are correctly capitalized. Could your piece use some headings to organize ideas? Recall capitalization rules as you add new headings.

SUM IT UP Capitalize the first, last, and all the important words in titles and headings. Check your abbreviations, as many require capital letters, too!

Assess the Learning

- Look through students' writing folders for pieces with titles and headings. Assess for correct use of capital letters.
- Confer with small groups to assess understanding of abbreviations. While both letters in the abbreviation for a state are capitalized *(IL, OR, MN),* other abbreviations may have only initial capital letters.

Link the Learning

- Provide an informational text without headings. Have students confer, using sticky notes to add headings to organize the text. Remind them to include correct capitalization.
- As students create a "works cited" page for a researched report, remind them to include correct capitalization in titles. (You can find a Works Cited reference tool in the Tools file on the Resources CD.)
- Many writers mistakenly use lowercase letters for short words in titles, such as "Go Tell it on the Mountain" or "Love is a Song." Remind students that all nouns, pronouns, adjectives, verbs, adverbs, and subordinate conjunctions of four letters or more in titles need capital letters.
- Help students understand the difference between acronyms and abbreviations. In an acronym, capitalize to indicate which letters form the acronym. NASA, for example, is the acronym for National Aeronautics and Space Administration. All the letters in NASA require capital letters.

Cycles for Lifting Punctuation

Thoughtful punctuation controls the flow of a message, helps the reader understand nuances of meaning, and makes the texts we construct more interesting. Punctuation should not be limited to end-of-process corrections. Rather, we believe it should be recast as a tool we use to shape our thoughts and elevate craft. Complex sentences, for example, are not possible without punctuation. Our objective is to support writers in understanding that punctuation, when thoughtfully used, can lift the quality of writing.

With this in mind, we coach writers to think about punctuation at two significant points in the writing process.

1. During drafting: Here, punctuation turns our thinking toward creating interesting phrasing, combining ideas and sentences, stimulating emotion in our readers (as with exclamation marks), creating an interesting opener to follow with a comma, and so on.
2. During editing: This is where we reread for the proper use of conventions and ensure that we have applied punctuation that will help a reader navigate our work.

Above all, we focus on helping students apply their knowledge of punctuation in a wide variety of contexts.

Cycles for Lifting Punctuation

End Punctuation: Period, Question Mark, and Exclamation Point

DAY 1 Model the Focus Point

Modeled Writing Sample

Memories danced across my mind as we grew closer to our destination. Hurry, Dad, drive faster! We rounded the final corner, and the resort came into view. Was this really the same place I'd visited before? So much had changed!

Can you imagine reading a text in which all the sentences were similar? That kind of text would be boring to read! Writers have a variety of sentences at their fingertips that they can use to make writing more interesting for readers. I'm starting my personal narrative: *Memories danced across my mind... destination.* This sentence is a simple statement—watch as I place a period at the end. I am continuing: *Hurry, Dad, drive faster.* To put a sense of urgency in this imperative sentence, I'm ending the sentence with an exclamation point. Less urgent imperative sentences can end with periods. I'm continuing the writing: *We rounded... before?* Notice that my last sentence ends with a question mark. All interrogative sentences, or questions, need to end with this punctuation. I'm finishing up my writing with a strong statement: *So much had changed!* I'm including an exclamation point to show that this sentence expresses a strong feeling.

TURN AND TALK **Partners, take a look at my writing as you evaluate the effect of using a variety of sentences. Recall the four types of sentences—declarative, interrogative, exclamatory, imperative—and work with your partner to name an example of each type.**

SUM IT UP **Having command of a variety of sentence types makes our writing more interesting for our readers. Be sure that each sentence type you write includes correct end punctuation.**

DAY 2 Guided Practice

TURN AND TALK **What makes Visit Phillips Park! a great persuasive text? Identify sentences of each type. Find a place where you could change a declarative sentence into an interrogative or exclamatory sentence. What is the effect of your change?**

SUM IT UP Display the class editing chart. Add "Use a variety of sentence types with correct end punctuation."

Using different types of sentences adds variety to your writing. Each type of sentence requires a particular type of end punctuation.

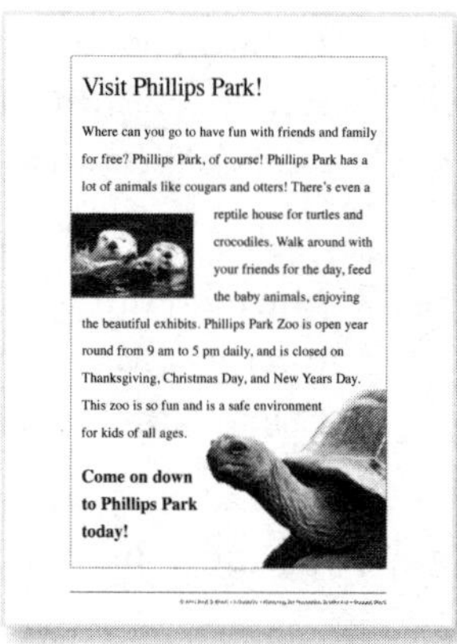

Visit Phillips Park!

Where can you go to have fun with friends and family for free? Phillips Park, of course! Phillips Park has a lot of animals like cougars and otters! There's even a reptile house for turtles and crocodiles. Walk around with your friends for the day, feed the baby animals, enjoying the beautiful exhibits. Phillips Park Zoo is open year round from 9 am to 5 pm daily, and is closed on Thanksgiving, Christmas Day, and New Years Day. This zoo is so fun and is a safe environment for kids of all ages.

Come on down to Phillips Park today!

Resources CD: Visit Phillips Park!

DAY 3 Independent Practice

Select a writing sample from a student's writing folder. Think aloud as you scan the piece for sentence types and check for appropriate end punctuation. Model as you change a declarative sentence into a sentence of another type to make the writing flow more smoothly and to add variety. Allow time for students to survey pieces of text for end punctuation and sentence variety. Encourage them to make thoughtful changes.

PEER EDIT Think together as you pinpoint a sentence or two that you can change from one sentence type to another. Explain how this change enhances your writing. Double-check your end punctuation.

SUM IT UP Using different sentence types makes your writing more interesting. Look for opportunities to break up strings of declarative sentences with different sentence types. Be sure that each sentence includes correct end punctuation: periods for declarative, question marks for interrogative, periods or exclamation points for imperative, and exclamation points for exclamatory.

Assess the Learning

- Collect students' writing to look for sentence variety and punctuation matched to sentence type. Note which students may need additional instruction.
- During writing conferences, ask students to note places where they might change sentences from one type to another. Discuss the effect on the writing.

Link the Learning

- Have students comb through mentor texts to find effective examples of sentence variety, groups of declarative sentences broken up with exclamatory and interrogative sentences, and so on. Have students share passages in small groups.
- Have students survey texts for imperative sentences. They might look at school or class guidelines, recipes, instruction manuals, and so on. What do they notice about the beginnings of imperative sentences? (They usually start with verbs: *Turn the handle to the right. Mix the ingredients together. Stand quietly as you wait to enter the bus.*)
- Divide the class into groups and assign each group a sentence type. Have groups create rubrics focused on their sentence types. A rubric for declarative sentences, for example, might include: *includes subject and verb, includes active verb, ends with a period,* and so on. Students can use completed rubrics to evaluate their own sentences.

Punctuating Dialogue

DAY 1 Model the Focus Point

Modeled Writing Sample

"Are you sure Sherry is on her way home?" whispered Alec.

"Absolutely," I replied. "It does feel like we've been crouched behind this chair forever, though."

The front door burst open.

As we jumped from our hiding place, we shouted, "Surprise!"

"This is so unexpected," Sherry gasped. "My birthday isn't until <u>next</u> week."

Dialogue—both real and imagined—lifts a narrative by allowing us to be in on the action and by providing windows into what characters say and think. But we need to give speakers credit for their words by using quotation marks to enclose exact words. My first sentence is "Are you sure. . . . " As I write this, notice that I begin with quotation marks. This bit of dialogue is a question. Watch how I place the quotation mark after the question mark. That is really important. Dialogue isn't finished until you identify the speaker and indicate the manner in which the words were delivered. Were the words screamed? In this case, they are hiding so I will write *whispered Alec.* Now I am continuing with my reply: *"Absolutely,". . .* Notice again that I place the word in quotation marks, and follow it with a comma. I place a period at the end of the word *replied.* Notice that I am starting a new sentence—words that I spoke. Because I spoke these words, I place them in quotation marks. I make sure that the period at the end of the sentence is inside the quotation marks.

Share your thinking as you continue, showing how you place dialogue tags at the beginning and middle of sentences and enclose punctuation within the quotation marks.

TURN AND TALK **Partners, work together to recall the rules for correct punctuation of dialogue. Apply what you know about dialogue to write another sentence for this narrative. Check your punctuation to be sure it makes sense.**

SUM IT UP **Dialogue is made up of the exact words of speakers. Follow punctuation rules to be sure you give speakers credit!**

DAY 2 Guided Practice

TURN AND TALK **Reread Concert in the Park very closely to take a look at the dialogue. Explain how the dialogue helps you better understand the article. Then evaluate the writer's use of punctuation rules for dialogue. What feedback might you offer the writer?**

SUM IT UP Display the class editing chart. Add "Follow rules for punctuating dialogue."

Dialogue is the speaker's exact words. When you write dialogue, enclose the speaker's words as well as appropriate punctuation marks in quotation marks.

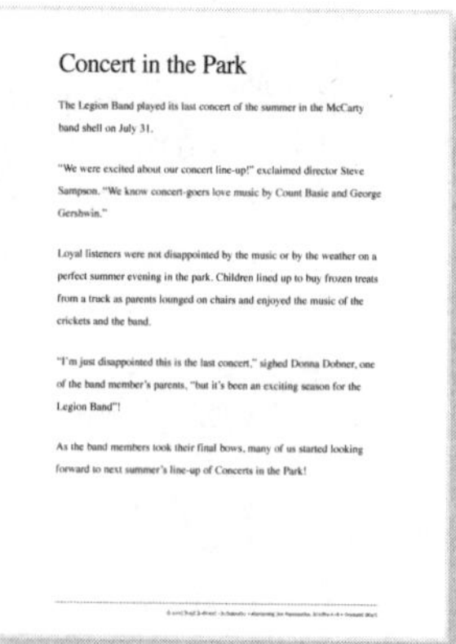

Concert in the Park

The Legion Band played its last concert of the summer in the McCarty band shell on July 31.

"We were excited about our concert line-up!" exclaimed director Steve Sampson. "We know concert-goers love music by Count Basie and George Gershwin."

Loyal listeners were not disappointed by the music or by the weather on a perfect summer evening in the park. Children lined up to buy frozen treats from a truck as parents lounged on chairs and enjoyed the music of the crickets and the band.

"I'm just disappointed this is the last concert," sighed Donna Dobner, one of the band member's parents, "but it's been an exciting season for the Legion Band"!

As the band members took their final bows, many of us started looking forward to next summer's line-up of Concerts in the Park!

Resources CD: Concert in the Park

DAY 3 Independent Practice

Look through a student's writing folder to find a piece of writing that includes dialogue or could benefit from its addition. Think aloud as you check punctuation and look for places to insert dialogue to add interest or insight to the narrative. Then have writers select pieces of their own writing into which they can insert dialogue.

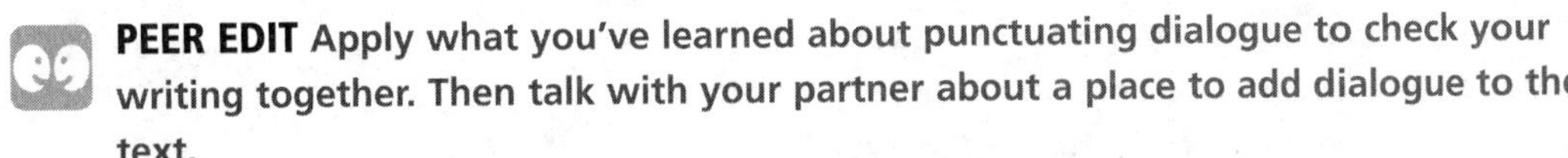

PEER EDIT Apply what you've learned about punctuating dialogue to check your writing together. Then talk with your partner about a place to add dialogue to the text.

SUM IT UP Be sure that dialogue in your writing is appropriately placed and includes the correct punctuation.

Assess the Learning

- Collect student writing samples that include dialogue. Scan for correct use of punctuation, exact words enclosed, and a variety of verbs used to introduce dialogue.
- Ask students to use sticky notes to mark especially powerful dialogue in a reading selection. Discuss the dialogue with them—how does it add to the text? What does it reveal about the speaker? How is it punctuated?

Link the Learning

- Have students create Readers Theater scripts based on content area studies. Point out the differences in punctuating dialogue in a text with the way that we punctuate dialogue in a script. Allow time for students to read scripts aloud with expression.
- Students can create explanatory posters with rules for punctuating dialogue. They should include rules that show how to punctuate different types of dialogue—exclamations, questions, statements, commands—as well as rules for dividing quotations and for paragraphing with dialogue. Have them support each rule with an illustrative sentence.
- Be sure that students know they should not use quotation marks with an indirect quotation. (*Mr. Butcher warned, "Our test tomorrow will be the most challenging yet!"* versus the indirect statement, *Mr. Butcher warned that our test tomorrow will be the most challenging yet.*)

Apostrophe: Contractions

DAY 1 Model the Focus Point

Watch as I write dialogue between an older brother and younger sister. When we speak—and when we write—we shorten some phrases by creating contractions. I'm starting with my first piece of dialogue: *My little sister... try?"* Notice the word *can't*—that is a contraction for *cannot*. I removed two letters—*no*—and replaced them with an apostrophe to show that letters are missing. Now I continue: *"Because you are not... scolded.* Hmmm. When I speak, I usually don't sound this formal! Especially with my little sister. Watch as I revise: *"Because you're....* " I am combining *you* and *are*, taking out the letter *a* and replacing it with an apostrophe to show that I have removed a letter.

> **Modeled Writing Sample**
>
> My little sister Kelly whined, "Why can't I try?"
>
> "Because you're not old enough!" I scolded.
>
> "But weren't you about my age the first time you rode your bike to a friend's house?"
>
> "I wasn't allowed to do that until I was 8."
>
> "You've forgotten something," Kelly smiled. "I'm 8!"

Continue modeling, sharing your thinking as you create contractions for *were you not, was not, you have,* and *I am.* Point out that the word *friend's* has an apostrophe—but it's not a contraction. The "test" for a contraction is that a contraction is a shortened form of a word or words. *Friend's* shows possession.

TURN AND TALK **Partners, read the dialogue together, each taking a role. Read the dialogue once with the contractions and once with the phrases that the contractions replace. Evaluate the effect of using contractions in the writing.**

SUM IT UP **A contraction is a shortened form of one or two words (one of which is often a verb). An apostrophe takes the place of the missing letter or letters.**

DAY 2 Guided Practice

TURN AND TALK **Identify contractions in the piece. Reread, substituting the words that make up the contraction. What is the effect of using a contraction rather than the words that make it up?**

SUM IT UP To the class editing chart, add "To make a contraction, put an apostrophe in place of the missing letter or letters."

Contractions can make our writing sound more natural and less formal. When you form a contraction, use an apostrophe in place of the letter or letters you remove.

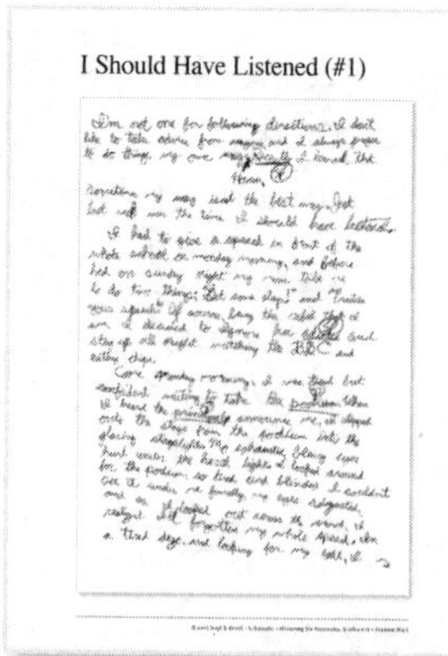
I Should Have Listened (#1)

Resources CD: I Should Have Listened

DAY 3 Independent Practice

Select a piece of writing from a student's folder and model rereading to check that contractions in the writing are correct, and that she has combined words with contractions when needed. Then have students look at their own writing, encouraging them to add contractions and checking that the contractions they use are correct.

PEER EDIT Apply what you've learned to be sure contractions are properly punctuated and to add another contraction to the piece if appropriate.

SUM IT UP Contractions make dialogue sound more natural and can give informal writing a "friendlier" voice. When you put two words together to form a contraction, replace the letter or letters you've omitted with an apostrophe.

Assess the Learning

- Ask students to share contractions from their writing and explain what words make up each contraction.
- Scan student writing for contractions. Note errors, such as omitting the wrong letters, putting the apostrophes in the wrong places in the words, combining words that aren't usually combined in contractions, and so on.

Link the Learning

- Have students work in teams to create posters that show "contraction families." They can group contractions: *be (I'm, you're, he's,* and so on), *will (I'll, you'll she'll...), would (I'd, he'd, they'd...) have/has (I've, you've, what's, where's...), had (I'd, he'd, they'd...),* and contractions that negate a verb *(isn't, aren't haven't, couldn't, mightn't,* and so on).
- Point out that in a few cases, contractions shorten nouns. *O'clock*, for example, is a contraction for "of the clock."
- Discuss when it might not be appropriate to use contractions, such as in very formal papers. Many current writing experts believe that, while writing, we should be guided by what "sounds right." Writing sounds warmer and more personal when we use contractions. In more formal writing and speaking, however, we should use contractions sparingly.
- Share a poem with contractions, such as Dwight Okita's "In Response to Executive Order 9066." Discuss the effect of the contractions.

Apostrophe: Singular Possessive Nouns

DAY 1 Model the Focus Point

A possessive noun shows ownership. If I say, for example, "That is Eliot's desk," I am saying that the desk belongs to Eliot. We form possessive nouns to show ownership in writing. To create a singular possessive noun, add an apostrophe and the letter *s*, even if the singular noun ends with *s*. I am writing about Egypt: *During its... smoothly*. Notice that I added an apostrophe and *s* to the word *Egypt*—that shows that the citizens belong to the country. Now I am writing about one of the jobs. I want to show the duties that belong to a scribe, so I am forming a singular possessive noun: *A scribe's duties....*

> Modeled Writing Sample
>
> Jobs in Ancient Egypt
>
> During its Golden Age, Egypt's citizens had jobs that helped their society run smoothly. A scribe's duties, for example, included creating necessary legal documents and teaching. A city's workforce might include artisans such as metal workers, potters, tailors, and carpenters. Each worker's role was clearly defined.

Continue modeling, writing the last two sentences and sharing your thinking as you create the possessive nouns *city's* and *worker's*.

TURN AND TALK **Partners, think together as you identify the singular possessive nouns in my writing. What clues can you identify that show you the nouns are singular? Restate the possessives: *the ___ belonging to ____*.**

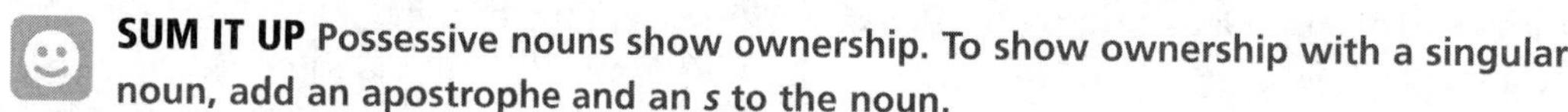

SUM IT UP **Possessive nouns show ownership. To show ownership with a singular noun, add an apostrophe and an *s* to the noun.**

DAY 2 Guided Practice

TURN AND TALK **Partners, analyze the writer's use of possessives in The Stanley Cup. Are the possessive nouns punctuated correctly? Can you see a place in the writing that would benefit from the addition of a singular possessive?**

SUM IT UP Display the class editing chart. Add "Add *'s* to singular possessive nouns."

A singular possessive noun shows ownership by one person, place, or thing. Add an apostrophe and an *s* after the noun to show ownership.

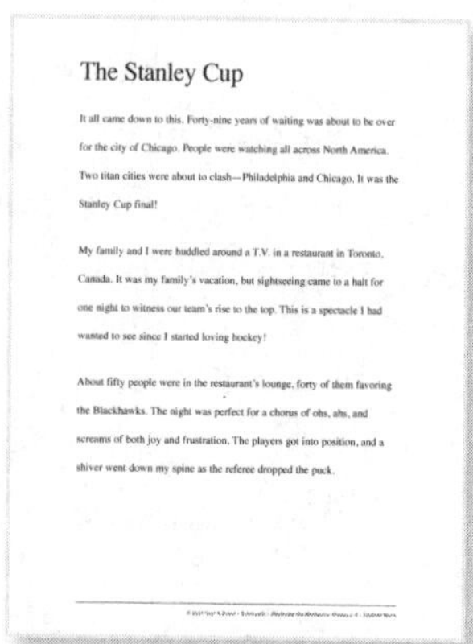

The Stanley Cup

It all came down to this. Forty-nine years of waiting was about to be over for the city of Chicago. People were watching all across North America. Two titan cities were about to clash—Philadelphia and Chicago. It was the Stanley Cup final!

My family and I were huddled around a T.V. in a restaurant in Toronto, Canada. It was my family's vacation, but sightseeing came to a halt for one night to witness our team's rise to the top. This is a spectacle I had wanted to see since I started loving hockey!

About fifty people were in the restaurant's lounge, forty of them favoring the Blackhawks. The night was perfect for a chorus of ohs, ahs, and screams of both joy and frustration. The players got into position, and a shiver went down my spine as the referee dropped the puck.

Resources CD: The Stanley Cup

DAY 3 Independent Practice

Locate a student writing sample that includes singular possessive nouns and think aloud as you model how to proofread for *'s* at the end of singular possessive nouns. Then have writers thumb through their writing folders to select a piece to proofread for singular possessive nouns.

PEER EDIT Verify with your partner that you have correctly formed singular possessive nouns in your work. Identify a place in your partner's writing that might benefit from adding a singular possessive noun.

SUM IT UP Adding *'s* to the end of a singular noun shows ownership by just one person, place, thing, or idea.

Assess the Learning

- Scan student writing for singular possessive nouns. Note common errors, such as adding apostrophes only, making singular nouns plural before adding the apostrophe, confusing possessives with contractions, and so on. As you chart errors, use your findings to inform your instruction.
- Confer with individual writers, asking them to show you singular possessive nouns in their work and explaining why they used them and how they formed them. Provide additional support as necessary.

Link the Learning

- In some cases when possessives are used, we aren't showing literal ownership. For example, we call the wages for a week *a week's wages.* The week does not "own" the wages. The possessive takes the place of the word *of* or *for* (another example: the worth of a dollar is *a dollar's worth*). Have students note examples of possessives they find in which the possessive demonstrates *of* or *for.*
- Share example of possessive nouns in poetry. You might share Robert Frost's "Nothing Gold Can Stay" (*Nature's first green is gold…Her early leaf's a flower…*) or Ralph Waldo Emerson's "Concord Hymn" (*Their flag to April's breeze unfurled…*). Have students write poems related to content. Challenge them to include several singular possessive nouns.

Apostrophe: Plural Possessive Nouns

DAY 1 Model the Focus Point

If one student has a locker, we show ownership of the locker by adding an apostrophe and *s* to the end of the noun—*student's locker*. But what if we wanted to talk about the lockers that belong to all the students in the school? The plural of *student* is *students*. To make the possessive form of a plural noun ending in *s*, we simply add an *apostrophe* after the *s*—*one student's locker, all the students' lockers*. Not all plural forms end in *s*, though. That changes the rule. I am writing about healthy diets. Watch as I begin: *Experts believe that....* Notice that I have an irregular plural—*children*. I am treating the word *children* the same way I would a singular noun, by adding an apostrophe and *s*. Now I am continuing by writing about the fact that all parents can plan to help kids make healthier choices. I start the sentence by making the word *parent* plural by adding an *s* and then adding an apostrophe after the *s*: *Parents' careful planning....*

> **Modeled Writing Sample**
>
> Experts believe that children's health is at stake because many don't eat enough healthy foods. Parents' careful planning helps their kids make healthier choices. No one can deny vegetables' benefits for good health—be sure that your refrigerator is stocked with them! It seems that families' schedules are incredibly busy, but making time for meals together may create healthier, happier families.

Share your thinking as you write the last two sentences, deliberately changing singular nouns into plural ones before adding the ending apostrophes to *vegetables* and *families.*

TURN AND TALK Writers, think together as you reread for plural possessive nouns in my model. How would these words look different if I were writing about only one vegetable and one family?

SUM IT UP To make a plural possessive noun, add an apostrophe to a plural noun that ends with an *s*. Add an apostrophe and an *s* to a plural noun that does NOT end in *s*.

DAY 2 Guided Practice

TURN AND TALK Identify the plural possessive nouns in this piece. Explain how you know that they are plural possessive nouns rather than singular possessive nouns or contractions.

SUM IT UP To the class editing chart, add "To make a plural possessive, add an apostrophe to plural nouns ending in *s*. Add *'s* to plural nouns not ending in *s*.

To show ownership with a plural possessive noun, simply add an apostrophe if the plural noun ends with *s*. If the plural noun does not end with *s*, add *'s*.

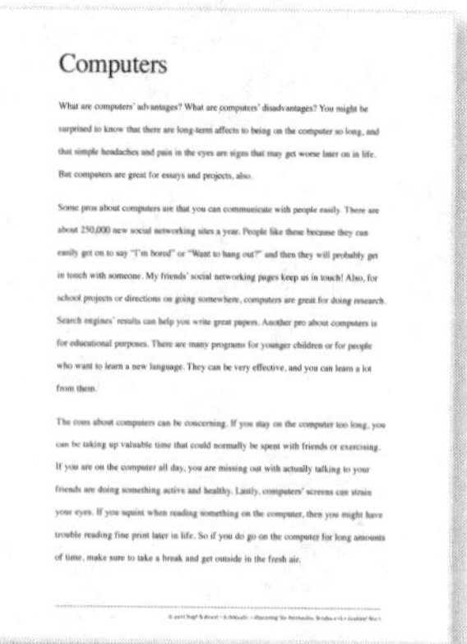
Computers

What are computers' advantages? What are computers' disadvantages? You might be surprised to know that there are long-term affects to being on the computer so long, and that simple headaches and pain in the eyes are signs that may get worse later on in life. But computers are great for essays and projects, also.

Some pros about computers are that you can communicate with people easily. There are about 250,000 new social networking sites a year. People like these because they can easily get on to say "I'm bored" or "Want to hang out?" and then they will probably get in touch with someone. My friends' social networking pages keep us in touch! Also, for school projects or directions on going somewhere, computers are great for doing research. Search engines' results can help you write great papers. Another pro about computers is for educational purposes. There are many programs for younger children or for people who want to learn a new language. They can be very effective, and you can learn a lot from them.

The cons about computers can be concerning. If you stay on the computer too long, you can be taking up valuable time that could normally be spent with friends or exercising. If you are on the computer all day, you are missing out with actually talking to your friends are doing something active and healthy. Lastly, computers' screens can strain your eyes. If you squint when reading something on the computer, then you might have trouble reading fine print later in life. So if you do go on the computer for long amounts of time, make sure to take a break and get outside in the fresh air.

Resources CD: Computers

DAY 3 Independent Practice

Locate a student writing sample that includes plural possessive nouns or one that would benefit from adding them. Think aloud as you proofread for the correct use of the apostrophe and, if applicable, the apostrophe and *s*. Then turn responsibility over to student editors to work on the plural possessive nouns in their own writing.

PEER EDIT Apply what you know about possessive nouns to verify that your partner has correctly punctuated them. Make sure you've correctly punctuated both singular and plural possessives and not confused possessives with plurals and contractions.

SUM IT UP To make a plural noun possessive, add an apostrophe if the plural noun ends with *s*. If the plural noun does not end with *s*, add an apostrophe and an *s* to the word.

Assess the Learning

- Survey students' writing folders for pieces that include singular and plural possessive nouns. Note error patterns to provide targeted instruction.
- During writing conferences, ask students to point out possessives in their writing. Have them explain how they created the possessives and what those possessives mean.

Link the Learning

- Have students create illustrated posters that show the singular and plural possessive forms of irregular nouns, such as *one goose's egg/ten geese's eggs, the mouse's tail/the mice's tails, the man's car/the men's cars.*
- Encourage students to locate possessive nouns in mentor texts and then sort them—plural possessives and singular possessives.
- Share additional rules for forming possessive nouns:

  If a compound noun shows ownership of the same thing, place an apostrophe and an *s* only after the second noun. For example, in the phrase "Tom and Linda's vacation plans," Tom and Linda both "own" the same vacation plans.

  Individual ownership with a compound noun requires that both nouns have *'s* added. For example, in the phrase "Jake's and Kia's bicycles," Jake and Kia each have a bicycle.

Comma: In a Series

DAY 1 Model the Focus Point

Commas help us separate items in a series or a list. The items can be single words, phrases, or clauses. A *phrase* is a group of words that do not make a sentence on their own, while the group of words creating a *clause* could stand on its own as a sentence. Let's take a close look at using commas in different kinds of series. In my first sentence, I'm listing the materials out of which sedimentary rock can form—sand, shells, and pebbles. Notice that, as I write, I include a comma between each item to separate them from one another. I used the conjunction *and* to connect the items in the list. In my next sentence, I'm writing phrases in a series. Without commas, it would get confusing trying to figure out which words go together! Adding commas between the phrases organizes my thoughts and makes them easier for readers to understand.

> **Modeled Writing Sample**
>
> Sedimentary rock is formed from particles of sand, shells, and pebbles. Sediment is carried through different processes, such as the blowing of wind, the slow movement of glaciers, or the flow of water. Over time, the sediments gather in layers, gradually harden, and turn into rock.

Write the last sentence of the modeled writing.

TURN AND TALK **Partners, carefully reread the last sentence. Explain how I punctuated the sentence and included a conjunction.**

SUM IT UP **We separate items in a series with commas. We usually connect items in series with a coordinating conjunction and include a comma before the conjunction.**

DAY 2 Guided Practice

TURN AND TALK **Apply what you know as you focus on commas. Identify places in The Grassy Savanna in which the writer successfully used commas. Suggest a place in the writing that would benefit from combining items to form a series connected with commas and a conjunction.**

SUM IT UP Display the class editing chart. Add "Use commas to separate words, phrases, and clauses in a series."

Remember, commas separate words, phrases, and clauses in a series. Commas help us organize ideas for readers.

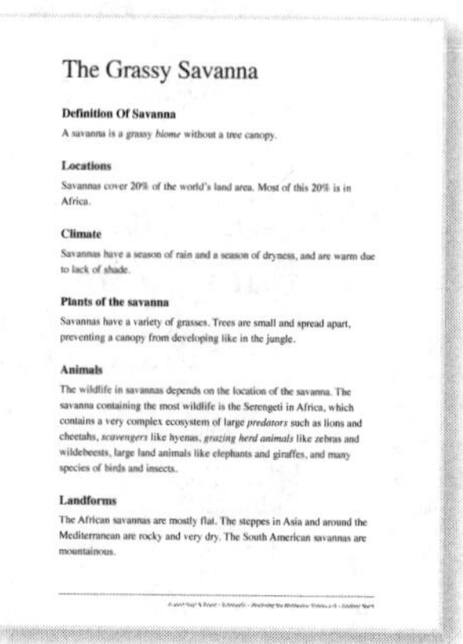

The Grassy Savanna

Definition Of Savanna

A savanna is a *grassy biome* without a tree canopy.

Locations

Savannas cover 20% of the world's land area. Most of this 20% is in Africa.

Climate

Savannas have a season of rain and a season of dryness, and are warm due to lack of shade.

Plants of the savanna

Savannas have a variety of grasses. Trees are small and spread apart, preventing a canopy from developing like in the jungle.

Animals

The wildlife in savannas depends on the location of the savanna. The savanna containing the most wildlife is the Serengeti in Africa, which contains a very complex ecosystem of large *predators* such as lions and cheetahs, *scavengers* like hyenas, *grazing herd animals* like zebras and wildebeests, large land animals like elephants and giraffes, and many species of birds and insects.

Landforms

The African savannas are mostly flat. The steppes in Asia and around the Mediterranean are rocky and very dry. The South American savannas are mountainous.

Resources CD: The Grassy Savanna

DAY 3 Independent Practice

Model how to proofread a piece of text (yours or a student's) for commas in a series. Think aloud as you check that commas are properly inserted to separate items. Think aloud also as you include commas in any items in a series that you combine or add to the text. Then give students time to select a piece of their own writing to proofread and edit for commas in a series.

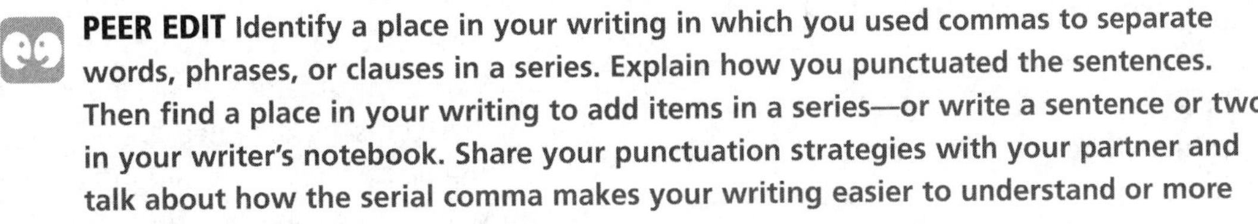

PEER EDIT **Identify a place in your writing in which you used commas to separate words, phrases, or clauses in a series. Explain how you punctuated the sentences. Then find a place in your writing to add items in a series—or write a sentence or two in your writer's notebook. Share your punctuation strategies with your partner and talk about how the serial comma makes your writing easier to understand or more interesting to read.**

SUM IT UP **Words, phrases, and clauses can all be placed in a series in sentences. Place a coordinating conjunction before the last item, and be sure to separate the items with commas.**

Assess the Learning

- Add a space on your Class Record-Keeping Grid (in the Assessment and Record Keeping file on the Resources CD) to note which students have mastered placing commas in series for phrases, clauses, and words. Provide additional instruction as necessary.
- Have students write explanations, telling how to place commas in sentences that include items in a series. Assess explanations for understanding.

Link the Learning

- Extend the lesson by discussing parallelism, a common error in series of phrases and clauses.
- In some writing, students may find the last comma in the series—the comma between the final item and the conjunction—has been omitted. Newspaper style often allows this comma to be omitted for column space, and some writers have adapted this rule. Most style guides, however, advocate keeping that last comma in place to avoid ambiguity.
- Have students use sticky notes to mark sentences in mentor texts that include items in series. They can copy sparkling examples onto sentence strips to display in the room. Have them use highlighters to showcase the commas.

Comma: With Opening Element

DAY 1 Model the Focus Point

I find the story of Amelia Earhart fascinating! Watch as I introduce her to readers: *Amelia Earhart is probably the world's most famous female pilot. She attempted to become the first woman to fly around the world.* As I take a closer look, I realize that flying around the world today is something many people do. But Earhart did it in 1937! Watch as I add an opener, *In 1937*. Notice that I place a comma after the opener. When a sentence begins with an opener—a phrase, subordinate or dependent clause, transition, or prepositional phrase—writers place a comma after the opener to organize ideas for readers and to help them understand the message. When we read aloud, a comma also indicates an organizational pause. Now I am writing a sentence that opens with a dependent clause that starts with the word *When*. The clause functions as an adverb, telling when and where Earhart disappeared. Where am I placing the comma? It comes right before the independent clause, the main part of the sentence.

> **Modeled Writing Sample**
>
> Amelia Earhart is probably the world's most famous female pilot. In 1937, she attempted to become the first woman to fly around the world. When she was 100 miles from a tiny Pacific island, her plane disappeared. Although searchers immediately started looking for her and her navigator, no one ever found a trace of them or their aircraft.

Add a final sentence that includes an opening element that starts with a subordinating conjunction. Share your thinking as you place the comma after the opening element.

TURN AND TALK **Partners, take a look at the sentences with the commas. How do you know that these are not compound sentences?**

SUM IT UP **Introductory phrases and clauses add interest and variety to writing. Be sure to include a comma after the phrase or clause, before the main clause in the sentence.**

DAY 2 Guided Practice

TURN AND TALK **Identify a sentence with an opening element in the piece Transportation. How does the opening element function in the sentence? How did the writer punctuate it? Identify another place in the writing that could be stronger with an opening element. Decide where you would add the opener and what punctuation you would use.**

SUM IT UP To the class editing chart, add "Insert a comma after the opening element in a sentence."

When you write an introductory phrase or clause in a sentence, include a comma after the opener and before the main independent clause.

Transportation

Resources CD: Transportation

DAY 3 Independent Practice

Select a piece of writing from a student's writing folder and share your thinking about the introductory elements you find in that piece. Point out the placement of commas and talk about how the introductory elements function in the sentences. If there are no sentences with opening elements, model how to create them, making sure you add commas to the sentences. Turn over responsibility to students to focus on introductory elements in their own writing.

PEER EDIT **Share your sentences with opening elements to check for correct placement of commas. Then reread and think together:** ***How might this writing benefit from the addition of an introductory phrase or clause?*** **As you identify a place to add an opener, be sure to include a comma between the opener and the sentence.**

SUM IT UP **Opening elements can add important information to sentences, such as** ***who, what, when, where, why,*** **and** ***how many*****. Be sure to include a comma after an introductory element.**

Assess the Learning

- Scan student writing for sentences with opening elements. Note error patterns, such as omitting commas, using independent clauses for openers, and including coordinating conjunctions.
- As you confer with individual students, ask them to point out sentences with openers. Have them explain the thinking behind their inclusion of the opening elements and point out the punctuation they used.

Link the Learning

- Have students collect openers from mentor texts, content area texts, and their own writing to categorize by opener type (dependent clause with subordinating conjunction, prepositional phrase, transitional word).
- Teach students subordinating conjunctions—*although, after, as, when, while, unless, before, because, if, since.* Have them write sample sentences with openers that use these conjunctions. Remind them to include commas after the openers.
- Find sentences with opening elements in mentor texts. Write the dependent phrases and clauses separately from the independent phrases and clauses. Have students identify which are sentences and which are fragments.

Comma: With Closing Element

DAY 1 Model the Focus Point

Closers allow us to add interesting information to sentences. Just as its name implies, a closer ends a sentence. When we add a closer to an independent clause, we use a comma to set it off from the rest of the sentence. I am starting my writing by describing the tundra environment: *Tundra animals. . . .* Now I am adding a sentence about owls: *Snowy owls hunt during the day*. This sentence gives information about snowy owls, but I want to add information about their hunting. Watch as I add a comma and then continue with a closer: *finding prey such as lemmings*. My next sentence will focus on arctic hares: *Arctic hares burrow into the sides of hills.* I am thinking I can add more information about hares, too. Why do they burrow? They burrow to protect themselves from strong winds. Watch as I replace the end of the sentence with a comma and add the closing element: *protecting themselves from strong winds.*

Modeled Writing Sample

Tundra animals thrive in an incredibly harsh, cold environment. Snowy owls hunt during the day, finding prey such as lemmings. Arctic hares burrow into the sides of hills, protecting themselves from strong winds. Musk oxen have coarse hair, their dense undercoats keeping them warm and dry.

Continue modeling, adding a closing element to the first sentence about tundra animals.

TURN AND TALK **Examine the closers in the writing sample and describe their effect on the writing. What kind of information do they add? Restate the rule for punctuating a sentence that includes a closer.**

SUM IT UP **A closer gives detailed information to your readers. Be sure that when you add a closer you precede it with a comma.**

DAY 2 Guided Practice

TURN AND TALK **Discuss the purpose of this piece as you decide what positives you might offer the writer. Then focus on the closers. What information do they add? What punctuation do they include? Explain where else you might add a closer.**

SUM IT UP Display the class editing chart. Add "Insert comma before sentence closers."

A closer can give readers important and detailed information about the independent clause. A closer is set off from the rest of the sentence by a comma.

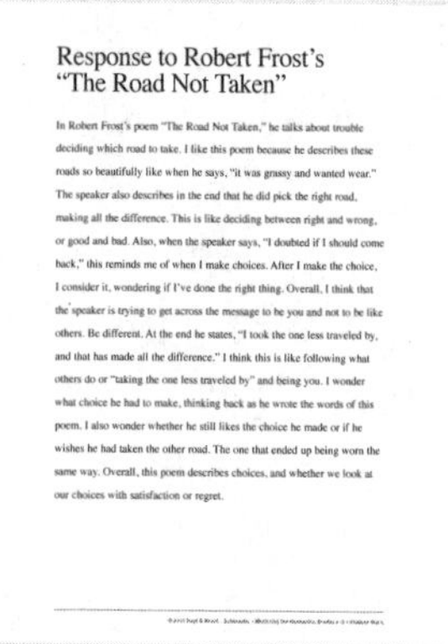

Response to Robert Frost's "The Road Not Taken"

In Robert Frost's poem "The Road Not Taken," he talks about trouble deciding which road to take. I like this poem because he describes these roads so beautifully like when he says, "it was grassy and wanted wear." The speaker also describes in the end that he did pick the right road, making all the difference. This is like deciding between right and wrong, or good and bad. Also, when the speaker says, "I doubted if I should come back," this reminds me of when I make choices. After I make the choice, I consider it, wondering if I've done the right thing. Overall, I think that the speaker is trying to get across the message to be you and not to be like others. Be different. At the end he states, "I took the one less traveled by, and that has made all the difference." I think this is like following what others do or "taking the one less traveled by" and being you. I wonder what choice he had to make, thinking back as he wrote the words of this poem. I also wonder whether he still likes the choice he made or if he wishes he had taken the other road. The one that ended up being worn the same way. Overall, this poem describes choices, and whether we look at our choices with satisfaction or regret.

Resources CD: Response to Robert Frost's "The Road Not Taken"

DAY 3 Independent Practice

Select a sample from a student's writing folder. Share your thinking as you check for commas preceding the closers. Model by finding a place in the writing that could benefit from adding a closer. Then turn the work over to student editors. Remind them that they don't want to add closers to every sentence. Instead, they should strive for a variety of sentence types and lengths.

PEER EDIT Read together, identifying closers and checking to be sure that commas precede them. Apply what you know about closers to suggest a place to add a closer. Be sure that it is correctly punctuated.

SUM IT UP A closer can add sophistication to writing and gives readers additional information. Be sure to insert a comma before you add a closer to a sentence.

Assess the Learning

- Scan student writing for sentences with closers. Check to be sure that students have not overused closers, that they use them to add further information, and that they offset closers with commas.
- Ask individuals to explain the punctuation rules for adding both openers and closers. What is the difference between the two? How are they similar? Assist students who need support.

Link the Learning

- Students might craft sentences with descriptive closers in poems about content area topics, such as habitats, historical events, and so on.
- Have students set aside space in their writer's notebooks to record sentences with powerful openers and closers to use as mentor texts. They can share particularly powerful and descriptive sentences in small groups or by writing them on sentence strips for display. Have them use highlighters to set off the sentence punctuation.
- Give students simple sentences to amp up with descriptive closers. Have them meet in small groups to discuss the information they added and to check for the inclusion of commas before closing elements.

Comma: With Conjunctions in Compound Sentences

DAY 1 Model the Focus Point

Our goal as writers is to convey ideas—but we also want to convey ideas in a way that sounds sophisticated. One way to make our writing more sophisticated is to connect equal ideas by combining independent clauses into compound sentences. We combine the clauses with coordinating conjunctions—*for, and, not, but, or, yet,* and *so*. You can remember them with the acronym FANBOYS. My first two sentences sound kind of short and choppy, and they both tell about kinds of businesses in Illinois. So I am going to connect them with *and—Illinois is a transportation hub, and the state is home to agriculture and industry*. Notice a very important punctuation mark in the sentence—I am placing a comma before the coordinating conjunction.

Modeled Writing Sample

Illinois is a transportation hub. The state is home to agriculture and industry. Settlers came to Illinois in the 1810s. It wasn't until the 1830s that Illinois became a state. Illinois has rich fertile land. John Deere's invention of a steel plow made the prairies of Illinois more valuable than ever.

Continue modeling. Combine the next two sentences with *but* and the last two sentences with *so.* Share your thinking for choosing specific conjunctions (*but* to show contrasting ideas and *so* to show cause and effect), and point out that, each time, you placed a comma before the conjunction.

TURN AND TALK **Partners, take a look at my sentences. Explain the effect of combining sentences with conjunctions. Identify the punctuation and state the rule for using commas to combine sentences with coordinating conjunctions.**

SUM IT UP **To create a compound sentence, combine two independent clauses with a coordinating conjunction. Place a comma before the conjunction in the sentence.**

DAY 2 Guided Practice

TURN AND TALK **Identify compound sentences in this piece. Decide which sentences could benefit from being joined together to create compound sentences. What connecting words would you use? Where would you place commas?**

SUM IT UP Display the class editing chart. Add "Combine two independent clauses with a coordinating conjunction and a comma to make a compound sentence."

Combining independent clauses to make compound sentences shows the relationship between ideas. Be sure to use coordinating conjunctions and precede your conjunctions with commas.

How Does Your Eye Work?

Your eyes seem really complicated, but they actually work in a simple way. It all begins when light rays are reflected off an object and the rays enter the eyes through the outer covering called the cornea. The cornea is kind of like a camera lens. The cornea bends the light rays that then pass through a round hole called the pupil. Behind the pupil, there is a colorless, transparent structure called the crystalline lens. Muscles called ciliary muscles surround the lens. These muscles are very important, because they hold the lens in place and these muscles work to allow you to see things up close and far away. The colored part of your eye, also called the iris, opens and closes to regulate the amount of light passing through. In bright light, the parts in the center of the retina, called cones, provide clear and sharp vision. Another job of the cones is to detect colors and fine details. The retina is a thin layer of tissue at the back of the eye embedded with millions of light sensitive cells. The other parts in the retina are called rods. Rods allow the eyes to detect motion, and they help us see in dim light and at night. Finally, a nerve called the optic nerve sends these impulses to the brain where an image is produced. So, that's how you are able to see things every day!

Resources CD: How Does Your Eye Work?

DAY 3 Independent Practice

Choose a sample from a student's writing folder that includes compound sentences and/or could benefit from sentence combining. Model checking for coordinating conjunctions and commas. Share your thinking as you decide which sentences to combine and which conjunction to use in each case. After modeling, turn responsibility over to student editors.

PEER EDIT Apply what you've learned about compound sentences to connect independent clauses with coordinating conjunctions. Try out different connecting words. Point out places where you successfully created compound sentences. Where did you place the commas?

SUM IT UP Create compound sentences by combining independent clauses with coordinating conjunctions. Place a comma before the conjunction in a compound sentence.

Assess the Learning

- Have students share compound sentences with you, pointing out the two clauses they combined, the conjunction they chose, and the comma. Assess understanding as you confirm that students are connecting sentences and not phrases or dependent clauses.
- Ask students to point out compound sentences in reading selections or content area texts, identifying the independent clauses and the conjunction.

Link the Learning

- Talk with students about comma splices, sentences in which two independent clauses are combined with commas but not with coordinating conjunctions, such as: *Settlers came to Illinois in the 1810s, it wasn't until the 1830s that Illinois became a state.* Writers can fix comma splices by inserting a coordinating conjunction into the sentence or by replacing the comma with a semicolon.
- Be sure that students understand the purposes of the coordinating conjunctions. *And* joins things that are alike or shows a continuation of thought. We use *but* and *yet* to contrast. *Or* shows a choice between two things, while *nor* continues a negative thought. The conjunctions *for* and *so* show cause-and-effect relationships.

Comma: With Nonrestrictive Elements

DAY 1 Model the Focus Point

Writers, for this explanation, I am starting with a sentence that defines *peninsula*: *A peninsula is connected to the mainland by an isthmus.* I wonder if that's enough information for my readers, though. This group of words definitely stands on its own as a sentence, but my readers may not understand my explanation without some additional information. I am adding a phrase that describes peninsulas and another phrase that defines *isthmus*. Notice as I write that I enclose these phrases with commas. These phrases are called nonrestrictive elements. Nonrestrictive elements are not necessary in a sentence, so I am setting off this "extra information" with commas. In my next sentence, I want to include more information about the Italian Peninsula. I start with a complete sentence: *The Italian Peninsula has a unique shape*. Watch as I insert the extra information and enclose it in commas.

Modeled Writing Sample

A peninsula, a piece of land surrounded by water, is connected to the mainland by an *isthmus*, a strip of land. The Italian Peninsula, jutting into three different seas in southern Europe, has a unique shape. Its appearance from above gives it its special nickname, *Lo Stivale* (the boot).

Continue modeling with an additional sentence that includes a nonrestrictive element.

TURN AND TALK Put your heads together as you identify the nonrestrictive element in the last sentence. What does the nonrestrictive element describe or rename? How is the sentence punctuated?

SUM IT UP A nonrestrictive element can add more detail and description to your writing. When you add a nonrestrictive element, set it off with commas.

DAY 2 Guided Practice

Tubas

The sound of a tuba, a large brass instrument, is a warm deep rich sound that is my most favorite sound in this world. The moment I send air through it and I can make it in tune I feel safer than before. I feel loved and like no one can touch me. I know I become invincible when I can play a song like Gustav Holst's First Suite in E-flat for Military Band. The low brasses, the most important instruments in a band, are the foundation for the sound. Being a tuba player I have much control of the volume of the entire band. It is a great feeling. I also get to play the sousaphone which is another version of the tuba that gives you the opportunity to march comfortably. I love running around with it in. You can do so many creative and interesting moves with it that really awes people. Which makes me really happy.

Resources CD: Tubas

TURN AND TALK Think together as you identify a place in Tubas where the writer has included a nonrestrictive element. How can you test that it's nonrestrictive? Then describe a place where you could add another nonrestrictive element. What extra information would it provide? Look for a place where you can rename a noun or give more information that describes it.

SUM IT UP To a class editing chart, add "Frame nonrestrictive elements with commas."

We use nonrestrictive elements to make our writing richer and to include more information for our readers. We frame nonrestrictive elements with commas in our sentences.

DAY 3 Independent Practice

Think aloud as you select a sample from a student's writing folder and consider adding nonrestrictive elements. Model how you check to make sure that commas frame the nonrestrictive elements. Read sentences without such interrupters to be sure the sentences still make sense—that's the true test of whether the additions are truly "nonrestrictive." Next, students can follow your lead as they add nonrestrictive elements to their own work.

PEER EDIT Analyze your work to determine a place you can add a group of words to rename a noun or tell more about it. Check to be sure that you've used the correct punctuation.

SUM IT UP Adding nonrestrictive elements to sentences gives your readers extra information and description. Be sure that you set off nonrestrictive elements with commas.

Assess the Learning

- Have students go through their own writing to highlight sentences that include nonrestrictive elements. Assess their understanding as you examine the sentences.
- As you confer with students individually, ask them to find a place in their writing that would benefit from including a nonrestrictive element. Observe as they add the nonrestrictive element and the punctuation. Provide assistance for those needing extra support.

Link the Learning

- Have students write sentences about content area studies that include nonrestrictive elements. Examples: *Jazz, a music genre that began in the early twentieth century, has roots in both African and European music. Mountains, taller than the land around them, are more plentiful under water than on land! Monsoons, bringing moisture in summer and drought in winter, are unpredictable and severe.*
- Give students simple sentences and ask them to add nonrestrictive elements. Discuss the kinds of information students added.
- Invite students to write character sketches or biographies that include nonrestrictive elements to enhance descriptions.

Dashes

DAY 1 Model the Focus Point

As I write about Apollo 13, a dramatic space mission, I want to add some excitement to the writing. I am writing about the explosion on board the craft: *On April 13, an explosion on board put the entire crew in danger*. I want to add some more drama and excitement to this sentence. The astronauts were in space for just two days when this catastrophe struck. So I am adding that phrase—*just two days after the launch*—to the middle of the sentence. Notice the punctuation I used around the phrase. I could have used commas and the punctuation would have been correct. But, instead, I used dashes. We use dashes to set off information in a sentence when we want to create real emphasis or dramatic flair. In this sentence, the dashes set off information in the middle. My idea for the next sentence is to show the drama of all the things that went wrong, so watch as I include a dash that gives the reader a dramatic pause: *The crew faced....* Dashes can indicate a list as well as an interrupter.

> **Modeled Writing Sample**
>
> The spacecraft Apollo 13 launched in April 1970. On April 13—just two days after the launch—an explosion on board put the entire crew in danger. The crew faced many hazards—a lack of power, freezing temperature in the cabin, a shortage of water, and an overabundance of carbon dioxide that made it hard to breathe. After a nail-biting four days in space, the astronauts returned safely to Earth on April 17. Many called the mission a "successful failure."

TURN AND TALK **Partners, take a look at my writing as you evaluate the effect of using dashes. Explain the effect of using a dash rather than using commas to set off a nonrestrictive element or, conversely, using a dash rather than a colon to set off a list.**

SUM IT UP **Dashes are best used sparingly—but they are great for dramatic effect! You can use dashes to set off nonrestrictive elements, lists, openers, and closers. Just be sure to use them when you want to emphasize the content that follows the dash.**

DAY 2 Guided Practice

TURN AND TALK **Explain what the writer set off with dashes in Goals. Evaluate the dashes' effect. Can you think of another place where dashes can be used to set aside a nonrestrictive element—with drama and excitement?**

SUM IT UP Display the class editing chart. Add "Use dashes to set off information in a sentence with drama and excitement."

Dashes, when used sparingly, can add interest to your writing. Use dashes to set off information in your writing or to introduce a list.

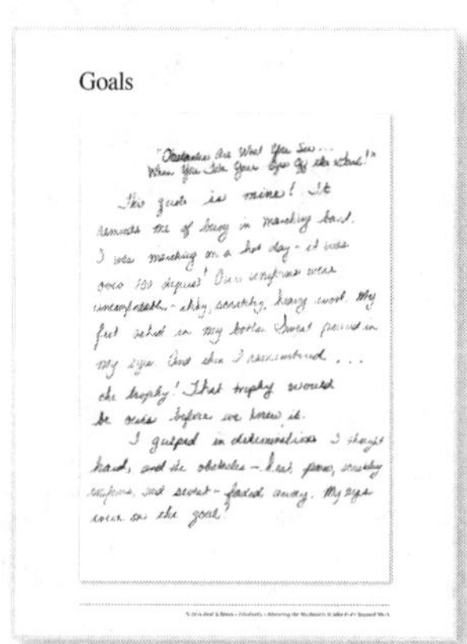
Goals

Resources CD: Goals

DAY 3 Independent Practice

Select a sample from a writing folder that includes dashes or one that might benefit from their addition. Think aloud as you proofread for dashes or as you add them to the piece. Be sure your think-aloud includes making a choice between dashes and commas (or a colon). Then turn responsibility over to student editors.

PEER EDIT Think together as you pinpoint a sentence that might benefit from the addition of dashes. How will the dashes affect the writing? What do you need to remember about using them?

SUM IT UP Using dashes can add a touch of dramatic excitement to your writing. Dashes can set off information in a sentence or introduce a list. Be sure not to overuse them, though.

Assess the Learning

- Collect students' writing folders to look for dashes. Note patterns of errors—not using dashes at all, overusing dashes, and mixing dashes with commas. Provide additional instruction as needed.
- During writing conferences, ask students to note places where they might use dashes for dramatic effect.

Link the Learning

- Hyphens join words and mark separate syllables. In electronic text, tell students to type two hyphens to create a dash.
- Have students create tables in their writer's notebooks to record sentences with dashes. Have them categorize—sentences in which the dash sets off an opener, sentences in which the dash sets off a closer, sentences in which the dash sets off a list, and sentences in which dashes set off an interrupter.
- Provide students sentences with commas that set off nonrestrictive elements and colons that indicate lists. Have students work in small groups to determine in which sentences it would be appropriate to replace those punctuation marks with dashes.
- Examine with students the use of dashes in a text such as Lincoln's Gettysburg Address.

Colons and Semicolons

DAY 1 Model the Focus Point

Modeled Writing Sample

There are six simple machines that make work easier: lever, inclined plane, wheel and axle, screw, wedge, and pulley. Simple machines have few or no moving parts; they use energy to work.

As I write about simple machines, I want to list all six types. I am starting with a sentence: *There are six simple machines....* I am creating a list in a sentence, so I am using a special punctuation mark, a colon. A colon is two dots with one dot above the other. Notice that the colon comes at the end of a complete sentence—the group of words before it could stand on their own as a sentence. I am including the colon to start a list. The colon is almost like a pause. It tells the reader, "Pay attention, here comes the list!" A colon can introduce a list, a summary, or a new idea. Here, I'm writing the names of the machines: *lever, inclined plane....* Watch as I continue: *Simple machines have few or no moving parts. They use energy to work.* I'd like to combine these sentences to include variety and make my writing sound fluent. But I do not want to include a coordinating conjunction here. Instead, I'm using a semicolon, a comma-shaped mark with a dot over it. A semicolon can join two sentences without using a coordinating conjunction. We also use semicolons to separate items in a series if some of the items contain commas.

TURN AND TALK Partners, think of another sentence in which you would use a colon. What about a semicolon? Explain the rule for using each type of punctuation.

SUM IT UP Use a colon to introduce a list, a summary, or a new idea in a sentence. Use a semicolon to join two independent clauses or to separate items in a series.

DAY 2 Guided Practice

TURN AND TALK Take a look through the writing for colons and semicolons. Explain how you know they are used correctly. If the piece does not contain either of these punctuation marks, identify a place where you can introduce a summary, an idea, or a list with a colon. Identify a place where you might combine two sentences with a semicolon.

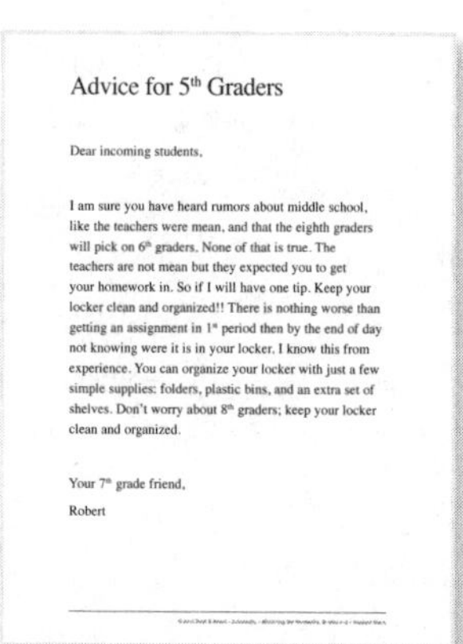
Advice for 5th Graders

Dear incoming students,

I am sure you have heard rumors about middle school, like the teachers were mean, and that the eighth graders will pick on 6th graders. None of that is true. The teachers are not mean but they expected you to get your homework in. So if I will have one tip. Keep your locker clean and organized!! There is nothing worse than getting an assignment in 1st period then by the end of day not knowing were it is in your locker. I know this from experience. You can organize your locker with just a few simple supplies: folders, plastic bins, and an extra set of shelves. Don't worry about 8th graders; keep your locker clean and organized.

Your 7th grade friend,

Robert

Resources CD: Advice for 5th Graders

SUM IT UP Display the class editing chart. Add "Use colons to introduce ideas, lists, and summaries. Use semicolons to join independent clauses."

Colons cue readers to watch for a list or a summary or a new idea. Semicolons combine sentences without coordinate conjunctions.

DAY 3 Independent Practice

Look through a student's writing folder and identify a piece of writing that includes colons or semicolons. Showcase your thinking as you proofread for correct use of these punctuation marks and as you add a colon and a semicolon to your writing. Then turn work over to student editors.

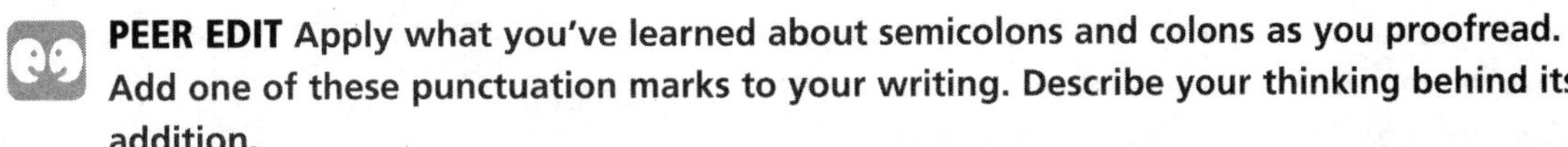

PEER EDIT Apply what you've learned about semicolons and colons as you proofread. Add one of these punctuation marks to your writing. Describe your thinking behind its addition.

SUM IT UP A colon cues the reader to pause and then pay attention to what's coming next: a list, a summary, or a new idea. A semicolon can join two independent clauses, and you can you leave out the coordinating conjunction. Semicolons are great fixes for comma splices!

Assess the Learning

- Collect writing samples and scan for semicolons and colons. Chart error patterns for future instruction and plan to engage students in using these punctuation marks.
- Ask students to mark passages in mentor texts or content area textbooks that include semicolons and colons. Listen in to their explanations of how these punctuation marks are used.

Link the Learning

- Reinforce the use of semicolons in lists, such as *On our trip, we visited the following cities: Traverse City, Michigan; Minocqua, Wisconsin; and St. Paul, Minnesota.*
- Semicolons are often used in sentences with the transitions *in addition, however, otherwise,* and *therefore,* such as: *Our dog Butch fetched a Frisbee from the creek; in addition, he dragged out a lot of sand and mud! Renee studied hard for her exam; therefore, she expects that she'll receive a high grade.*
- Introduce other uses of colons, such as in greetings of business letters (*Dear Mr. Adams: To Whom It May Concern:*), to separate hour and minutes in a time notation (*12:15 P.M.*), and to introduce a quotation.

Underlining and Quotation Marks

DAY 1 Model the Focus Point

Writers, I've started a response to an article I read in a magazine: *The Known World is a great article in Muse magazine*. I know that I need to set off titles with special punctuation so that my readers will understand that I am talking about pieces of text. "The Known World" is a short article. Short articles and chapter titles need to be enclosed with quotation marks. We've used quotation marks in the past to enclose the exact words of speakers, but this is another way to use this punctuation mark. What about the title of the magazine? If I were typing with a word processor, I'd put the title in italics. But I know there's no way to do that in my handwriting. So I underline the title—underlining is the same as using italics in handwriting. Writers underline the titles of all longer pieces of text—magazines, nonfiction books, novels, long poems, and so on.

> **Modeled Writing Sample**
>
> "The Known World" is a great article in <u>Muse</u> magazine! It explains how scientists name new discoveries. I've always wondered how each animal gets its name. Some of them are so unusual!
>
> I found <u>Math Mania</u> a repeat of information I already know. The only new information was in Chapter 6, "Easy Tricks for Turning Decimals Into Fractions."

Write the beginning of another response (see second paragraph) for students to analyze.

TURN AND TALK **Partners, take a look at the beginning of my second response. Analyze the response using what you know about underlining and quotation marks. What can you tell about *Math Mania* and *Easy Tricks for Turning Fractions Into Decimals*?**

SUM IT UP **Use quotation marks to enclose the titles of short works or parts of short works. Underline the titles of longer texts, such as books and magazines.**

DAY 2 Guided Practice

TURN AND TALK **Take a close look at Character Sketch: Ponyboy, scanning for titles. What titles do you see in the text? Are they punctuated correctly? Explain how you know.**

SUM IT UP To the class editing chart, add "Use quotation marks for titles of short texts; underline titles of long texts."

When you write the title of a text, think about its length. The title of a book chapter, for example, should be in quotation marks, while the title of an entire book should be underlined. Using these punctuation marks clarifies information for our readers.

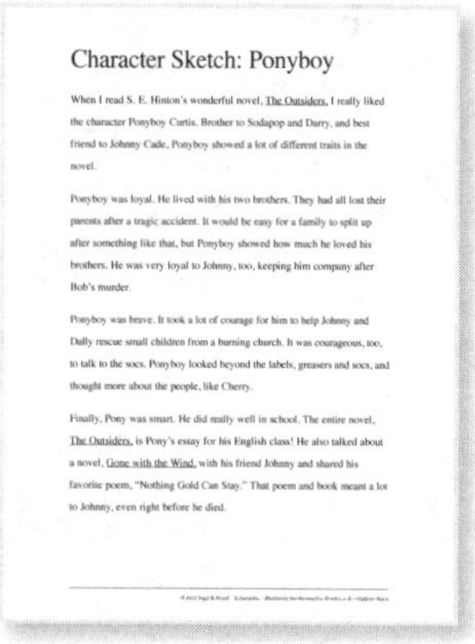

> Character Sketch: Ponyboy
>
> When I read S. E. Hinton's wonderful novel, <u>The Outsiders</u>, I really liked the character Ponyboy Curtis. Brother to Sodapop and Darry, and best friend to Johnny Cade, Ponyboy showed a lot of different traits in the novel.
>
> Ponyboy was loyal. He lived with his two brothers. They had all lost their parents after a tragic accident. It would be easy for a family to split up after something like that, but Ponyboy showed how much he loved his brothers. He was very loyal to Johnny, too, keeping him company after Bob's murder.
>
> Ponyboy was brave. It took a lot of courage for him to help Johnny and Dally rescue small children from a burning church. It was courageous, too, to talk to the socs. Ponyboy looked beyond the labels, greasers and socs, and thought more about the people, like Cherry.
>
> Finally, Pony was smart. He did really well in school. The entire novel, <u>The Outsiders</u>, is Pony's essay for his English class! He also talked about a novel, <u>Gone with the Wind</u>, with his friend Johnny and shared his favorite poem, "Nothing Gold Can Stay." That poem and book meant a lot to Johnny, even right before he died.

Resources CD: Character Sketch: Ponyboy

DAY 3 Independent Practice

Select a piece of writing from a student's writing folder and model editing for correct use of quotation marks and underlining with titles. Students may become confused when examining quotation marks, as they use them also to enclose direct quotations from speakers. Once you have shared your thinking as you edit, allow students to scan for pieces that might benefit from a closer look at quotation marks and underlining.

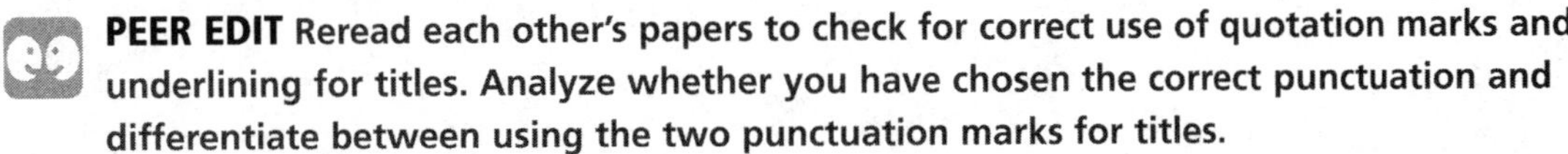

PEER EDIT Reread each other's papers to check for correct use of quotation marks and underlining for titles. Analyze whether you have chosen the correct punctuation and differentiate between using the two punctuation marks for titles.

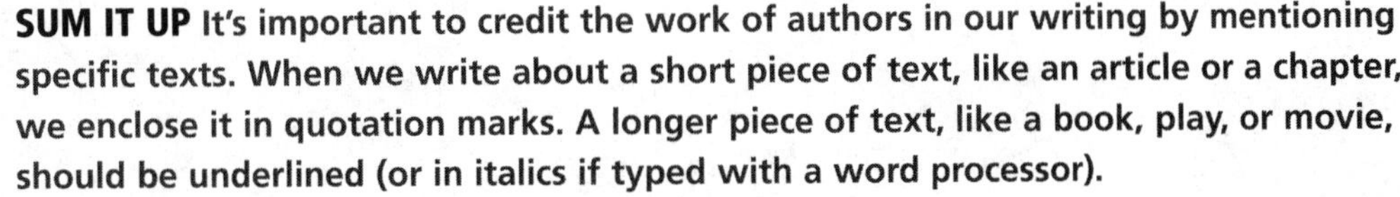

SUM IT UP It's important to credit the work of authors in our writing by mentioning specific texts. When we write about a short piece of text, like an article or a chapter, we enclose it in quotation marks. A longer piece of text, like a book, play, or movie, should be underlined (or in italics if typed with a word processor).

Assess the Learning

- Show students a "works cited" page from an informational report. Ask them to use the punctuation marks to determine which of the works are short pieces of text and which are longer works.
- Scan student writing for punctuation of titles. Note error patterns as you plan small-group instruction.

Link the Learning

- Titles are important in works cited pages. When students write informational reports, make sure they create lists of works cited and include correct punctuation. See the Guide to Works Cited (in the Tools file on the Resources CD) for additional assistance.
- Have students list titles of books, articles, essays, and so on that they have read in a response log. Be sure that students not only craft rich responses, but that they also correctly punctuate the titles of the works they've examined.

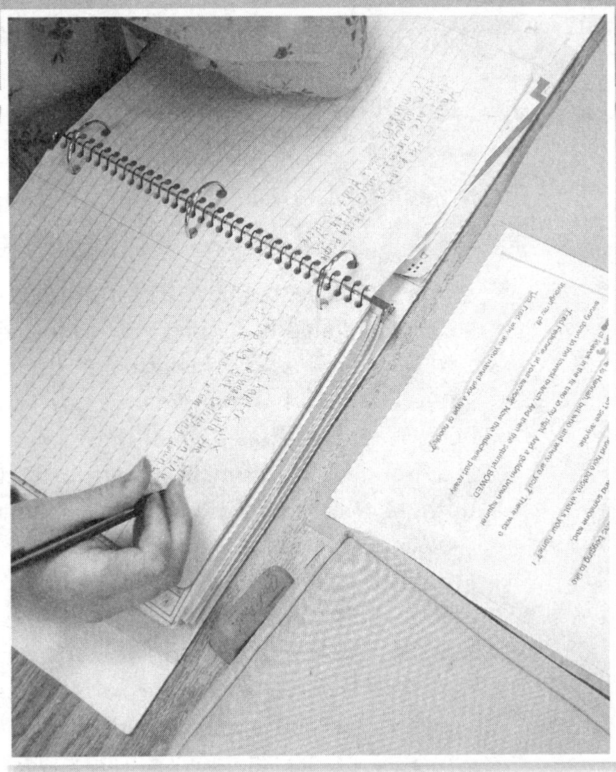

Cycles for Success With Sentence Structure

Of utmost important in the writing toolbox of our middle school writers is the ability to craft sophisticated sentences. While younger writers might strive to be sure that every sentence has a subject and a verb, writers further along in their development focus on sentence fluency and variety. They learn that punctuating groups of long sentences with short sentences in a text heightens drama and interest. They look for ways to combine ideas in sentences to eliminate repetition and redundancy and to make the writing flow for their readers. Sophisticated writers use fragments sparingly and deliberately.

As teachers, it's important to model a variety of strategies to combine sentences:

- combine smaller related sentences into compound sentences using conjunctions
- embed an adjective, adverb, or clause within a sentence
- make multiple embeddings with adjectives, adverbs, and adverbial clauses

Recent studies support the notion that teaching adolescents how to write increasingly complex sentences enhances the overall quality of their writing.

Cycles for Success With Sentence Structure

Complete Sentences and Fragments

DAY 1 Model the Focus Point

Display the modeled writing sample, maintaining the fragments.

> **Modeled Writing Sample**
>
> I read a great book—*Bud, Not Buddy* by Christopher Paul Curtis. During the Great Depression. Ten-year-old Bud Caldwell lives in an orphanage in Flint, Michigan. Escapes from an abusive foster family. Bud sets out on an adventure to find his father. He doesn't find what he expects, but he does find a family!

Complete sentences have at least two parts—a subject and a verb. A great way to find them is to ask, *Who or what did something?* That tells the subject. Then ask, *What did they do?* That tells the verb. A sentence has both of these parts. A fragment is a group of words missing the subject, verb, or both. My first group of words in my summary is *I read.....* Let's check for a subject. Who did something? I did! Now let's look for a verb. What did I do? I read a book. This group of words is a sentence. Now let's look at the second group of words. Who or what did something? What did they do? I can't find either one of these parts in this group of words! It's obviously a fragment. I need to fix the fragment by making it into a sentence or attaching it to another one. I didn't read the book during the Great Depression, so it wouldn't make sense to combine it with the first sentence! The story takes place during the Great Depression. So I'll add the information from the fragment to the next sentence: *Ten-year-old Bud Caldwell lives in an orphanage in Flint, Michigan, during the Great Depression*.

TURN AND TALK Partners, take a look at my writing as you check for sentences and fragments. Explain how you can tell the difference. Then suggest a way to correct any fragments in the writing.

Be sure that students understand the fragment *Escapes from*. . . is missing a subject. Writers can fix the fragment by adding the "who," or the subject, of the sentence.

SUM IT UP A sentence requires two parts—a subject and a verb. If you have a fragment, add the missing part or parts or combine the fragment with another sentence.

DAY 2 Guided Practice

TURN AND TALK Talk about the content in Tubas before you identify any fragments. Discuss how you might turn those fragments into sentences or combine them with other groups of words.

SUM IT UP Display the class editing chart. Add "Complete sentence = subject + verb."

A complete sentence answers two questions: *Who or what did something? What did they do?* A group of words that does not answer both or either of these questions is a fragment. Fragments are usually undesirable in our writing.

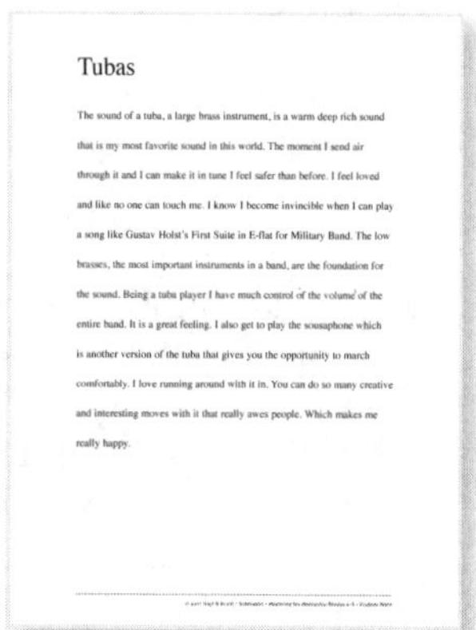

Tubas

The sound of a tuba, a large brass instrument, is a warm deep rich sound that is my most favorite sound in this world. The moment I send air through it and I can make it in tune I feel safer than before. I feel loved and like no one can touch me. I know I become invincible when I can play a song like Gustav Holst's First Suite in E-flat for Military Band. The low brasses, the most important instruments in a band, are the foundation for the sound. Being a tuba player I have much control of the volume of the entire band. It is a great feeling. I also get to play the sousaphone which is another version of the tuba that gives you the opportunity to march comfortably. I love running around with it in. You can do so many creative and interesting moves with it that really awes people. Which makes me really happy.

Resources CD: Tubas

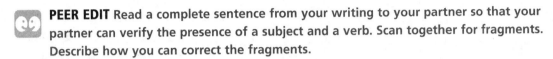

DAY 3 Independent Practice

Select a writing sample from a student's writing folder. Share your thinking as you check that groups of words are sentences rather than fragments. Model fixing fragments by adding missing parts or by combining fragments with other sentences or fragments. Have students select pages from their own writer's notebooks to review for complete sentences.

PEER EDIT Read a complete sentence from your writing to your partner so that your partner can verify the presence of a subject and a verb. Scan together for fragments. Describe how you can correct the fragments.

SUM IT UP A complete sentence has two parts: a subject and a verb. The subject tells the "who" of the sentence, while the verb tells what the subject does or did. If you have only one of these parts—or neither of them—the group of words is a fragment.

Assess the Learning

- Have students use an Editing Checklist (in the Assessment and Record Keeping file on the Resources CD) and check for the presence of complete sentences. Observe students' checklists to see which students need additional help with the strategy.
- During individual writing conferences, show students fragments and ask them to identify what parts are missing. Challenge them to add information to create sentences.

Link the Learning

- Have students flag interesting and descriptive sentences that they find in mentor texts. Share sentences that sparkle! Partners can identify the subjects and verbs.
- Provide sentences that include dependent clauses, prepositional phrases, opening and closing elements, and so on. Challenge students to pare the sentences down to simple subject and verb.
- Explain that some sentences can be made up of only two words—and still be complete sentences! Save a spot on your wall for students to post powerful two-word sentences they find in mentor texts. Share an example first, such as these sentences from Nancy Farmer's *House of the Scorpion:* "Matt winces." "Maria flinched." "Matt froze." Discuss the effect of these two-word sentences on the writing.

Compound Sentences With Coordinating Conjunctions

DAY 1 Model the Focus Point

Before the lesson, write the coordinating conjunctions—*for, and, nor, but, or, yet, so*—on a chart to display for student reference.

> **I strive for sentence variety to keep my readers engaged in my messages. One way to add variety to writing is to think carefully about the structure of my sentences and vary structures as I write. Watch as I write about a wonderful wintry day with the goal of combining some of my sentences to add variety. I'm writing two statements: *The snow and the wind had sculpted some amazing hills in the front yard. I couldn't wait to sled down them.* I stop to check that both of these groups of words are sentences. Since they both have subjects and verbs, I'm confident they're complete sentences. But I'm thinking about combining them to vary my writing a bit. I'm choosing *and* as a conjunction, because the ideas are related to each other. If they were different, I might choose *but*. Watch as I combine them with a comma and the coordinating conjunction *and: The snow and the wind....* Notice I'm placing the comma *before* the coordinating conjunction.**

Modeled Writing Sample

The snow and the wind had sculpted some amazing hills in the front yard, and I couldn't wait to sled down them! I tramped out to the garage to retrieve my sled, but I discovered that the snow had covered the garage door. Shoveling had to come before sledding!

Continue modeling, highlighting your thinking as you deliberately choose the conjunction *but* to show a contrasting relationship—*I tramped out to the garage to retrieve my sled,* but *I discovered that the snow had covered the garage door.*

TURN AND TALK **Partners, describe the effect of combining independent clauses to create compound sentences. What does this do to your writing?**

SUM IT UP **Connect two independent clauses with a coordinating conjunction to form a compound sentence. Double-check that you've chosen a coordinating conjunction that makes sense in the sentence, and be sure to place a comma before the conjunction.**

DAY 2 Guided Practice

TURN AND TALK **Writers, take a close look at the sentences in The Stanley Cup. What sentences could you combine to add variety to your sentence structures? What coordinating conjunction would you use? Explain why.**

SUM IT UP Display the class editing chart. Add "Combine independent clauses to make compound sentences."

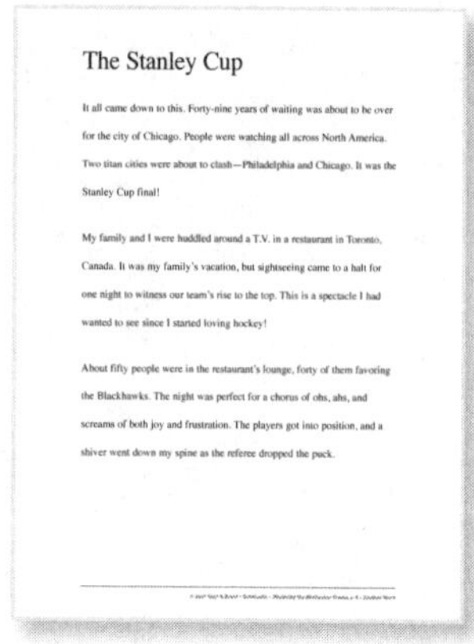

The Stanley Cup

It all came down to this. Forty-nine years of waiting was about to be over for the city of Chicago. People were watching all across North America. Two titan cities were about to clash—Philadelphia and Chicago. It was the Stanley Cup final!

My family and I were huddled around a T.V. in a restaurant in Toronto, Canada. It was my family's vacation, but sightseeing came to a halt for one night to witness our team's rise to the top. This is a spectacle I had wanted to see since I started loving hockey!

About fifty people were in the restaurant's lounge, forty of them favoring the Blackhawks. The night was perfect for a chorus of ohs, ahs, and screams of both joy and frustration. The players got into position, and a shiver went down my spine as the referee dropped the puck.

Resources CD: The Stanley Cup

Compound sentences are tools for changing up the structures of our sentences and adding variety to our writing. We don't want to combine *every* sentence. We need to think carefully about how combining sentences enhances our messages and which coordinating conjunction best suits the meaning.

DAY 3 Independent Practice

Select a piece of writing from a student folder that would benefit from thoughtful sentence combining. Think aloud as you look for opportunities to combine independent clauses, choosing a coordinating conjunction that matches the meaning. Then turn responsibility over to student editors to combine sentences in meaningful ways.

PEER EDIT Apply what you've learned to identify a place where you can combine sentences. Consider what coordinating conjunction will work best to show the relationship between the ideas.

SUM IT UP Compound sentences add interest and variety to our writing while also showing the relationship between ideas. Be sure to think carefully about which coordinating conjunction to use to enhance meaning.

Assess the Learning

- Look through students' writing folders for evidence of powerful sentence construction with compound sentences. Note those students who combine sentences but don't use conjunctions that make sense with the message.
- Show students a passage from a mentor text and ask which sentences they might combine to add variety in sentence structure. Which conjunction would they use? Why?

Link the Learning

- Remind students that they can also combine sentences by placing a semicolon between independent clauses. Provide practice with semicolons.
- Provide compound sentences in which punctuation is missing and ask students to explain their thinking behind adding commas and/or semicolons.
- Be sure students know that commas only belong before coordinating conjunctions when they are used to join two independent clauses or when they connect the last item in a series.

Introductory Elements

DAY 1 Model the Focus Point

My goal as I write an explanation today is to add variety to my sentence structures and give specific information by including opening elements. I want my readers to visualize this sport as they read, so watch as I write *If you see someone vaulting. . . .* My opening phrase is adverbial—adverbs tell how, when, where, why, to what extent, or under what conditions. The word *if* is a signal that I'm telling "under what conditions." Before I continue with the independent clause, I place a comma after the opener. I'm telling my readers that athletes who do *parkour* are called *traceurs*. Now I want to describe traceurs. Watch as I include an opening element that adds descriptive details: *Gracefully leaping over. . . .* Just like in my first sentence, I'm placing a comma before the independent clause to set aside the opening element.

> **Modeled Writing Sample**
>
> If you see someone vaulting over walls or jumping over park benches, you may be witnessing a thrilling sport called *parkour*. Parkour athletes are called *traceurs*. Gracefully leaping over obstacles in their paths, traceurs display amazing athleticism as they carry out their goal—to move forward. In moves called speed vaults, traceurs launch themselves over walls without slowing down.

Continue modeling, writing the final sentence that includes an opening element and a comma.

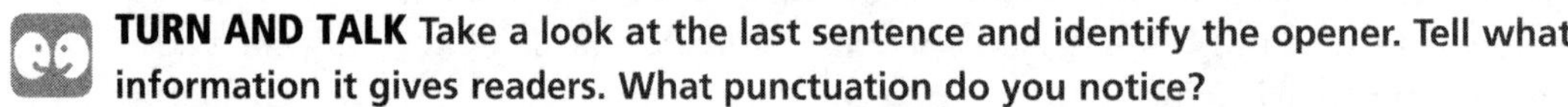

TURN AND TALK Take a look at the last sentence and identify the opener. Tell what information it gives readers. What punctuation do you notice?

SUM IT UP Creating sentences with openers adds variety to writing as well as exciting information and descriptions. When you add an opener, be sure to follow it with a comma to set it aside from the independent clause.

DAY 2 Guided Practice

TURN AND TALK Talk about the content of I Should Have Listened and then identify an opener and explain what information this opener adds to the sentence. Can you find a place where an opener would add variety in sentence structure while offering specific information for readers?

SUM IT UP To the class editing chart, add "Include openers to add variety to sentences. Openers are often followed by commas."

Openers create variety in sentence structure and add valuable information, helping your readers visualize or giving information such as how, when, where, why, to what extent, or under what conditions.

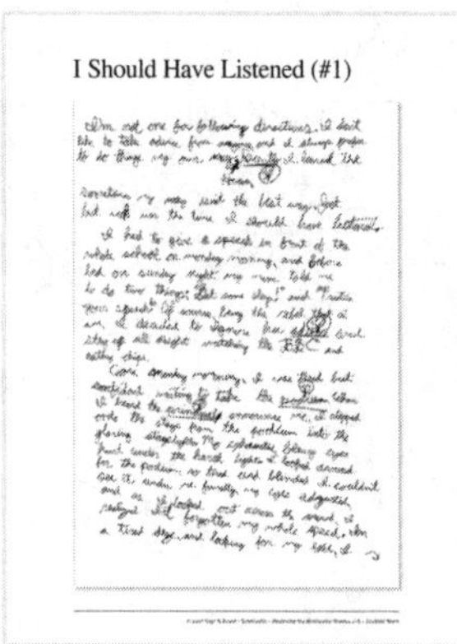
I Should Have Listened (#1)

Resources CD: I Should Have Listened

DAY 3 Independent Practice

Have students search through their writing folders for sentences that they can enhance with openers. Allow a few minutes for proofreading and editing.

PEER EDIT **Apply what you've learned about openers to offer your partner a suggestion for adding an opener. Explain how to punctuate it. What kind of information would this opener give readers?**

SUM IT UP **Sentences with openers help create sentence variety while also offering powerful descriptions that engage readers in your message. Remember to follow openers with commas.**

Assess the Learning

- Survey student writing to determine which writers understand how to create sentences with openers. For those who are using these sophisticated sentence structures, check to be sure they are not overusing them. Provide additional support for students who need it.
- As you observe writers at work, ask them to share their thinking about openers they are adding to their writing. What kind of information are they trying to convey? How do the openers help their readers? Check for punctuation as well.

Link the Learning

- Point out to students that, while many adverbs end in *ly,* not all words that end in *ly* are adverbs (e.g., *lovely, lonely, friendly,* and so on).
- Help students understand that adverbs and adverbial phrases can modify both verbs and adjectives.

  Manner: The dog moved <u>quickly</u> and barked <u>loudly</u>.

  Place: I've lived <u>in this city</u> for years. My best friend lives <u>here,</u> too.

  Frequency: Mia <u>often</u> studies at the library. She tries to read <u>every day.</u>

  Time: Be sure that you're back <u>before dark.</u> Don't worry—I'm on my way <u>now.</u>

  Purpose: We drove slowly <u>to look for our lost dog.</u> He left our yard <u>to chase a butterfly.</u>
- Provide students with copies of Create Your Own Resource: Understanding Adverbs and Prepositional Phrases (in the Tools file on the Resources CD) and have students add it to their writer's notebooks, adding adverbs throughout the year.

Closing Elements

DAY 1 Model the Focus Point

Modeled Writing Sample

Bright stars shone, piercing the darkness. The radio's song blared, its tune matching the rhythm of the road. We were a long way from our destination, but I didn't mind. Nighttime is my favorite time in a car, cocooned in safety from the fast-paced world.

Varying the structures of our sentences is a sure-fire way to add variety to our writing and make our sentences engaging. Watch today as I write a description of a trip with a very specific goal: to add at least one closer to make my sentences more interesting. I'm describing the scene around my car: *Bright stars shone*. I want to help my readers visualize the brightness of the stars, so watch as I add a closer: *piercing the darkness.* Notice that when I add the closer, I first replace the period with a comma. See what a great effect that closer has? It describes how bright those stars are. I'm continuing my description: *The radio's song blared.* Again, I am thinking: *How can I make this scene come to life for my readers?* I don't want to add closers to every single sentence in my writing, but this is a great place to add one. First the comma, then the closer: *its tune matching. . . .* Now I can really picture this scene, a loud and rhythmic song matching our driving.

Continue writing, thinking aloud as you deliberately decide to include a compound sentence before another sentence with a closer. Be sure students understand that writers don't want to add closers to every sentence—closers have impact when they are strategically placed in the text.

TURN AND TALK Partners, think together about the closer in my last sentence. What information does it add to the sentence? What do you notice about the punctuation?

SUM IT UP Sentence closers add more information, such as sensory details. Add closers to sentences that could benefit from further description.

DAY 2 Guided Practice

TURN AND TALK Think together about this piece. focusing on closers. What sentence do you think might benefit from the addition of a closer? What information would the closer give to readers?

SUM IT UP Display the class editing chart. Add "Add closers to sentences to give additional information."

A closer adds information, often sensory details that help readers visualize. Before adding a closer to an independent clause, change the period to a comma.

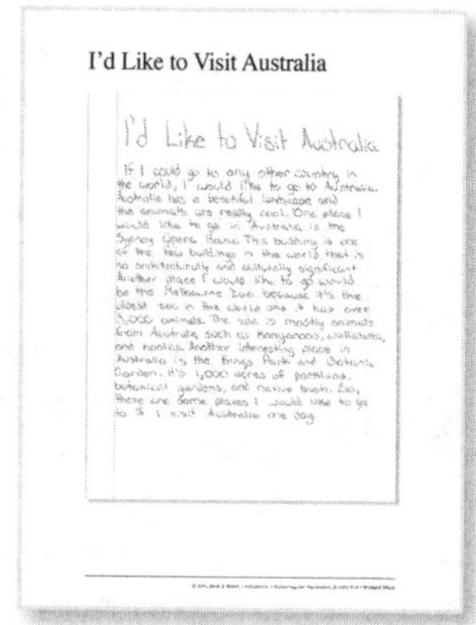
I'd Like to Visit Australia

I'd Like to Visit Australia

Resources CD: I'd Like to Visit Australia

DAY 3 Independent Practice

Locate a student writing sample that includes closers or would benefit from their addition. As you think aloud, focus on why you are adding a closer. Have students search through notebooks and writing folders for writing they can enhance with closers.

PEER EDIT Point out a place in your partner's writing where you might add a closer. What information would the closer include? How would adding the closer increase sentence variety?

SUM IT UP Closers allow you to include more information or sensory details. Place a comma before a closer.

Assess the Learning

- Notice which students have not attempted to add closers. Also, note those who have incorrectly punctuated closers. Assist those who need instruction.
- Ask students to point out closers in their writing. What guided their decision to add closers to those particular sentences? What information do those closers add?

Link the Learning

- Teach students to use absolutes as closers:

  The cat was stretching on the carpet. Its claws were extended./The cat was stretching on the carpet, its claws extended. (combining by removing the be verb in the second sentence)

  Kerry watched the scary move. Kerry was too nervous to open her eyes!/Kerry watched the scary movie, too nervous to open her eyes. (combing by removing the double subject and the be verb)

  Juan rocketed down the water slide. He was splashing and yelling./Juan rocketed down the water slide, splashing and yelling. (combining by turning the verbs into absolutes)

- Invite students to write character sketches or descriptions of family members. Encourage them to use sentence closers to add detail to their descriptions.

Interrupters

DAY 1 Model the Focus Point

> **Modeled Writing Sample**
>
> Fossa, cat-like mammals, live in Madagascar. They have cougar-like bodies, but their heads resemble those of the mongoose. Their tails, as long as their bodies, allow them to hang from tree limbs. Their *pelage*, or fur, is short, straight, and dense.

I want to make sure my readers understand the content of my writing. I am writing a description of an interesting animal called a fossa (FOSS-uh). My first sentence is: *Fossa live in Madagascar.* I am thinking that my readers need to know a bit more information, because many of them probably have no idea what a fossa is! So watch as I add an interrupter: *Fossa, cat-like mammals. . . .* What a big difference this will make for my readers' understanding! Now my readers will have some background information about what fossa are. I am continuing my description first by telling how they look and then focusing on their unique tails: *Their tails allow them to hang from tree limbs.* This is pretty fascinating information, but watch as I add another interrupter that will give readers more information about the animals' tails: *Their tails, as long as. . . .* Notice that each time I add an interrupter, I'm enclosing that interrupter with commas.

Continue modeling, thinking aloud as you deliberately place an interrupter to define a term, *pelage,* that readers may not know.

TURN AND TALK **Writers, think together about the interrupters I added to the explanation. What information do they give writers? What effect do they have on the structure of sentences?**

SUM IT UP **An interrupter can give valuable information, definitions, or descriptions to our readers. Be sure to enclose interrupters with commas.**

DAY 2 Guided Practice

TURN AND TALK **Writers, think together as you look for evidence of interrupters in this piece. What interrupters did the writer use? What was the effect on your understanding? Where else in this writing might you add an interrupter to beef up sentence variety and add essential information?**

SUM IT UP To a class editing chart, add "Include interrupters to add information and descriptions."

An interrupter is not only a great way to vary sentence structure—it may also add information or description that help your readers better understand your message.

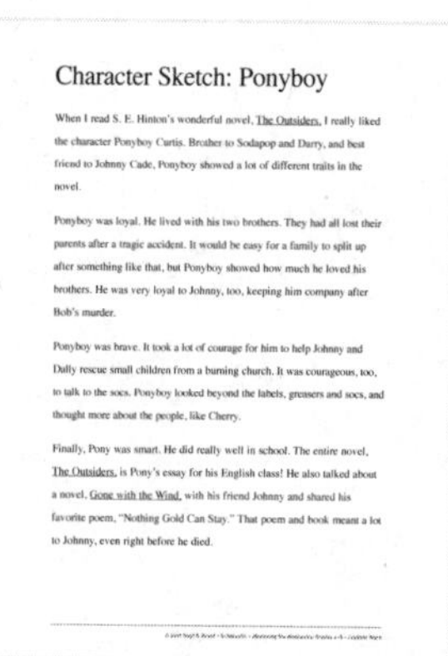
Character Sketch: Ponyboy

When I read S. E. Hinton's wonderful novel, The Outsiders, I really liked the character Ponyboy Curtis. Brother to Sodapop and Darry, and best friend to Johnny Cade, Ponyboy showed a lot of different traits in the novel.

Ponyboy was loyal. He lived with his two brothers. They had all lost their parents after a tragic accident. It would be easy for a family to split up after something like that, but Ponyboy showed how much he loved his brothers. He was very loyal to Johnny, too, keeping him company after Bob's murder.

Ponyboy was brave. It took a lot of courage for him to help Johnny and Dally rescue small children from a burning church. It was courageous, too, to talk to the socs. Ponyboy looked beyond the labels, greasers and socs, and thought more about the people, like Cherry.

Finally, Pony was smart. He did really well in school. The entire novel, The Outsiders, is Pony's essay for his English class! He also talked about a novel, Gone with the Wind, with his friend Johnny and shared his favorite poem, "Nothing Gold Can Stay." That poem and book meant a lot to Johnny, even right before he died.

Resources CD: Character Sketch: Ponyboy

DAY 3 Independent Practice

Locate a student writing sample that includes interrupters or that would benefit from adding them. Think aloud as you identify the information included in the interrupter and/or find a place that would improve by adding information or description. Have students comb through their own writing to find a piece that would benefit from a closer look at interrupters.

PEER EDIT Apply what you know about interrupters to proofread your piece—do the interrupters add more information? Are interrupters punctuated with commas? Now identify a place in your partner's writing that might benefit from an interrupter. What purpose would that interrupter serve?

SUM IT UP An interrupter can add more information or description to a sentence. These powerful additions to sentence structure need to be enclosed in commas.

Assess the Learning

- Survey students' writing folders for pieces that include interrupters. Scan to be sure that students are able to insert interrupters that make sense in context and that they punctuate them correctly.
- During writing conferences, ask students to point out places in their writing where they could have attempted to place interrupters. What additional information did the interrupters add to the sentence?

Link the Learning

- If students need more practice in understanding how to punctuate interrupters, see Comma: With Nonrestrictive Elements (page 78).
- Point out that sometimes interrupters appear at the beginnings or endings of sentences if they function as appositives. An *appositive* is a noun or noun phrase that renames a noun near it in a sentence. The appositive may appear in multiple places:

  Maggie, a loveable floppy-eared mutt, quickly became part of our family.

  A loveable floppy-eared mutt, Maggie quickly became part of our family.

  Our family adopted Maggie, a loveable, floppy-eared mutt.
- Help students understand that they should *not* use commas to set off essential elements, such as a relative clause: Mom jumped when she heard the noise that echoed through the house. (The clause *that echoed through the house* is not an appositive.)

Sentence Fluency and Variety

DAY 1 Model the Focus Point

We've learned that a variety of sentence structures can make our writing engaging and interesting to read. Using multiple sentence structures also makes our writing fluent, which means that the sentences flow and are easy to read. I am capturing a focused moment—my debut in a musical—as I strive for fluency and sentence variety. Notice that my first sentence is setting the scene! I want my readers to be right in the moment with me, so I'm including an opening: *As the curtain drew back....* I don't want my second sentence to use exactly the same structure, so notice that I am combining two independent clauses with a coordinating junction, *and*.

> **Modeled Writing Sample**
>
> As the curtain drew back, I gulped. I had never been in a musical before, and I had a lead! Would I forget the lyrics? The music began, providing my cue. One last breath. I warbled just a bit, but then I was comfortably singing. My debut, at least so far, was a success!

Think aloud as you model, deliberately choosing to insert an interrogative sentence to break up the flow of declarative sentences and including a closing element to describe the moment the music began.

Now I'm writing: *One last breath*. That group of words tells who or what—one last breath. But there's no verb. That means the group of words is a fragment. Although we normally don't want to include fragments in our writing, a deliberate fragment can provide a dramatic pause. You're right there with me as I take one last breath before trying to sing!

Share your thinking as you use *but* to join two clauses and end with a sentence that includes an interrupter.

TURN AND TALK **Partners, carefully reread the model I wrote. What does this model tell you about sentence variety? What generalizations can you make about sentence fluency from this model?**

SUM IT UP **Use a variety of sentence structures to make writing interesting and more fluent. Use sentence fragments sparingly and deliberately.**

DAY 2 Guided Practice

TURN AND TALK **What types of sentences do you see in Computers? What sentences might you change to add even more variety and to make the sentences flow more smoothly?**

SUM IT UP Display the class editing chart. Add "Use a variety of sentence structures. Use fragments sparingly and deliberately."

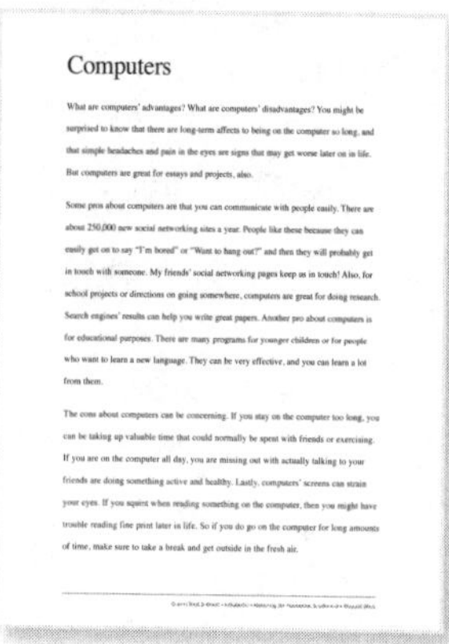

Computers

What are computers' advantages? What are computers' disadvantages? You might be surprised to know that there are long-term affects to being on the computer so long, and that simple headaches and pain in the eyes are signs that may get worse later on in life. But computers are great for essays and projects, also.

Some pros about computers are that you can communicate with people easily. There are about 250,000 new social networking sites a year. People like these because they can easily get on to say "I'm bored" or "Want to hang out?" and then they will probably get in touch with someone. My friends' social networking pages keep us in touch! Also, for school projects or directions on going somewhere, computers are great for doing research. Search engines' results can help you write great papers. Another pro about computers is for educational purposes. There are many programs for younger children or for people who want to learn a new language. They can be very effective, and you can learn a lot from them.

The cons about computers can be concerning. If you stay on the computer too long, you can be taking up valuable time that could normally be spent with friends or exercising. If you are on the computer all day, you are missing out with actually talking to your friends are doing something active and healthy. Lastly, computers' screens can strain your eyes. If you squint when reading something on the computer, then you might have trouble reading fine print later in life. So if you do go on the computer for long amounts of time, make sure to take a break and get outside in the fresh air.

Resources CD: Computers

Remember, having a variety of sentence structures at your fingertips allows you to craft fluent writing that your readers will appreciate. Be careful not to overuse fragments, if you use them at all.

DAY 3 Independent Practice

Share your thinking as you survey a piece of writing (yours or a student's) to check for variety in sentence structure. Model adding an opener, closer, or interrupter to give the work more variety. Turn responsibility over to student editors.

PEER EDIT Identify places in your writing where you have used a variety of sentence structures—compound sentences and sentences with openers, closers, and interrupters. Identify any fragments in the writing. Are they intentional, used to create drama or show emphasis? If not, how can you correct them?

SUM IT UP Our writing toolbox includes sentences with many structures—compound sentences and sentences with openers, closers, and interrupters. Using a variety helps us deliver content and make our writing fluent. In general, eliminate fragments in favor of complete sentences. Use fragments deliberately, only for dramatic effect or for emphasis.

Assess the Learning

- Add a space on your Class Record-Keeping Grid (in the Tools file of the Resources CD) to note which students have mastered sentence structures. Pull together students in small groups who may need additional instruction.
- Have students write letters to their peers in another class explaining the various sentence structures. Assess for understanding.

Link the Learning

- Share mentor texts in which writers have deliberately used fragments for emphasis or dramatic effect, such as E. B. White's essay "Once More to the Lake," Gary Paulsen's *Dogsong*, or nonfiction texts such as Cynthia Rylant's *The Journey: Stories of Migration*.
- Be sure that students do not confuse short sentences with fragments. Short sentences—often just two words, a subject and verb—can be powerful punctuations in the middle of groups of longer sentences. Writers must proceed much more cautiously with fragments.
- Have students find examples in mentor texts of passages in which variety in sentence structure punches up writing. Invite them to share their findings.

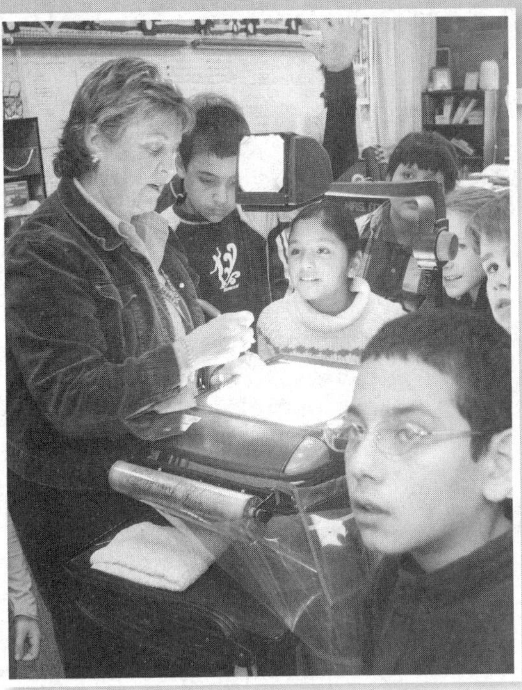

Cycles for Improving Grammar Awareness

We need to expose middle school students to quality read-alouds and have rich conversations with them that promote the grammar we expect them to emulate in their writing. With these strong building blocks—modeling in conversations and mentoring from authors they love—their ears become tuned to what "sounds right." They will come to expect certain sentence structures and notice when nouns and verbs do not agree, when plurals are missing, or when tense is misplaced.

Modeled writing enables students to hear us wonder aloud about pronoun choices, verb tenses, word order, and so on. When students can see a proficient language user in action, they begin to see how to integrate the focused grammar strategies we're teaching into their work as writers.

Parallel Structure

DAY 1 Model the Focus Point

Modeled Writing Sample

Lewis Latimer was a prized member of Thomas Alva Edison's team, responsible for inventing carbon filaments for light bulbs. In 1881, Latimer supervised the installation of electric lights in New York, Philadelphia, London, and Montreal. Latimer was not only an inventor, he also enjoyed writing, playing music, and drafting.

Writers, I'm crafting a short biography of Lewis Latimer, an African American inventor who helped Thomas Edison by creating an important element of electric light bulbs. Watch as I begin with a sentence about Latimer: *Lewis Latimer was a prized member. . . .* I think it's important to know that Latimer helped light up cities! So I'm writing: *In 1881, Latimer supervised the installation of electric lights in New York, Philadelphia, London, and Montreal.* Notice that I placed commas between the items in series. Did you also notice that all the items in the series are cities? Because each item is a city, this means that the sentence has parallel structure. I want to write more about Latimer: *Latimer was not only an inventor, he also enjoyed writing, played music, and to draft*. Now I see a bit of a problem. Take a look at the end of the sentence. The items are in a series, but they are not parallel. *Writing* is a gerund, *played music* is a verb phrase, and *to draft* is an infinitive. To make this parallel, I need to change the items so they are all one type of word or phrase. I'm going to make them all gerunds: *writing, playing music, and drafting*. Now the sentence has parallel structure.

TURN AND TALK **Partners, take a look at this sentence: *Rita was a successful cook because she measured ingredients carefully, mixed thoroughly, and her equipment was precise*. Explain why this sentence does not have parallel structure. Describe how you might fix it. (*Rita was a successful cook because she measured ingredients carefully, mixed thoroughly, and used precise equipment.*)**

SUM IT UP **Parallel structure means using the same word pattern to show that two or more ideas have the same level of importance.**

DAY 2 Guided Practice

TURN AND TALK **Apply what you know about parallel structure as you read the sentences in Visit Phillips Park! Identify a place where the structure is not parallel. Explain what you would do to revise the sentence to achieve parallelism.**

SUM IT UP Display the class editing chart. Add "Create parallel structure by checking for equal words, phrases, and clauses."

When we combine ideas in a series, it's important to check for parallelism. All the words in a series, for example, need to be nouns, gerunds, infinitives, and so on.

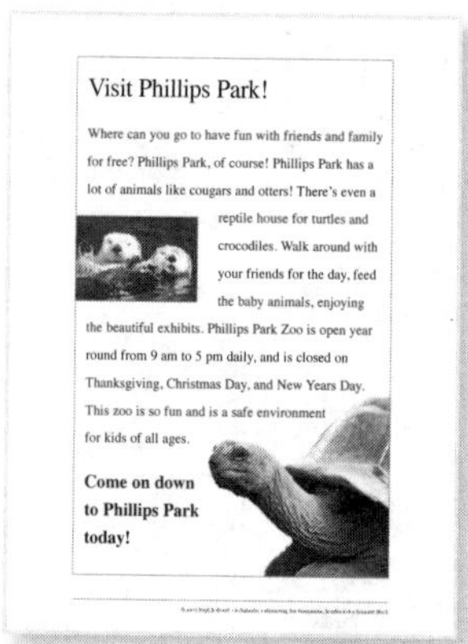

Visit Phillips Park!

Where can you go to have fun with friends and family for free? Phillips Park, of course! Phillips Park has a lot of animals like cougars and otters! There's even a reptile house for turtles and crocodiles. Walk around with your friends for the day, feed the baby animals, enjoying the beautiful exhibits. Phillips Park Zoo is open year round from 9 am to 5 pm daily, and is closed on Thanksgiving, Christmas Day, and New Years Day. This zoo is so fun and is a safe environment for kids of all ages.

Come on down to Phillips Park today!

Resources CD: Visit Phillips Park!

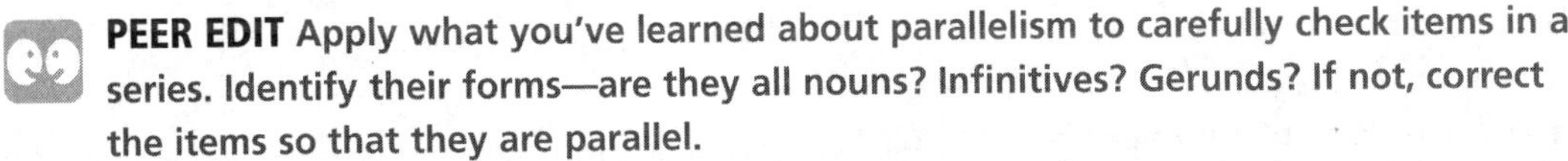

DAY 3 Independent Practice

Choose a sample from a student writing folder that includes items in a series. Share your thinking as you check for parallelism and correct errors. Have student editors choose writing and do the same.

PEER EDIT Apply what you've learned about parallelism to carefully check items in a series. Identify their forms—are they all nouns? Infinitives? Gerunds? If not, correct the items so that they are parallel.

SUM IT UP When two or more items have the same level of importance (like items in a series), the items need to be parallel—all words, all phrases, or all clauses—and of the same type. Join parallel structures with coordinating conjunctions.

Assess the Learning

- Scan student writing for serial commas and for parallelism. Note which students may need extra assistance.
- In individual writing conferences, provide students with writing models in which items in series are not parallel. Assess students' ability to identify the lack of parallelism and to revise for parallelism.

Link the Learning

- Infinitives in series can be parallel in two ways:

  When Hector is at camp, he likes to hike, boat, and swim.

  When Hector is at camp, he likes to hike, to boat, and to swim.

- Give students some tips for checking for parallelism:
  - Stop at the conjunction *and* and *or* to examine the elements on either side of the conjunction.
  - Reread and listen carefully to be sure that the writing sounds correct.
  - Rewrite the parallel items in a list. Do they seem similar? In the sentences above, for example, the lists would read *hike, boat, swim* and *to hike, to boat, to swim*. The elements in each list are similar.

Verb Tenses: Present, Past, and Future

DAY 1 Model the Focus Point

Verbs are powerful words that carry the action of the sentence. They can also show us when something happens. The "when" of a verb is called *tense*. I'm carefully considering tense today as I write about an amazing invention! In my first sentence, I'm writing about something I do now. Notice that I use the verbs *exercise* and *fasten*. These verbs are in the present tense. In my next sentence, I am writing about something I did in the past. I researched. Because I did this in the past, I use a past-tense verb. I create the past tense of many verbs by adding *–ed* to the verb: *I researched*. In the third sentence I use past-tense verbs to show that events happened in 1941—the year is a clue to the tense. I wonder, too, about the future. I am ending my writing with my wondering: *I wonder what inventors will create in the future. . . .* Notice that I changed tense! To talk about future events, we keep the verb, like *create*, and then add the word *will*.

Modeled Writing Sample

When I exercise, I fasten my running shoes with Velcro. I researched this amazing device! In 1941, a Swiss engineer noticed the burrs that stuck to his dog's fur. He examined them under a microscope and created a fastener that had the same kind of hooks. I wonder what inventors will create in the future based on their discoveries in nature.

TURN AND TALK Partners, look back through the writing to identify verbs in the present, past, and future tenses. Use the verbs as examples as you explain how to form the past and future tenses.

SUM IT UP Correct use of verb tense allows us to show whether action in a sentence has taken place in the past, present, or future.

DAY 2 Guided Practice

TURN AND TALK Examine the verbs in Advice for 5th Graders. Do they show action in the past, present, and future? How does the writer show when the action takes place? What advice would you give to this writer about verb tense?

SUM IT UP To the class editing chart, add "For regular verbs, make the past tense by adding *–ed*. Use *will* or *shall* to show future tense."

Writers carefully consider verb tense to show when the action in a sentence takes place. For regular verbs, show the past by adding *–ed*. Show the future by adding *will* or *shall* before the verb.

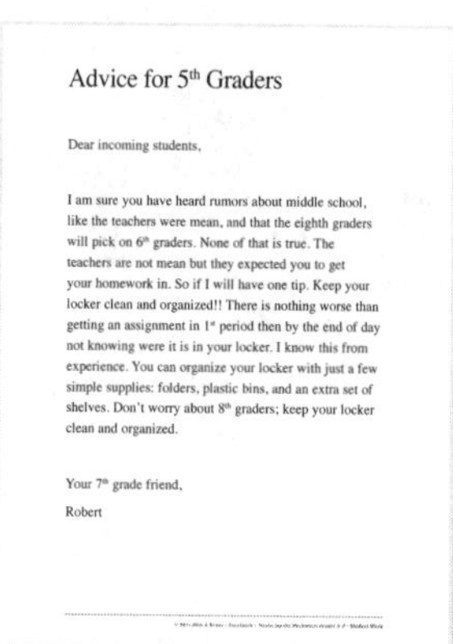
Advice for 5th Graders

Dear incoming students,

I am sure you have heard rumors about middle school, like the teachers were mean, and that the eighth graders will pick on 6th graders. None of that is true. The teachers are not mean but they expected you to get your homework in. So if I will have one tip. Keep your locker clean and organized!! There is nothing worse than getting an assignment in 1st period then by the end of day not knowing were it is in your locker. I know this from experience. You can organize your locker with just a few simple supplies: folders, plastic bins, and an extra set of shelves. Don't worry about 8th graders; keep your locker clean and organized.

Your 7th grade friend,

Robert

Resources CD: Advice for 5th Graders

DAY 3 Independent Practice

Select a sample from a writer's notebook to model proofreading for verb tenses. Share your thinking as you look for clues in context that signal the use of past, present, and future tenses. Model changing verbs as necessary. Then turn responsibility over to students.

PEER EDIT Point out verbs and talk about the tenses. Explain how you knew which tense to use and how you formed the tense. Identify any sentences in which the verb should change. Describe how to change the tense and why you need to change it.

SUM IT UP Verb tense indicates when the action in a sentence takes place—past, present, or future. Add *–ed* to regular verbs to indicate past tense. To show future tense, add the helping verb *shall* or *will*.

Assess the Learning

- Scan students' writing folders to assess for use of past, present, and future tenses. Note error patterns in choosing correct tense and in forming tense correctly.
- Pinpoint a sentence and ask the writer to explain how he or she chose and formed the verb tense. Ask the writer to change the verb to a different tense, explaining his or her thinking during the revision.

Link the Learning

- Explain to students that verb tense in one piece of writing generally remains the same. Share and model these tips:
  - Use the past tense in narratives to write about events in the past.
  - Use the present tense to tell facts, to discuss your own ideas, to talk about things that happen every day, and to write about the action in books and movies.
  - Indicate the future tense by using helping verbs such as *will, shall, is going to,* and *are about to.*
  - Point out that adverbs in sentences are often good clues about which verb tense to use—and that adverbs and tense need to be consistent. The adverb *tomorrow,* for example, indicates future tense, while the adverb *now* indicates present tense.
  - Let students know that *shall* is used to show future tense with pronouns such as *I* or *we.*

Verb Forms: Regular and Irregular

DAY 1 Model the Focus Point

When we write about things that happened in the past, we use past-tense verbs. For many verbs, we add *–ed* to form the past tense. We call those verbs regular verbs. I am writing about Frederick Douglass. Since he lived in the past, I am using past-tense verbs. Watch as I begin: *Frederick Douglass. . . . Unlike many slaves, Douglass learned. . . .* Notice that *learn* is a regular verb. I added *–ed* to the verb *learn* to form the past tense. Now I'm continuing: *His owner's wife teached him the alphabet.* As I write that, it doesn't sound right. *Teach* must be an irregular verb. The past-tense of *teach* is *taught*. The only way to know the past tense forms of irregular verbs is to memorize them or use a reference to double-check.

> **Modeled Writing Sample**
>
> Frederick Douglass was born a slave in Maryland around 1818. Unlike many slaves, Douglass learned to read when he was young. His owner's wife taught him the alphabet. Through reading, Douglass found out more about the world, and he was determined to seek freedom. He tried to escape several times, finally succeeding in 1838. Douglass became a leader in the movement to free other slaves.

Continue modeling, sharing your thinking as you form the past tenses of the regular verb *try* and the irregular verbs *find* and *become.*

TURN AND TALK **Partners, look back through the writing to identify a regular verb. Explain how I formed the past tense of that regular verb. Then identify an irregular verb. Explain how you know that the verb is irregular.**

SUM IT UP **Regular verbs form their past tense by adding *–ed* to the main verb. Irregular verbs form their past tense in different ways. To know which form of an irregular verb is correct, you need to memorize the forms or use a reference.**

DAY 2 Guided Practice

TURN AND TALK **Discuss the meaning of No Power! Proofread the paper for past-tense verbs, making sure they are formed correctly. Classify the verbs as regular or irregular verbs.**

SUM IT UP To the class editing chart, add "Add *–ed* to form the past tense of regular verbs. For irregular verbs, check a reference."

We construct the past-tense forms of most verbs by adding *–ed*. Irregular verbs may completely change their spellings, or they may simply stay the same.

No Power!

Resources CD: No Power!

DAY 3 Independent Practice

Select from a student writing folder a sample that you can proofread for correct forms of verbs. Share your thinking as you identify the verbs and check that their tenses are formed correctly. Give students a reference for irregular verbs and have them choose a piece of writing to proofread for verb tenses.

PEER EDIT Read your writing together, identifying verbs and classifying them as regular or irregular. Check that you've correctly formed past-tense verbs. Use a reference to check your irregular verbs.

SUM IT UP Verbs carry the action of sentences. We can classify verbs as regular or irregular. Regular verbs form the past tense by adding *–ed*. Irregular forms change spellings or may remain the same.

Assess the Learning

- Scan students' writing folders to assess their use of past tense of both regular and irregular verbs. Look for patterns of errors, such as not making necessary the spelling change when adding *–ed,* adding *–ed* to irregular verbs, using the wrong verb tense, making mistakes in subject-verb agreement, and so on.
- Have a student pinpoint both regular and irregular verbs in a piece of writing and contrast how he or she formed the past tense of the verb.

Link the Learning

- Provide students with the Regular and Irregular Verbs reference (in the Tools file on the Resources CD). Encourage them to keep the tool in their writer's notebooks and add to it when they encounter other irregular verbs in their reading or their writing.
- Have students write mentor sentences that show the different forms of irregular verbs that you can post for student reference. Pairs of students, for example, could each write sentences for one of the irregular verbs.
- Invite students to scour mentor texts for examples of irregular verbs. They will find them in a variety of texts, from poems, essays, novels and short stories to articles, content area textbooks, and nonfiction picture books.

Verbs: Linking and Auxiliary

DAY 1 Model the Focus Point

Some verbs carry the action of sentences, but other verbs connect the subject to information—they rename the subject or give information or a description. In my first sentence about Salvador Dali, I am using a verb like that—a linking verb. Watch as I write: *Salvador Dali was an artist.* After the linking verb, *was*, the rest of the sentence renames Dali, an artist. Notice that in my next sentence, I'm using the same linking verb: *None of the teachers... were*. This time, the first part of the sentence doesn't rename the subject; it's a description. Linking verbs can introduce descriptions. Watch as I continue:... *because Dali had shown talent at an early age*. What do you notice about this second part of the sentence? The verb is two words: *had shown*. We call the verb *had* an auxiliary verb. Auxiliary verbs, sometimes called helping verbs, help form the tense or the mood of a verb.

Modeled Writing Sample

Born in Spain in 1904, Salvador Dali was a talented artist. None of the teachers at his art academy were surprised at his ability, because Dali had shown talent at an early age. Surrealists were famous for visual surprises in their work. Dali was known for including elements of dreams in his paintings.

Continue modeling, sharing your thinking as you use the linking verb *were* and use an auxiliary form of *to be* with the word *known* to form the verb *was known*.

TURN AND TALK Writers, reread the model. Identify the linking verbs and the action verbs that have auxiliary, or helping, verbs.

SUM IT UP Linking verbs connect subjects with more information or description. Auxiliary verbs form verb phrases with action verbs.

DAY 2 Guided Practice

TURN AND TALK Discuss the purpose of the writing. Identify linking verbs and explain what information they link back to the subject. Explain how the writer used auxiliary verbs in the writing.

SUM IT UP Display the class editing chart. Add "Use linking verbs to connect information and descriptions to subjects; use auxiliary verbs to help to form verb phrases."

While some verbs provide action to sentences, other verbs link ideas or "help" main verbs to create tense, mood, or voice.

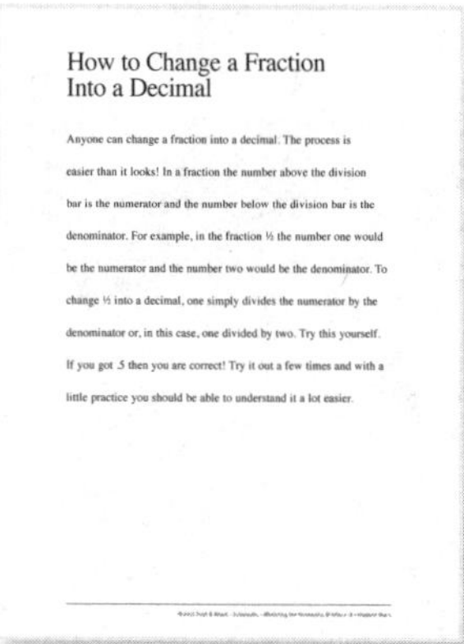

How to Change a Fraction Into a Decimal

Anyone can change a fraction into a decimal. The process is easier than it looks! In a fraction the number above the division bar is the numerator and the number below the division bar is the denominator. For example, in the fraction ½ the number one would be the numerator and the number two would be the denominator. To change ½ into a decimal, one simply divides the numerator by the denominator or, in this case, one divided by two. Try this yourself. If you got .5 then you are correct! Try it out a few times and with a little practice you should be able to understand it a lot easier.

Resources CD: How to Change a Fraction Into a Decimal

DAY 3 Independent Practice

Select a piece of student writing to use to model proofreading for linking and auxiliary verbs. Share your thinking as you check that both types of verbs are used correctly. Have students review their own writing for both linking and auxiliary verbs.

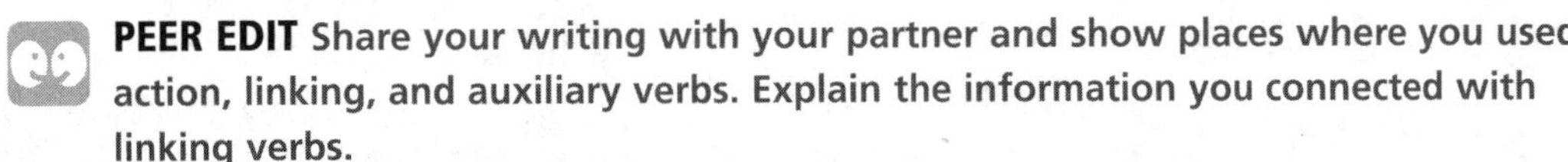

PEER EDIT **Share your writing with your partner and show places where you used action, linking, and auxiliary verbs. Explain the information you connected with linking verbs.**

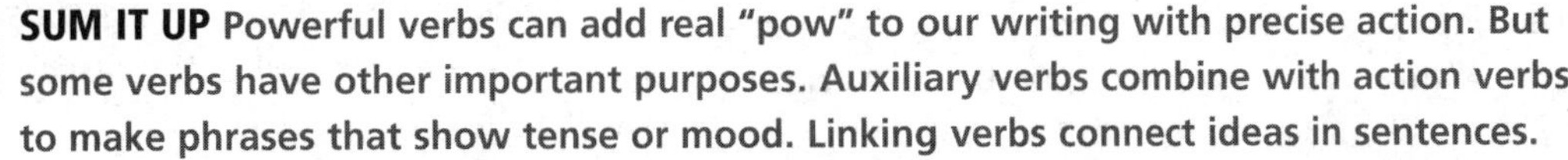

SUM IT UP **Powerful verbs can add real "pow" to our writing with precise action. But some verbs have other important purposes. Auxiliary verbs combine with action verbs to make phrases that show tense or mood. Linking verbs connect ideas in sentences.**

Assess the Learning

- Scan student writing for linking and auxiliary verbs. Note error patterns with choosing the wrong form of linking verbs, using the wrong tense of auxiliary verbs, and so on. Provide extra assistance for those who need it.
- In individual conferences, have students point out linking verbs and auxiliary verbs and explain their purposes in the writing.

Link the Learning

- Teach students the linking verbs—*be, am, is, are, was, were, being, been, become,* and *seem*—as well as verbs that may be linking verbs OR action verbs: *appear, feel, grow, look, prove, remain, smell, sound, taste,* and *turn*. Example:

  Maria tasted the stew after she added more spices.

  The cinnamon made it taste good!
- Let students know that if they can substitute the word *is, am,* or *are* for one of the action verbs in the list, then that action verb is functioning as a linking verb.
- Share additional auxiliary verbs with students: *will, shall, may, might, can, could, must, ought to, should, would, used to, need.* Let students know that sometimes adverbs are inserted into verb phrases. In the sentence *I had already begun my project,* for example, the auxiliary verb is *had,* and the main verb is *begun. Already* is an adverb that reveals time.

Verbs: Active and Passive Voice

DAY 1 Model the Focus Point

Modeled Writing Sample

A path of destruction was left by the ravaging tornado. Our garage was crushed by a massive tree limb. The debris in our town was being picked up by groups of exhausted but enthusiastic volunteers.

Create a model ahead of time that uses passive voice to provide practice with changing passive voice to active voice.

> **Writers, take a look at my description of destruction in the wake of a tornado. These sentences aren't wrong—they include subjects, verbs, and great descriptive words. Yet this style is one that writers usually try to avoid. These verbs are in the passive voice. In sentences with active voice, verbs show that the subject does something. But passive voice shows that something is acted upon by something else. I try to change passive voice to active voice whenever I can. In the first sentence, I notice that the path was left by the tornado. Who or what did the acting? The tornado! So watch as I move the tornado to the subject part of the sentence: *The ravaging tornado left a path of destruction*. Now the sentence is in active voice, and its style is much clearer for readers.**

Continue modeling with the second sentence, thinking aloud as you move the tree limb to the subject position of the sentence: *A massive tree limb crushed our garage.*

TURN AND TALK Writers, put your heads together as you read the last sentence. Identify who or what is doing the acting in this section. Explain how you would change the sentence from passive to active voice.

SUM IT UP While passive voice is desirable in technical or scientific reports, in most of our writing, we want to avoid it. You can avoid passive voice by placing your subject first and choosing a strong action verb for the sentence.

DAY 2 Guided Practice

TURN AND TALK Take a close look at the sentences in The Didgeridoo. Which include verbs in the passive voice? Explain how to change the passive voice into active voice.

SUM IT UP To a class editing chart, add "Avoid passive voice with subject-first, active-verb sentences."

> **Although passive voice is useful for some types of science and technical writing, we should strive whenever possible to use active voice in our writing.**

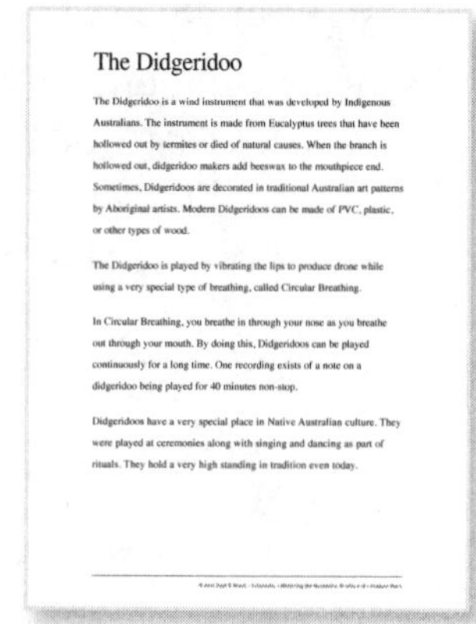

The Didgeridoo

The Didgeridoo is a wind instrument that was developed by Indigenous Australians. The instrument is made from Eucalyptus trees that have been hollowed out by termites or died of natural causes. When the branch is hollowed out, didgeridoo makers add beeswax to the mouthpiece end. Sometimes, Didgeridoos are decorated in traditional Australian art patterns by Aboriginal artists. Modern Didgeridoos can be made of PVC, plastic, or other types of wood.

The Didgeridoo is played by vibrating the lips to produce drone while using a very special type of breathing, called Circular Breathing.

In Circular Breathing, you breathe in through your nose as you breathe out through your mouth. By doing this, Didgeridoos can be played continuously for a long time. One recording exists of a note on a didgeridoo being played for 40 minutes non-stop.

Didgeridoos have a very special place in Native Australian culture. They were played at ceremonies along with singing and dancing as part of rituals. They hold a very high standing in tradition even today.

Resources CD: The Didgeridoo

DAY 3 Independent Practice

Think aloud as you select a sample from a student writing folder and check for passive voice. Model how to turn a sentence with passive voice into a sentence with active voice. Students can then follow your lead as they scan their own work for verbs.

PEER EDIT Apply what you know about passive voice by identifying areas in this writing in which you used passive voice rather than active voice. Work with your partner to change your sentence so that it uses active rather than passive voice.

SUM IT UP Sentences with active voice are strong and powerful. You can achieve active voice by making your subjects do the action rather than being acted upon.

Assess the Learning

- Scan through student writing to be sure that students have used active voice in their writing, except for sentences in which the subject would truly be unclear if they did.
- Give students a sentence written in passive voice. Ask them to write an explanation, telling how to change the sentence to active voice. Assess for understanding.

Link the Learning

- Provide sentences written in passive voice (examples: *This mess was made by our dirty dog! Many life-changing inventions were created by Thomas Alva Edison. This book was penned by my favorite author.).* Ask students to change them to active voice.
- Let students know that they can use passive voice when they are unsure who did the action. It would be fine, for example, to use passive voice in a sentence such as *The good news was delivered at 1:00 P.M.* if the writer did not know who specifically delivered the news—or if the writer wanted to emphasize the good news!
- Have students look for examples of passive voice in advertisements or propaganda. *(This cereal was rated as the best! Over 11 new taxes were passed in our city.)* Sometimes passive voice can be used to obscure the facts. Who rated the cereal the best? Who passed the taxes?

Singular Subject-Verb Agreement

DAY 1 Model the Focus Point

Subjects are the "who" of a sentence, while a verb tells what the subject does or did. Verbs need to agree with subjects in number. In other words, a sentence with a singular subject (only one person, place, or thing) has a verb that agrees with the singular subject. Watch as I write a description of working in a busy café. I am starting with the singular subject *I*. I choose the verb *work* to follow *I*: *As I work. . . .* Now I am continuing: *. . . so much happens around me!* This noun phrase, *so much*, functions as a singular noun. The verb, *happens*, agrees with a singular noun. I am continuing my description: *A woman nearby chats on her phone. . . .* Wait a minute—that doesn't sound quite right! The verb does not agree. Watch as I revise: *A woman nearby chats. . . .* Now the singular subject, *woman*, agrees with the singular verb, *chats*.

Modeled Writing Sample

As I work in the café, so much happens around me! A woman nearby chats on her phone, thrilled to hear from a long-lost friend. A toddler begs his mom for a delicious cookie after lunch. In the back corner, a group of girls giggles as they tell jokes. I bend over the keyboard, focusing on my writing.

Continue the model, pausing to share your thinking with the singular subject-verb pairs: *toddler/begs, group/giggles, I/bend.*

TURN AND TALK Partners, take a look at my writing as you identify subject-verb pairs. Then think of something else you might see or hear in a busy café. Write a sentence with a singular subject and a verb that agrees with it.

SUM IT UP If you write a sentence with a singular subject, you need to be sure to use a verb that agrees with it in number. *Is, was,* and *has,* for example, are verbs that agree with singular subjects.

DAY 2 Guided Practice

TURN AND TALK Read the text together. Then identify singular subjects in the writing. Do the verbs agree? Explain why or why not and describe how you would make subjects and verbs agree.

SUM IT UP Display the class editing chart. Add "Singular subjects need singular verbs."

Remember to carefully check that singular subjects have singular verbs.

Response to Robert Frost's "The Road Not Taken"

In Robert Frost's poem "The Road Not Taken," he talks about trouble deciding which road to take. I like this poem because he describes these roads so beautifully like when he says, "it was grassy and wanted wear." The speaker also describes in the end that he did pick the right road, making all the difference. This is like deciding between right and wrong, or good and bad. Also, when the speaker says, "I doubted if I should come back," this reminds me of when I make choices. After I make the choice, I consider it, wondering if I've done the right thing. Overall, I think that the speaker is trying to get across the message to be you and not to be like others. Be different. At the end he states, "I took the one less traveled by, and that has made all the difference." I think this is like following what others do or "taking the one less traveled by" and being you. I wonder what choice he had to make, thinking back as he wrote the words of this poem. I also wonder whether he still likes the choice he made or if he wishes he had taken the other road. The one that ended up being worn the same way. Overall, this poem describes choices, and whether we look at our choices with satisfaction or regret.

Resources CD: Response to Robert Frost's "The Road Not Taken"

DAY 3 Independent Practice

Model how to look for agreement of singular subjects and verbs in a piece of writing you select from a student's writing folder. Then allow students time to identify singular subjects in their writing and check that verbs agree.

PEER EDIT Partners, work together to identify subjects and verbs. Be sure that singular subjects have singular verbs. If you find verbs that don't agree, be sure to revise for agreement.

SUM IT UP Subjects and verbs must agree. A singular subject requires a singular verb. Check your verbs carefully to be sure they agree.

Assess the Learning

- Use a Class Record-Keeping Grid (in the Assessment and Record Keeping file on the Resources CD) to note which students are having difficulty with subject-verb agreement. Provide extra support with additional practice.
- During individual writing conferences, ask students to point out singular subjects and verbs. Have them generalize about the verbs that agree with singular subjects.

Link the Learning

- Point out that verb forms not only change when subjects are plural, but also may depend on whether pronouns are in first or third person, such as: *I live in Oswego. She lives in Oswego, too!*
- Students may drop the inflectional ending *–s: He ask the teacher where to find an extra book.* Note which students make this error both in writing and in speech. You may want to pull them together for additional instruction.
- Have students identify sentences with powerful verbs in mentor texts and mark with sticky notes passages that exemplify agreement between singular nouns and verbs. Allow time for sharing in small groups.

Plural Subject-Verb Agreement

DAY 1 Model the Focus Point

Modeled Writing Sample

Beatboxers make music using their mouths, lips, tongues, and voices. Their noises sound like horns, strings, or drums. Many artists around the world promote this unique form of music making!

Singular nouns name only one person, place, or thing; plural nouns name more than one. When we write, it's important to identify whether subjects are singular or plural because their verbs must agree. Watch as I write about a unique form of music, beatboxing: *Beatboxers make music. . . .* Let's take a close look at the subject. The *s* at the end shows that the subject is plural—I'm writing about more than one beatboxer. I chose the verb *make*, because this verb agrees with a plural subject. Now I am writing about the noises that beatboxers make: *Their noises sound. . . .* I deliberately chose the verb *sound*, because it agrees with a plural subject. If the subject were *noise*, I'd choose the verb *sounds*.

Introduce the last sentence for students to examine with partners.

TURN AND TALK Partners, take a close look at this sentence and identify the subject. Is it singular or plural? How can you tell? Examine the verb. How can you tell it agrees with the subject?

SUM IT UP Subjects that name more than one noun or use pronouns like *we* and *they* are plural subjects. Make sure verbs agree with them in number. You might use verbs like *are, were, have,* or action verbs without the inflectional ending *–s*.

DAY 2 Guided Practice

TURN AND TALK Read Transportation to identify plural subjects. Check to be sure that their verbs agree. Then choose a subject to change from plural to singular. Talk about how the form of the verb would change with the new subject.

SUM IT UP Display the class editing chart. Add "Plural subjects require plural verbs."

Subjects and verbs must agree. Plural subjects require plural verbs.

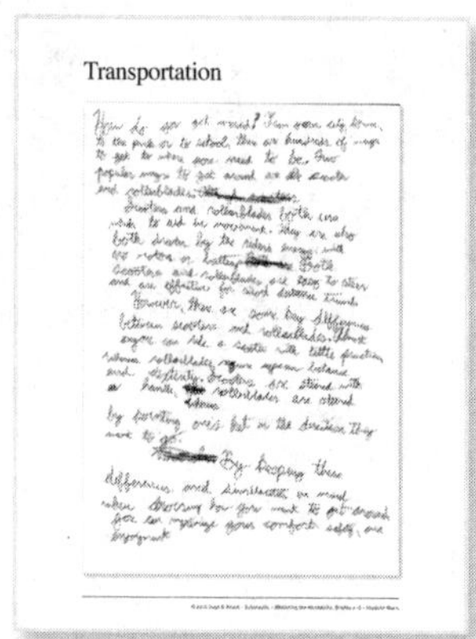
Transportation

Resources CD: Transportation

DAY 3 Independent Practice

Look through a student's writing folder to locate a piece of writing that includes plural subjects. Share your thinking as you model how to revise verbs to be sure that verbs and subjects agree. Then turn the editing process over to students so they can be sure that verbs agree with plural subjects.

PEER EDIT Apply what you've learned about subject-verb agreement to be sure that plural subjects and verbs agree. Explain to your partner how to revise verbs so that they agree.

SUM IT UP Subjects and verbs in sentences must agree. Plural subjects require plural verbs.

Assess the Learning

- Observe students at work, observing who edits verbs for subject-verb agreement. Note which students may need further instruction in identifying and correcting errors in subject-verb agreement.
- Provide students with sentences with singular subjects and verbs. Ask them to change the subjects to plural and make the verbs agree.

Link the Learning

- Share rules for subject-verb agreement with tricky subjects. Write these rules on a chart and have students write illustrative sentences or find sentences that exemplify the rules in mentor texts. Here are just a few of the many rules of subject-verb agreement. Use a reference to find others, and invite students to find additional examples in reference sources and in mentor sentences.
  - Two singular subjects connected by *or* or *nor* require a singular verb: *Neither my mom nor my sister knows the answer to this math problem.*
  - Two singular subjects connected by *either/or* or *neither/nor* require a singular verb: *Either Wes or Josh will help paint the scenery.*
  - When a singular subject is connected by *or* or *nor* to a plural subject, put the plural subject last and use a plural verb: *The serving bowl and the plates go on the table.*
  - Use a plural verb with two or more subjects when they are connected by *and: A puzzle and stuffed bear are toys from my childhood I won't give up.*

Pronouns and Their Antecedents

DAY 1 Model the Focus Point

Pronouns can keep our writing from being repetitive, but we must be sure that they have clear antecedents. An antecedent is the noun or nouns to which a pronoun refers. As I write today about the Gettysburg Address, I am paying careful attention to the antecedents. I start with an opening sentence about the speech: *President Lincoln delivered. . . .* Now to add more details: *He wasn't even scheduled. . . .* I want to take a careful look at my pronoun, *he*. Is it clear to what the pronoun is referring? The pronoun refers to President Lincoln, so the antecedent is clear. Watch as I continue: *Organizers had asked Lincoln to speak two weeks before. The organizers didn't give him much time to prepare the speech!* I'm stopping because something sticks out—two sentences in a row start with the same noun. I could replace the second noun with a pronoun, because the antecedent will be clear. I am revising: *Organizers had asked Lincoln to speak two weeks before. They didn't. . . .* Writers, I've noticed a pronoun in the last sentence that doesn't have an antecedent: *they*. I know that I meant *photographers*, but that's not clear in the writing. So watch as I revise: *In fact, it went by so quickly, photographers did not. . . .*

> **Modeled Writing Sample**
>
> President Lincoln delivered his Gettysburg Address in 1863. He wasn't even scheduled to be the main speaker at the dedication of the Soldiers' National Cemetery. Organizers had asked Lincoln to speak two weeks before. They didn't give him much time to prepare the speech! It was only 300 words long. In fact, it went by so quickly, they did not even have time to take a photograph of Lincoln uttering his now-famous words.

TURN AND TALK **Partners, work together to identify each pronoun I used. Then identify their antecedents and explain how you determined which words were the antecedents.**

SUM IT UP **Each pronoun in your writing must clearly refer to a noun. The noun to which a pronoun refers is called an antecedent.**

DAY 2 Guided Practice

TURN AND TALK **Identify the pronouns in Today's Schedule and check that each pronoun has an antecedent. If any of the pronouns are unclear, be sure to replace the pronouns or make the antecedents clearer.**

SUM IT UP Display the class editing chart. Add "Pronouns need clear antecedents."

Pronouns are great tools for writing, but they need to be clear for our readers. Be sure that each pronoun in your writing has a clear antecedent.

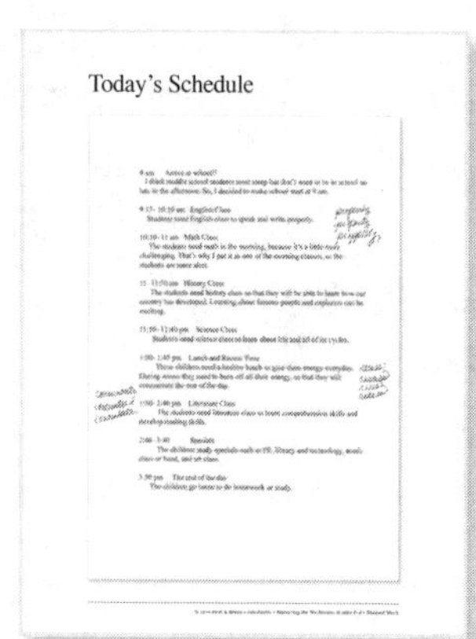

Resources CD: Today's Schedule

DAY 3 Independent Practice

Select a piece of writing from a writing folder. Proofread the piece, modeling your thinking as you identify both pronouns and their antecedents. Have students choose pieces to reread for a closer eye on pronouns.

PEER EDIT Partners, apply what you know about pronouns to locate pronouns and their antecedents. Are there any pronouns for which the antecedents are unclear? Revise your writing by adding an antecedent or replacing the pronoun with a noun.

SUM IT UP Pronouns can make our writing lean and fluent, but each pronoun needs a clear antecedent. Otherwise, the writing will be confusing! Check for antecedents. If antecedents are missing, add them or replace the pronoun with a noun.

Assess the Learning

- During writing conferences, ask students to point out pronouns in their writing. Then have them identify the antecedents. Provide additional instruction for those who need it.
- Provide a content area passage or a passage from a mentor text. Ask students to identify pronouns and name their antecedents. Note those who need assistance.

Link the Learning

- Remind students that pronouns need to agree with their antecedents in both gender and number. For example, the pronoun *her* refers to only a female, while *they* can refer to a group of males, females, or both. Some nouns are tricky. Although a club is a group of people, for example, a club is considered singular and uses a singular pronoun, *it*.
- Take a passage from a mentor text and replace the nouns with pronouns. As students read the passage, ask them to consider the effect of pronoun overuse. Encourage them to revise the sentences you provide.
- Ask students to write explanations detailing how to identify pronouns and their antecedents. They can trade explanations with partners, try out the procedures, and work together to identify pronouns and antecedents in their writing.

Pronouns: Possessive

DAY 1 Model the Focus Point

Modeled Writing Sample

Packing up at the end of a camping trip is never easy! Is that your sleeping bag? No, it's his. Did you accidentally pick up my beach towel? No, this one is mine! What about this mess kit? I'm sure it's yours! But all these pesky mosquito bites? Sadly, they are *ours*!

Possessive pronouns show ownership. As I write about trying to sort out camping gear, I'm going to focus on showing ownership with pronouns. I'm beginning with: *Packing up at the end of a camping trip is never easy! Is that your sleeping bag? No, it's the sleeping bag belonging to Harry*. What if I want to shorten this writing a bit? Instead of writing *the sleeping bag belonging to Harry*, I could shorten it to *Harry's sleeping bag*. If I wanted to shorten it even further, I could replace the phrase with a possessive pronoun: *his*. Watch as I continue: *Did you accidentally pick up my beach towel? No, this one is mine!* I used the possessive pronoun, *mine*, to take the place of the words *my beach towel*. It's succinct and clear.

Continue modeling, focusing on the possessive pronouns *yours* and *ours*.

TURN AND TALK **Partners, think together as you identify the possessive pronouns. Describe how using possessive pronouns affects the writing.**

SUM IT UP **Possessive pronouns take the place of phrases, showing ownership. Note that we don't use apostrophes with possessive pronouns. Possessive pronouns include *mine, ours, his, hers*, and so on. Some are singular, and some are plural. Some refer specifically to male or female, while some refer to either or both!**

DAY 2 Guided Practice

TURN AND TALK **Focus on possessive pronouns. What possessive pronouns do you see? What noun phrases do you think the writer replaced? Identify a place where a possessive pronoun might smooth out the writing.**

SUM IT UP To the class editing chart, add "Possessive pronouns show ownership and do not include apostrophes."

You can use possessive pronouns to take the place of possessive phrases. Be sure possessive pronouns are correct in number and gender.

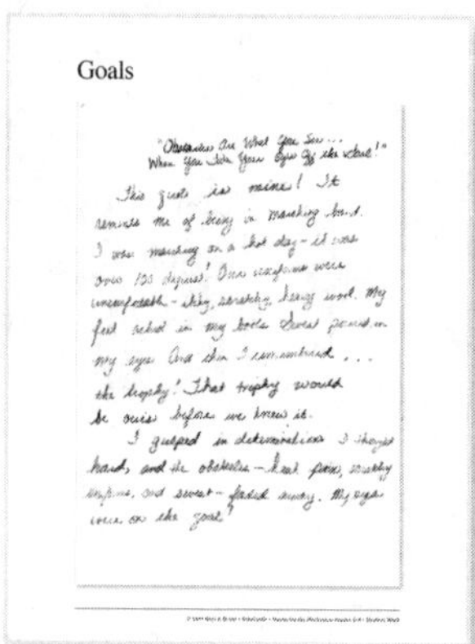
Goals

Resources CD: Goals

DAY 3 Independent Practice

Select a piece of writing from a writing folder and share your thinking as you proofread for correct use of possessive pronouns. Have students continue the process with pieces of their own.

PEER EDIT Explain what possessive pronouns do in writing. Then look together at each other's writing. Identify possessive pronouns and discuss whether they are clear in the writing.

SUM IT UP Possessive pronouns allow you to replace longer possessive noun phrases in your writing. Possessive pronouns include *his, ours, yours,* and so on.

Assess the Learning

- Review student writing samples for evidence of understanding of possessive pronouns. Note those who need assistance to add possessive pronouns to writing and those who need assistance to make sure they have used the correct gender and case of possessive pronoun.
- In small groups, ask students to classify possessive pronouns as singular or plural. Check for understanding.

Link the Learning

- Help students understand the difference between a possessive adjective and a possessive pronoun. Possessive adjectives modify nouns, while possessive pronouns take the place of noun phrases. Possessive adjectives come before nouns. Possessive pronouns can appear as subjects and objects.

  Possessive adjective: That is <u>my</u> pencil.

  Possessive pronoun: That pencil is <u>mine</u>.

- Share a chart for student reference for possessive pronoun number and gender. Ask them to look in mentor texts for examples of each of these possessive pronouns.

Number	Person	Gender	Possessive Pronoun
Singular	1st	both	mine
	2nd	both	yours
	3rd	masculine	his
	3rd	feminine	hers
	3rd	common	its
Plural	1st	both	ours
	2nd	both	yours
	3rd	both	theirs

Pronouns: Indefinite

DAY 1 Model the Focus Point

We know that many pronouns refer to a specific gender—we use *his* to refer to a male, for example. But what if we're talking about a group or we aren't sure of the antecedent? We can use indefinite pronouns, or pronouns that are vague. Watch as I begin my writing: *Anyone can mail....* The word *anyone* does not refer to a specific person, so it's an indefinite pronoun. I'll continue my writing: *Many claimed....* My research on postage stamps showed me that there are at least eight different countries and inventors who claimed being "first." Rather than listing them all, I'm capturing them with the indefinite pronoun *many*. Continue writing: *People... online*. Did you notice yet another indefinite pronoun in the writing? I used the indefinite pronoun *some* to refer to *people*. One important thing to know is that some indefinite pronouns are singular and some are plural. The pronoun *some* is considered plural, so I used the plural verb, *send*.

> **Modeled Writing Sample**
>
> Anyone can mail a letter, as long as the letter has a postage stamp. Many claimed to have invented the stamp, but the first stamps appeared in Great Britain in 1840. People have alternatives to sending mail today. Some send e-mails or pay bills online. Stamps, however, are fun to collect. Several in my collection feature musicians, artists, and scientists.

Write the last two sentences of the model.

TURN AND TALK **Partners, take a close look at the last sentence. Identify the indefinite pronoun. What is its antecedent? Does the indefinite pronoun act like a singular or a plural pronoun? Explain how you know.**

Students should identify *several,* a plural indefinite pronoun that uses the plural verb *feature*, and identify the antecedent as *stamps.*

SUM IT UP **An indefinite pronoun does not refer to any specific person, thing, or amount. Be careful that indefinite pronouns agree with verbs in number.**

DAY 2 Guided Practice

TURN AND TALK **Scan the piece together for indefinite pronouns. Why do you think the writer used indefinite pronouns? Check to be sure that they agree with verbs.**

SUM IT UP Display the class editing chart. Add "Use indefinite pronouns when you do not know a specific person, thing, or amount."

***All*, *another*, *any*, *anybody*, *anything*, *each*, and so on are all indefinite pronouns. When you use them in your writing, check for subject-verb agreement and for antecedents.**

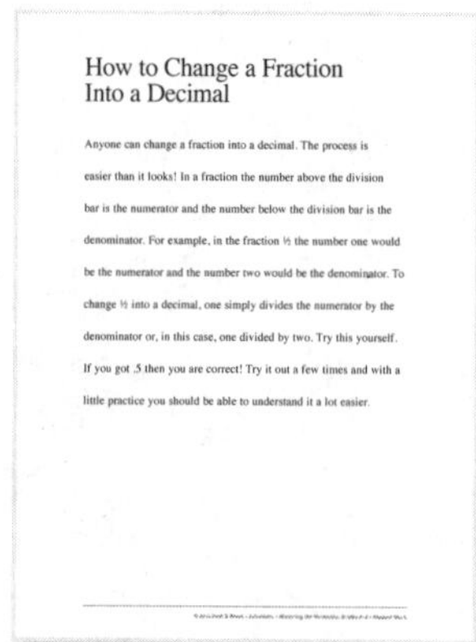

How to Change a Fraction Into a Decimal

Anyone can change a fraction into a decimal. The process is easier than it looks! In a fraction the number above the division bar is the numerator and the number below the division bar is the denominator. For example, in the fraction ½ the number one would be the numerator and the number two would be the denominator. To change ½ into a decimal, one simply divides the numerator by the denominator or, in this case, one divided by two. Try this yourself. If you got .5 then you are correct! Try it out a few times and with a little practice you should be able to understand it a lot easier.

Resources CD: How to Change a Fraction Into a Decimal

DAY 3 Independent Practice

Share your thinking as you take a piece of writing from a writing folder and then reread it with an eye toward indefinite pronouns. Check to be sure that they are appropriate, that they make sense in gender and number, and that they agree with verbs. Then have students take over the process, choosing pieces to reread for indefinite pronouns.

PEER EDIT Take a close look at your writing to identify indefinite pronouns. Apply what you know to make sure that they make sense in the sentences and that they are correct in gender, number, and subject-verb agreement.

SUM IT UP Indefinite pronouns allow you to refer to things that aren't specific. Use them sparingly, and be sure that you've considered number and gender when you've chosen an indefinite pronoun for your writing.

Assess the Learning

- Scan student writing for indefinite pronouns. Note those students who may need assistance to choose the appropriate pronouns and to make sure they agree with verbs.
- Provide a passage with indefinite pronouns and ask students to identify them. How do they know they are indefinite pronouns? As you listen to their explanations, you can assess which students need further instruction.

Link the Learning

- Provide a list of indefinite pronouns for students to keep in their writing folders. The list might include: *all, another, any, anybody/anyone, anything, each, enough, everybody/everyone, everything, few, little, many, nobody, none, one, several, some, somebody/someone.* Have students sort them into singular and plural and look for examples of them in mentor texts.

  Remind students that many indefinite pronouns also function as adjectives:

  Pronoun: <u>Each</u> of the players was ready to go.

  Adjective: I watched <u>each</u> player warm up.
- Provide cloze sentences from which indefinite pronouns are missing. Ask students to work with partners to choose the correct pronouns. What clues did they use to determine which pronoun(s) fit best?

Nouns and Pronouns: Subjective and Objective Cases

DAY 1 Model the Focus Point

Provide students with a list of subjective and objective case pronouns for their reference during the lessons.

> **You know that pronouns can take the place of nouns, but when we write, we must carefully consider the position of a pronoun in the sentence. Subjective-case pronouns, like *I*, *you*, and *he*, belong in the subjects of sentences. Objective-case pronouns, like *them* and *him*, are subjects of verbs or subjects of prepositions. I am carefully considering whether to use subjective or objective pronouns in my sentences. I'm writing about my brother Eliot: *My little brother....* I'm writing my next sentence about Eliot, but how do I start my sentence, with *he* or with *him*? A pronoun at the beginning of the sentence is in the subject position, so watch as I write with the subjective pronoun: *He spends hours there....* I continue: *Once a frog is safely in his bucket, he observes it*. I'm thinking very carefully about the pronouns. *He* is in the subject position, so I know that's correct. What about *it*? Checking my chart, I see that *it* can be used for either the subject or the object. And I know that I need a singular pronoun, because the antecedent is *a frog*.**

Modeled Writing Sample

My little brother thinks the backyard is an amazing place to explore. He spends hours there, scouting for frogs. Once a frog is safely in his bucket, he observes it. Eliot gently places them back in the grass when his frog observations are complete. We love reading his science journals!

Continue modeling, thinking deliberately about the pronouns *them* and *we*. Model choosing the correct pronoun for case, gender, and number.

TURN AND TALK **Partners, reread my model. Identify the pronouns. Which are objective case? Which are subjective case? Explain how you know.**

SUM IT UP **Pronouns help our writing flow more smoothly, but be sure to use the correct pronouns—think carefully about whether the pronouns in the sentences are subjects or objects.**

DAY 2 Guided Practice

TURN AND TALK **Identify pronouns in the piece Tsunamis. Classify them as subjective-case or objective-case pronouns. Classify nouns as well.**

SUM IT UP Display the class editing chart. Add "Use subjective-case pronouns for subjects; use objective case for objects of verbs and prepositions."

> **Subjective-case pronouns, like *I* and *she*, belong in the subjects of sentences. Objective-case pronouns, like *me* and *her*, are subjects of verbs or subjects of prepositions.**

Tsunamis

A tsunami is a large ocean wave that is caused by sudden motion on the ocean floor. This sudden motion could be anything from an earthquake, a powerful volcanic eruption, an underwater landslide, or even the impact of a large meteorite. Most tsunamis are caused by earthquakes. What happens is that there are two plates that have a lot of friction between them. They then become "stuck." As the stuck plate continues to descend into the mantle, there becomes a large buildup of energy. It can be stored for long periods of time – decades or even centuries. Energy keeps building until it exceeds the amount the plate can hold. When there is too much energy, the stuck plate snaps back into a position where it is not stuck. This sudden release of energy is the beginning of the tsunami. The moving wave then starts to travel to where the earthquake occurred. The shoreline has lowered from the tsunami, so the waves rush toward land to flood the shore. The waves will travel swiftly through open waters. When it hits it is like a "wave train" because the multiple waves will follow the large wave. After the tsunami hits, it can cause a substantial amount of damage. Only one tsunami can destroy an entire coastal village and remove all the sand from the beach that took hundreds of years to create. Tsunamis can also destroy islands of all its natural habitats and can cause death to surrounding areas. Overall, tsunamis are very dangerous and its good to know how they occur.

Resources CD: Tsunamis

DAY 3 Independent Practice

Select a piece of writing from a student's writing folder and model rereading it with a close eye on pronouns. Consider whether the sentences correctly use objective- and subjective-case pronouns and make any changes that are necessary. Then have students reread for pronouns in their own writing.

PEER EDIT **Classify pronouns as subjective, objective, or possessive. If you find any errors in your pronouns, work with your partner to correct them.**

SUM IT UP **Use subjective-case pronouns in the subjects of sentences. Use objective-case pronouns for the objects of verbs or for the objects of prepositions.**

Assess the Learning

- Scan students' writing folders for pronouns. Use your Class Record-Keeping Grid (in the Assessment and Record Keeping file on the Resources CD) to note those who do not use the correct case of pronouns in sentences.
- During writing conferences, provide cloze sentences into which students should insert pronouns. Observe as they choose pronouns and note those who need more instruction.

Link the Learning

- Post this chart on a bulletin board and ask students to locate sentences in mentor texts that exemplify each pronoun case.

Subjective-Case Pronouns	Objective-Case Pronouns	Possessive-Case Pronouns
I	me	my (mine)
you	you	your (yours)
he, she, it	him, her, it	his, her (hers), its
they	them	their (theirs)
who	whom	whose

- Let students know about some special case problems.
  - In compound structures, if there are two pronouns or a pronoun and a noun, it sometimes helps to drop the noun or other pronoun to figure out which pronoun to use: *Bob and* ___ *play basketball.* Because you'd say, "I play basketball," you can write: *Bob and I play basketball.*
  - In comparisons, think about the part of the sentence that is "missing" and you'll be able to use the correct pronoun case: *She is taller than I (am tall). He is as worried as I (am worried). This will help you as much as (it helps) me.*
  - In formal writing, we use the subjective case after forms of *to be: It is I at the door. It was she who called.*

Gerunds

DAY 1 Model the Focus Point

Verbs often end in *–ing*, but some words ending with *–ing* function as nouns. These words are called *gerunds*. I am writing today about traveling: *Traveling is a great way....* I see the word with *–ing*. In this sentence, the word functions as a noun. *Traveling* is the subject of the sentence. I'm continuing my writing: *Preparing... but stocking....* Are the *–ing* words in this sentence gerunds or verbs? Each of these words is the beginning of a gerund phrase. Both *preparing for a trip* and *stocking your car* are subjects of clauses. Next, I'm writing about my packing list: *I'm packing a flying....* I'm including two words with *–ing*, but neither is a gerund. *Packing* is part of the verb phrase: *am packing*. *Flying* describes the disc, so it's an adjective.

Modeled Writing Sample

Traveling is a great way to see new places and meet new people! Preparing for a trip takes time, but stocking your car makes a journey fun. I'm packing a flying disc in the car. It's great for exercising at a rest stop, and it also makes a handy tray for eating a healthy snack! I love singing in the car, too. I always bring along my favorite music—and earplugs for my mom.

Continue modeling, thinking aloud about the gerunds *exercising* and *eating* (objects of prepositions) and *singing* (direct object).

TURN AND TALK Partners, work together to identify the gerunds in the passage. Classify them as subjects, direct objects, and objects of prepositions. Explain how you can tell whether a word ending in *–ing* is a noun, verb, or adjective.

SUM IT UP Gerunds add variety to our writing and succinctly capture ideas. A gerund ends with *–ing* and functions as a noun in a sentence.

DAY 2 Guided Practice

TURN AND TALK Focus on gerunds in this piece. What gerund can you find? How does it function in the sentence? Locate other words with *–ing* and tell what part of speech they are if they are not gerunds.

SUM IT UP Display the class editing chart. To it, add "Gerunds are verbs ending in *–ing* that function as nouns."

A gerund is a verbal—a verb ending in *–ing*. Alone or as part of a phrase, it can serve the function of a noun in a sentence.

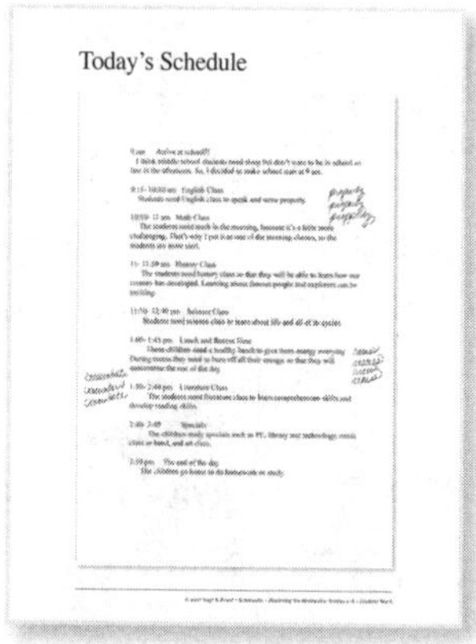

Resources CD: Today's Schedule

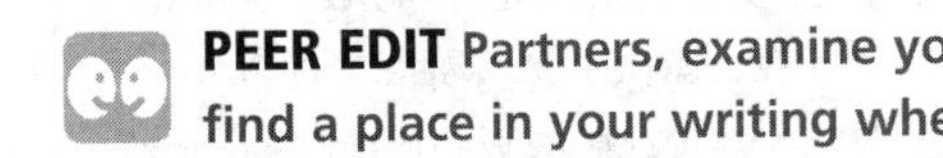

DAY 3 Independent Practice

Select a piece of writing from a student's folder. Share your thinking as you identify gerunds in the piece of text. If the writing does not have a gerund, consider adding one. If there is a gerund in the piece, consider adding descriptive words or turning the gerund into a gerund phrase. Then have students select pieces of their own writing and follow your lead to edit.

PEER EDIT Partners, examine your writing to identify gerunds. Then work together to find a place in your writing where a gerund might make your writing clearer or easier to understand. Differentiate between gerunds and other words that end with *–ing*.

SUM IT UP Words that end with *–ing* may function as verbs, adjectives, or nouns. The nouns are gerunds, and they can function as subjects or objects. A gerund phrase is made of a gerund plus its modifiers and objects.

Assess the Learning

- Have students identify gerunds in a mentor text. Encourage them to explain how they know the words are gerunds and not verbs or adjectives.
- As you observe writers at work, use a Class Record-Keeping Grid (in the Assessment and Record Keeping file on the Resources CD) to note any students who need assistance with gerunds. Provide extra support for those students.

Link the Learning

- Encourage students to write poems that capture content area learning and include gerunds and gerund phrases.
- For students who are ready, focus on the *–ing* construction with a verb that acts as an adjective, the participle. *(I bought new running shoes.)* When students use participles in phrases, remind them to take care that participles don't "dangle."
  - Dangling participle: *I saw the mountain looking through the window. Looking through the window* is a dangling participle because, in this sentence, it seems to be modifying *mountain*, as if the mountain is looking through the window.
  - Corrected: *Looking through the window, I saw the mountain.*

Infinitives

DAY 1 Model the Focus Point

When I write, I use a variety of structures to express ideas and to keep my writing fresh, As I wrote about a study plan, I focused on using infinitives. Infinitives are *verbals*—they are made of the word *to* plus a verb. Let's highlight the infinitive in the first sentence—*to learn*. The phrase starts with *to* and includes a verb. This phrase functions as an adverb. Why must we study? We must study to learn. In the second sentence, I used an infinitive, too. *My goal is to study*. In this sentence, the infinitive is the subject complement—it comes after a form of *to be*.

Modeled Writing Sample

We must study to learn! My goal is to study smarter this year. First, I'm setting aside a specific time to work each day. I'm more likely to take homework seriously if I schedule it. I might go to the library to study. Don't worry, though. I'm sure I'll still have plenty of time to play!

Focus on the next infinitives, *to work* and *to take homework seriously*, sharing your thinking as you identify the infinitives and explain how they function in sentences.

Let's take a look at this sentence: *I might go to the library to study*. It looks like there are two infinitives here—*to the library* and *to study*. I'm checking that each has a verb. Hmm. I realize that the first phrase is not an infinitive! The word *to* is a preposition here—it's followed by an article and a noun, *the library*. That's a great reminder. Not every phrase that starts with *to* is an infinitive.

TURN AND TALK Partners, take a look at the model and identify all the infinitives. Classify whether the infinitives are subjects, objects, adjectives, or adverbs.

SUM IT UP An infinitive is made of the word *to* with a verb. An infinitive can function as a subject, direct object, adjective, or adverb. It can also serve as a subject complement in a sentence with a linking verb, such as *My goal is to eliminate two seconds from my running time*.

DAY 2 Guided Practice

TURN AND TALK Focus on the message of the piece. Then see if you can identify an infinitive. Explain how you know this phrase is an infinitive. What function does it serve in the sentence?

SUM IT UP Display the class editing chart. Add to it "Infinitive = *to* + verb."

Composed of *to* and a verb, an infinitive is a phrase that can serve as a subject, object, adverb, or adjective in a sentence.

How Does Your Eye Work?

Your eyes seem really complicated, but they actually work in a simple way. It all begins when light rays are reflected off an object and the rays enter the eyes through the outer covering called the cornea. The cornea is kind of like a camera lens. The cornea bends the light rays that then pass through a round hole called the pupil. Behind the pupil, there is a colorless, transparent structure called the crystalline lens. Muscles called ciliary muscles surround the lens. These muscles are very important, because they hold the lens in place and these muscles work to allow you to see things up close and far away. The colored part of your eye, also called the iris, opens and closes to regulate the amount of light passing through. In bright light, the parts in the center of the retina, called cones, provide clear and sharp vision. Another job of the cones is to detect colors and fine details. The retina is a thin layer of tissue at the back of the eye embedded with millions of light sensitive cells. The other parts in the retina are called rods. Rods allow the eyes to detect motion, and they help us see in dim light and at night. Finally, a nerve called the optic nerve sends these impulses to the brain where an image is produced. So, that's how you are able to see things every day!

Resources CD: How Does Your Eye Work?

DAY 3 Independent Practice

Model with a sample you have selected from a student folder. Scan the writing for infinitives and identify their parts of speech. If you see a place where an infinitive might help a sentence make more sense, add the infinitive to the sentence as you share your thinking about it. Then have students select writing from their own folders to reread for infinitives.

PEER EDIT Partners, apply what you know about infinitives to your writing by identifying infinitives and explaining how they function in the sentences. If you find places in which infinitives are unclear, revise them to be sure they make sense in your sentences.

SUM IT UP Infinitive phrases can act as nouns, adverbs, or adjectives in sentences. To make an infinitive phrase, combine *to* with a verb. Remember, *to* can also be a preposition. Do not confuse infinitive phrases with prepositional phrases.

Assess the Learning

- During writing conferences, show students phrases that begin with *to.* Ask students to differentiate between prepositional phrases and infinitive phrases.
- Ask students to point out infinitive phrases in their writing. Have them explain how they formed the infinitives and how the infinitive phrases function in their writing.

Link the Learning

- Some verbs are more likely than others to be followed by infinitive phrases. Begin a list with such verbs as *decide, intend, plan, refuse, advise, encourage, instruct,* and so on. Have students create sentences in which the verbs are followed by infinitives.
- Most infinitives don't require special punctuation. An exception is an infinitive phrase that functions as an adverb at the beginning of a sentence: *To create healthier meals, we bought a new cookbook.*
- Have students be wary of split infinitives, in which additional words are added between *to* and the infinitive. They are usually unacceptable in formal writing.

  Unacceptable: I need to quickly leave the building.

  Acceptable: I need to leave the building quickly.

Adjectives: Comparative and Superlative Forms

DAY 1 Model the Focus Point

Adjectives lend precision to our writing by helping us craft amazing descriptions. Sometimes we use adjectives to compare—speeds, sizes, weights, and more. I am going to use adjectives to compare in my writing about world records: *I find world records....* Notice that I am using an adjective, *fascinating*. *I find world records one of the most fascinating topics of all.* I am adding the word *most* to show that I am comparing more than two things. Watch as I continue: *The other middle school....* Notice that I am using two different forms of the adjective, *large*. I add *–er* to show that I am comparing two things—my school to another school. I use *–est* to show that I am comparing one school to all the other schools in the world. With some words, we can add *–er* and *–est* to create the comparative form (comparing two things) and the superlative form (comparing more than two things). With longer adjectives, we usually need to add *more* or *most*. Continue thinking aloud as you write, deliberately using comparative and superlative forms of adjectives.

> **Modeled Writing Sample**
>
> I find world records one of the most fascinating topics of all. The other middle school in our town has a larger school population than mine, but the largest school in the world had more than 30,000 students in 2008. That school is more populous than our entire town! I think skateboarding is the most fun form of exercise. But can you imagine skateboarding on a board more than 35 feet long? That's the longest skateboard in the world.

TURN AND TALK What did you notice about my comparisons? Find a comparison of two objects. Then find a comparison of more than two objects. How do they differ? Explain to your partner.

SUM IT UP We can use the comparative and superlative forms of adjectives to describe nouns. Add *–er* or *most* to compare two nouns. Use *–est* or *most* to compare more than two nouns.

DAY 2 Guided Practice

TURN AND TALK Talk about the piece Tubas. Then read the selection with the idea of identifying interesting comparisons and including others using *–er, –est, more,* and *most.*

SUM IT UP To a class editing cart, add "Show comparisons with adjectives by adding *–er, –est, more, most.*"

Comparative adjectives compare two objects, while superlative adjectives compare more than two. With short adjectives, you can usually ad *–er* or *–est*. For longer adjectives, you may need to add *more* and *most* to the adjective.

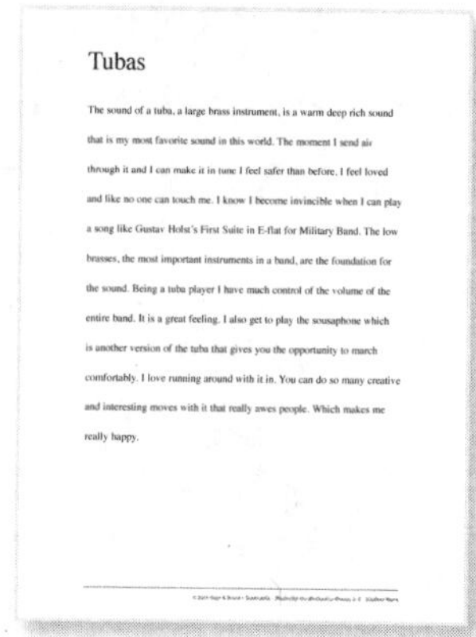

Tubas

The sound of a tuba, a large brass instrument, is a warm deep rich sound that is my most favorite sound in this world. The moment I send air through it and I can make it in tune I feel safer than before. I feel loved and like no one can touch me. I know I become invincible when I can play a song like Gustav Holst's First Suite in E-flat for Military Band. The low brasses, the most important instruments in a band, are the foundation for the sound. Being a tuba player I have much control of the volume of the entire band. It is a great feeling. I also get to play the sousaphone which is another version of the tuba that gives you the opportunity to march comfortably. I love running around with it in. You can do so many creative and interesting moves with it that really awes people. Which makes me really happy.

Resources CD: Tubas

DAY 3 Independent Practice

Share your thinking as you reread an existing piece of writing to insert comparisons. Allow time for writers to rethink and insert comparisons that make the writing more colorful and descriptive.

PEER EDIT Work together to find pieces in your writing folders where you can add comparative and superlative adjectives. Check to be sure that you use *–er* and *more* when you compare two objects and use *–est* and *most* when comparing more than two.

SUM IT UP Adjectives make writing colorful, descriptive, and more precise. You can compare objects with *–er, –est, more,* and *most.*

Assess the Learning

- Confer with writers and ask them to use a variety of comparative forms to compare objects they are learning about in their content area classes. Identify students who need extra assistance in knowing when to use the endings and when to use *more* and *most.*
- Have students write letters of explanation to classmates to tell how to compare objects with comparative and superlative forms. Assess letters for understanding.

Link the Learning

- Ask students to write an explanation in the form of a classification (see Pulling It All Together section page 192). Encourage them to use comparative and superlative adjectives in their classifications.
- Have students generalize about the spelling changes that occur when forming comparative and superlative adjectives.
- Share a chart that shows the comparative and superlative forms of irregular adjectives. Encourage students to use a variety of forms in their writing:

Adjective	Comparative Form	Superlative Form
good	better	best
bad	worse	worst
far	farther	farthest
little	less	least
many	more	most

Adverbs: Comparative and Superlative Forms

DAY 1 Model the Focus Point

Adverbs are a great tool for us to use, because they allow us to describe action with so much more precision! We can use adverbs to compare actions, too. I am writing about animals' speeds using a tale as a lead: *Maybe you've heard....* Notice I am including two adverbs in this sentence: both *fast* and *strategically* are adverbs that describe the verb *race*. To compare the two actions, I am adding *–er* to *fast* to make the comparative form, *faster*. To make the comparative form of *strategically*, I am adding the word *more*. After all, *strategicallyer* would be a bit awkward, not to mention incorrect! Watch as I continue: *Moving at....* I am including another adverb in my writing—*better*. *Better* is the comparative form of the adverb *well*. Now comes one more comparison: *But which animal moves most swiftly of all?* Notice that in this comparison, I used *most* and not *more*. The words *of all* are a clue—I am comparing all animals, not just two. So I use the superlative form of the adverb—*most swiftly*.

> **Modeled Writing Sample**
>
> Maybe you've heard the tale of the tortoise and the hare—the hare lost when the tortoise raced not faster but more strategically. Moving at about 35 miles per hour, a hare races better than a tortoise, which clocks in at less than 2/10 of a mile an hour. But which animal moves most swiftly of all? Peregrine falcons can reach speeds of over 200 miles per hour!

TURN AND TALK **Partners, take a close look at adverbs. Find an adverb that compares. Does the adverb compare two objects or more than two? Explain how you can tell. Describe how to create the comparative and superlative forms of adverbs.**

SUM IT UP **Comparative adverbs compare two or more actions while superlative adverbs compare more than two. Add *–er* or *–est* to form comparative and superlative forms of most one-syllable adverbs. Use *more* or *most* for adverbs with two or more syllables.**

DAY 2 Guided Practice

TURN AND TALK **Discuss the meaning of the writing as you determine what compliment you'd offer the writer. Then think about comparative and superlative adverbs. Where might a comparative or superlative adverb make the writing even stronger?**

SUM IT UP Display the class editing chart. Add "To compare adverbs, use *–er, –est, more,* and *most*."

> Dear principle,
> I do not think students should be going door-to-door or openly Fundraising for the school. It could be dangerous going door-to-door without supervision. I also think it takes hour focus away from school. I can't think about writing or doing home work while fundraising. So I think students should not fundraise for the school

Resources CD: Copyediting Principal

Remember, use *–er* and *–est* to form comparative and superlative forms of one-syllable adverbs. For adverbs of two or more syllables, use *more* and *most*. You can also use *less* and *least*.

DAY 3 Independent Practice

Show writers how to look through a writing folder (your own or a student's) to find writing with adverbs that compare. Share your thinking with students as you proofread for and add comparative and superlative adverbs. Now turn the task over to student editors.

PEER EDIT Take turns reading your writing. Point out adverbs that compare. Identify a place where the writing could benefit from new comparative or superlative adverbs. Explain the rules you followed to create those adverbs.

SUM IT UP Remember, comparative adverbs compare two actions. Superlative adverbs compare three or more. For most one-syllable adverbs, add *–er* and *–est* to form comparative and superlative adverbs. For longer adverbs, generally add *more, most, less,* or *least* to compare actions.

Assess the Learning

- Ask students to identify comparative and superlative adverbs in their own writing and explain the rules they used to form them. Note students who need additional small-group instruction.
- During writing conferences, supply students with cloze sentences from which comparative or superlative adverbs are missing. Have them supply the correct forms and explain how they formed them.

Link the Learning

- Some adverbs change form to compare. Share this chart with students so they have it as a reference:

Adverb	Comparative	Superlative
much	more	most
little	less	least
well	better	best
badly	worse	worst

- Give special attention to tricky adverbs:
  - *Good* is always an adjective. *Well* can be either an adjective or adverb.
  - *Bad* is always an adjective. *Badly* is an adverb.
  - *Real* is an adjective. *Really* is an adverb.
- Comparative and superlative adverbs are tricky, especially for your English language learners. Be sure to find and highlight great sentences in mentor texts and ask students to identify the adverbs, explain how many actions are being compared, and identify the rules that were used to create the comparative and superlative forms.

Prepositions and Prepositional Phrases

DAY 1 Model the Focus Point

Consider giving students a reference list of prepositions to have on hand during the lesson.

As I write an explanation today telling how a GPS works, I am paying special attention to using prepositions. Prepositions explain relationships between ideas in sentences. Watch as I begin: *No matter where you are... find your way*. Notice that I am inserting a preposition, *on*. A noun, *globe*, comes after the preposition. The phrase *on the globe* is called a prepositional phrase. The phrase describes location—*on the globe*. Now I am continuing to write more about how a GPS works: *A GPS works with....* Can you point out the preposition? *With* is a preposition that begins the phrase *with Earth-orbiting satellites*. The phrase is an adverb, because it tells how a GPS works. I always strive for a variety of sentences in my writing, so watch as I begin my next sentence with an opener that is a prepositional phrase: *At any time... four of these satellites*. Actually, this sentence is full of prepositional phrases! The dependent clause *at any time of the day or night* includes two prepositional phrases, and the entire clause is an opener that functions as an adverb.

Modeled Writing Sample

No matter where you are on the globe, a global positioning system (GPS) can help you find your way. A GPS works with Earth-orbiting satellites. At any time of the day or night, your GPS can find four of these satellites. Once your GPS figures out the distance to the satellites, the GPS can calculate your position on Earth.

Continue the modeling, writing the last sentence.

TURN AND TALK Partners, take a look at the last sentence. Identify the prepositions. Identify the articles and nouns that make up the prepositional phrases.

SUM IT UP Prepositions link nouns, pronouns, and noun phrases to other words in a sentence. Prepositions usually tell relationships in time and place.

DAY 2 Guided Practice

TURN AND TALK Discuss the purpose of the writing. Identify the prepositional phrases as you pinpoint the prepositions. Explain how they tell more about time or location. Then describe a place in the writing that might benefit from a prepositional phrase.

SUM IT UP To a class editing chart, write "Prepositional phrase = preposition + noun phrase or pronoun."

Prepositions can show relationships like time and place. A prepositional phrase includes a preposition, a noun or pronoun, and any articles or adjectives that come between them. Prepositional phrases often function as adverbs.

Tsunamis

A tsunami is a large ocean wave that is caused by sudden motion on the ocean floor. This sudden motion could be anything from an earthquake, a powerful volcanic eruption, an underwater landslide, or even the impact of a large meteorite. Most tsunamis are caused by earthquakes. What happens is that there are two plates that have a lot of friction between them. They then become "stuck." As the stuck plate continues to descend into the mantle, there becomes a large buildup of energy. It can be stored for long periods of time – decades or even centuries. Energy keeps building until it exceeds the amount the plate can hold. When there is too much energy, the stuck plate snaps back into a position where it is not stuck. This sudden release of energy is the beginning of the tsunami. The moving wave then starts to travel to where the earthquake occurred. The shoreline has lowered from the tsunami, so the waves rush toward land to flood the shore. The waves will travel swiftly through open waters. When it hits it is like a "wave train" because the multiple waves will follow the large wave. After the tsunami hits, it can cause a substantial amount of damage. Only one tsunami can destroy an entire coastal village and remove all the sand from the beach that took hundreds of years to create. Tsunamis can also destroy islands of all its natural habitats and can cause death to surrounding areas. Overall, tsunamis are very dangerous and its good to know how they occur.

Resources CD: Tsunamis

DAY 3 Independent Practice

Select a sample from a student's writing folder to scan for prepositions. Identify the prepositions and phrases and share your thinking as you make sure that these phrases make sense in the sentences. Then have students look in their own writing folders to find pieces to reread with a focus on prepositions.

PEER EDIT **Work with your partner to identify prepositions and prepositional phrases in the writing. Then find a place that might benefit from the addition of a prepositional phrase used as an opener or placed elsewhere in a sentence.**

SUM IT UP **Prepositions often indicate place or time. Form a prepositional phrase with a preposition, modifiers or adjectives, and a noun, pronoun, or gerund.**

Assess the Learning

- Confer with writers to have them identify in context prepositions and the words that make up prepositional phrases.
- Scan student writing in their folders to locate evidence of understanding of prepositional phrases. Note those students who need further instruction.

Link the Learning

- Provide a reference list of prepositions: *about, above, according to, across, after, against, along, among, apart from, around, as, at, because of, before, behind, below, beneath, beside, between, beyond, by, despite, down, during, except, for, from, in, in addition to, in back of, in front of, in place of, inside, instead of, into, near, next, of, off, on, onto, on top, of, out of, outside, over, past, regarding, through, throughout, till, to, toward, under, underneath, until, up, upon, with, within, without.*
- The word *but* usually acts as a coordinating conjunction, but if it means "except," it's a preposition. *(Everyone but Teri went to the beach. We went to the beach, but Teri went to the zoo.)* Be sure students understand to use a comma before *but* only when *but* is a conjunction.
- Some prepositions can also function as subordinate conjunctions in complex sentences: *after, as, before, since,* and *until.* Remind students that nouns, pronouns, or gerunds along with their modifiers follow prepositions.

  Conjunction: After we packed up our picnic, we headed home.

  Preposition: The movie is after lunch.

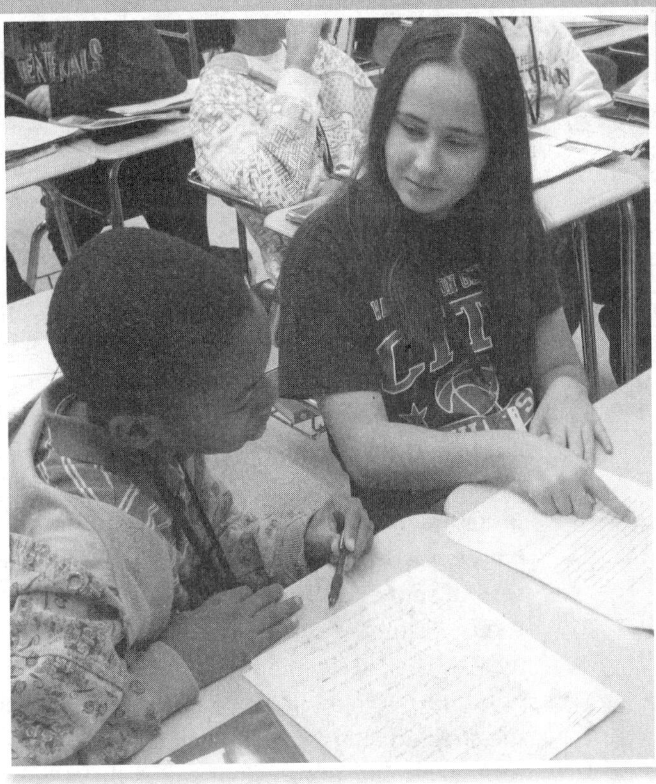

Cycles for Success With Spelling

Strategic spellers have a distinct sense of spelling consciousness that guides them in their writing. Spelling consciousness is the intuitive sense writers have that a word doesn't quite "look right." How do they know when a word doesn't look like it's correctly spelled? While students may rely on the spelling patterns they have learned, part of the secret is for a writer to trust his or her own intuition about words. If a word doesn't look right, it probably should be checked.

When writers approach spelling tasks strategically, they gain a sense of when they can use their own knowledge and when they need to consult a reference, such as a dictionary, a list of easily confused words, spell-checking software, and so on. To help your writers, lead them in developing spelling consciousness and effective strategies for spelling.

Cycles for Success With Spelling

Spelling Consciousness

DAY 1 Model the Focus Point

During my first draft, I'm really focused on ideas. I don't want to interrupt my thinking to correct spelling. When I'm writing, I make sure to underline words or put a little *sp* above them when I am not sure if I am spelling them correctly. It's a reminder to go back and check later, but it doesn't stop the flow of ideas. As I write my first sentence about recycling, I'm taking a close look at the word *separate*. Is the second vowel an *e* or an *a*? I'm not sure! So I'm underlining the word to remember to check it later. I'm wondering about *accumulates*, too, as I write my second sentence. It's such a great verb! I don't want to put a simple verb like *put* just because I'm not sure how to spell *accumulate*. So watch as I underline that word, too, to remind me to use a reference to check the spelling later. I'm using my spelling consciousness. That means that I pay attention to spelling and know when words don't quite "look right." I underline those words and then keep on writing to be sure that I've chosen the richest and most interesting words I can.

> **Modeled Writing Sample**
>
> When people first started recycling, they had to seperate their recyclables—plastics in one bin, glass in another, and so on. But my family accummulates all our recycling in one tub. How is it possible to sort them apart? Technology! Workers use magnets to remove the metal. Believe it or not, they can use lazers to sort papers and plastics. Each material gives back a different wavelength.

Share your thinking as you continue to model.

TURN AND TALK **Partners, think together as you evaluate this strategy. Why is it a good idea to underline words of which you're unsure and continue writing the first draft instead of using a reference during this stage?**

SUM IT UP **If a word doesn't look right, trust your spelling instincts and underline the word or mark it with *sp*. Return to it after you've drafted your content.**

DAY 2 Guided Practice

TURN AND TALK **Apply what you've learned about spelling consciousness as you reread this personal narrative. What words would you have underlined or marked with *sp*? Why?**

SUM IT UP Display the class editing chart. Add "Underline or write *sp* near any words with spellings you're unsure of."

While you're writing a first draft, focus on the ideas. If you write a word and are unsure you've spelled it correctly, underline it or mark it with *sp* so you'll remember to return to it later.

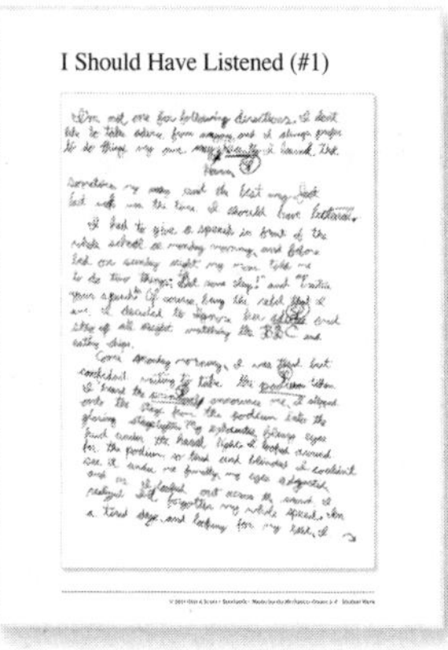

I Should Have Listened (#1)

Resources CD: I Should Have Listened

DAY 3 Independent Practice

Use a writing sample you've created to model spelling consciousness. Point out words that you've underlined and explain what about them didn't "look right." Then have students look through their own writing folders to reread with a closer eye on spelling.

PEER EDIT Define "spelling consciousness." Choose a piece of writing that shows you used your spelling consciousness. Clarify how it helps your work as a writer.

SUM IT UP If you are unsure of the spelling of a word, quickly underline it or mark it with *sp*. After writing, return to verify the spelling and, if necessary, correct it.

Assess the Learning

- As students write independently, observe which use spelling consciousness as evidenced by their use of underlines and *sp* on their papers.
- As you confer with writers, ask what "tips them off" that a word may be incorrectly spelled. Listen in to gauge understanding and provide extra support, if necessary.

Link the Learning

- Students might record the correct spellings of words that are tricky for them using the Word Bank form (in the Tools file on the Resources CD). Be sure they have used references to spell the words correctly!
- Encourage students to choose rich, robust words rather than words that are simply easy to spell. Use mentor texts to illustrate the effect of powerful words: Maya Angelou's *I Know Why the Caged Bird Sings,* Will Hobbs's *Down the Yukon,* Natalie Babbitt's *Tuck Everlasting,* Walter Wick's *A Drop of Water,* engaging articles from magazines such as *Muse* and *National Geographic,* and so on.
- Discuss resources for checking the spellings of words. Discus problems that might arise when using computer spell-checking.

Use Margin Spelling

DAY 1 Model the Focus Point

> **Modeled Writing Sample**
>
> **Night at the Opera**
>
> I have to admit, I was (sp) suspishous. A night at the opera? Isn't the opera long, boring, and ~~dreery~~ dreary? Maybe a great story set to music wouldn't be so bad. I ajusted my attitude and sank into the plush seat.
>
> suspicous
> suspicious
> suspishous
>
> drery
> dreery
> dreary
>
> adgustid
> adjusted

Today I am going to use a strategy called margin spelling to help me spell words correctly. A published piece would never include extra words on the page, but when I'm drafting, it's a great strategy to use! When I'm unsure of a spelling, I try out different spellings in the margin. If I figure out that one of them is correct, I cross out the misspelled word and write the correct spelling above it. What if I'm still unsure? In that case, I cross out all my attempts and put *sp* above the word. Then I can use a reference source to check the spelling after I'm done with the first draft. As I am writing about my night at the opera, I'm pausing as I write my first sentence: *I have to admit, I was suspishous.* I'm not sure I've spelled the last word correctly! I am trying some different spellings in the margin. None of these look quite right to me, so I'm putting an *sp* above the word to check it later. Watch as I continue: *A night at the opera? Isn't the opera long, boring, and dreery? Dreery* rhymes with *leery*, but they don't look like they are spelled the same way! Let me try a few margin spellings. Hmmm... now this looks familiar! I know to spell the word *dreary*. I'll correct it in my writing.

Continue to model, sharing your thinking as you use the margin to spell *adjusted*.

TURN AND TALK **Partners, evaluate the margin spelling strategy. How did it help me figure out the spellings of words?**

SUM IT UP **While you write, use margin spelling to try out different spellings of tricky words. Choose the correct spelling or mark the word to check it later.**

DAY 2 Guided Practice

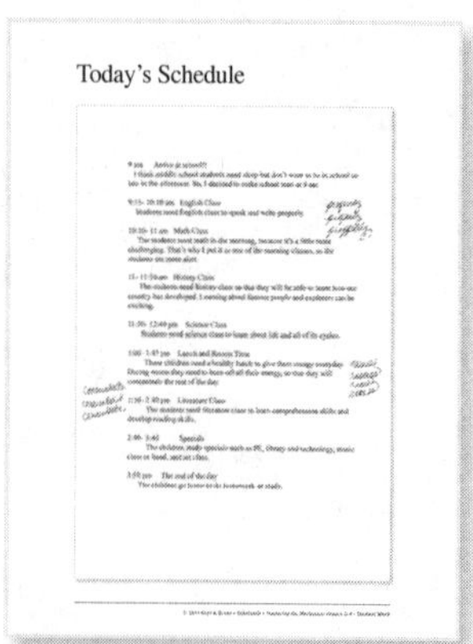
Resources CD: Today's Schedule

TURN AND TALK **Explain the writer's strategy for spelling words correctly in Today's Schedule. If you were this writer's editing partner, what feedback related to spelling would you share?**

SUM IT UP Display the class editing chart. Add "Use margin spelling to help with tricky words."

Margin spelling is a quick way to "try out" tricky words, using what you know about spelling strategies to see if any of the words "look right."

DAY 3 Independent Practice

Model scanning a paper for potential spelling errors. Try a few margin spellings, using a large piece of paper so students can see your attempts. After modeling, turn responsibility over to student editors.

PEER EDIT Compare margin spelling with your partner. Does margin spelling help you with spellings of tricky words? In what ways? Apply what you know about spelling to attempt a few more margin spellings for words that don't look quite right.

SUM IT UP Writers use margin spelling to help themselves identify correct spelling or remind them to check a word later.

Assess the Learning

- Have student editors each record one example of margin spelling attempts on sticky notes in their papers' margins. Collect the notes to analyze patterns of spelling errors and inform instruction.
- Emphasize with students the importance of making serious attempts at correct spelling in the margins rather than simply writing down groups of letters. As you confer with writers, note which may need additional support.

Link the Learning

- Talk about transferring the margin strategy to other content. For example, students might try different values of an unknown in an algebra problem or different solutions to a story problem in math class using "margin math."
- Share words with tricky spellings and have students write "margin spellings" on sticky notes to share with partners.
- Encourage students to use the Word Bank form (in the Tools file on the Resources CD) to record correct spellings of tricky words. Remind them to go back to the reference to choose robust words for their future writing.

Use Root Words

DAY 1 Model the Focus Point

Note: Reproduce the Word Parts reference (in the Tools file on the Resources CD). Display the complete model for students.

> **Modeled Writing Sample**
>
> What is the best kind of home for an amphibious pet? Animals like salamanders need aquariums so they can spend time on both water and land. Be careful to use a thermometer to monitor the temperature in the tank.

We can unlock both spellings and meanings of words when we break them into parts and take a closer look at each part. Salamanders are amphibious—they live on both land and water. But I wasn't sure how to spell *amphibious*. I tried starting with *amf*, but that didn't seem right to me. So I checked this reference, a chart with root words. *Amphibious* has a root, or word part—*amphi*. The root means "both sides." That makes sense in unlocking both spelling and meaning! Knowing the root helps me spell the word with *amphi* at the beginning and assures me that I've chosen the right word to classify salamanders. What if I didn't know how to spell *aquariums*? Could word parts give me a clue? My root list shows that *aqua* is a root that means "water." Checking the reference helps me spell the word and unlock its meaning.

TURN AND TALK **Partners, think together as you examine the chart. What can you find out about the word *thermometer*? How does the chart help you in unlocking both the meaning and the spelling?**

SUM IT UP **Root words have consistent spellings and meanings that can help us unlock the meanings and spellings of words. A root word reference can assist us with spelling and with choosing the correct word for our writing.**

DAY 2 Guided Practice

TURN AND TALK **Identify words in the text that have root words you can find on the chart. Clarify how the information on this chart may have assisted this writer with spelling. Define the words based on the meanings of the roots.**

SUM IT UP To the class editing chart, add "Use root words to unlock spellings and meanings."

Root words can help you with both the meanings and spellings of words in your writing. Use a root word reference to help you spell word parts.

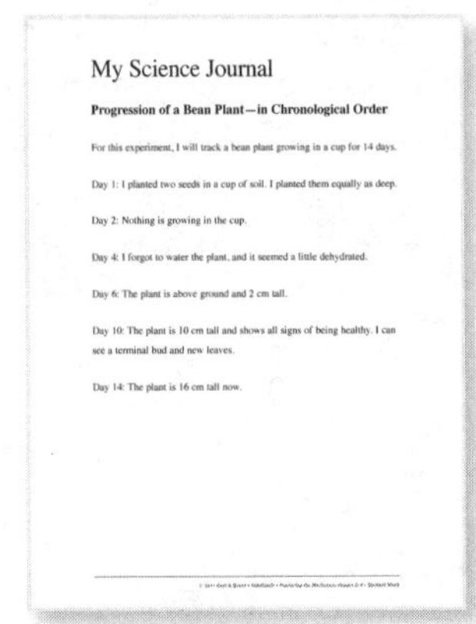
My Science Journal

Progression of a Bean Plant—in Chronological Order

For this experiment, I will track a bean plant growing in a cup for 14 days.

Day 1: I planted two seeds in a cup of soil. I planted them equally as deep.

Day 2: Nothing is growing in the cup.

Day 4: I forgot to water the plant, and it seemed a little dehydrated.

Day 6: The plant is above ground and 2 cm tall.

Day 10: The plant is 10 cm tall and shows all signs of being healthy. I can see a terminal bud and new leaves.

Day 14: The plant is 16 cm tall now.

Resources CD: My Science Journal

DAY 3 Independent Practice

Model how to scan a piece of writing for words that include roots, placing a sticky note near them. Use the Word Parts reference to check for both spelling and for meaning in context, making any necessary corrections. Then turn responsibility over to student editors, having them look through their own writing to check a word with a root or to add a powerful word that includes a root.

PEER EDIT **Share your work with your partner. Identify words with roots that you included in your writing. Identify as well any new words that you added. How did the Word Parts reference help you strengthen your writing?**

SUM IT UP **Many words contain roots that have specific meanings. Using a root word reference can help you with both correct spelling and precise meaning of words that include roots.**

Assess the Learning

- Collect student writing folders and scan for words with roots. Assess for correct spelling as well as for correct use of the words in context. Reteach as necessary.
- Give students words with roots and ask them to write sentences using the words in context. Be sure they have access to the Word Parts chart. Assess for understanding of root meaning.

Link the Learning

- Have students create posters of root word "families." For example, a poster with the root *graph* could include *telegraph, photograph, graphite, holograph, lithograph, calligraphy,* and so on.
- Students can scan mentor texts and content area texts for words with roots, add them to the Word Parts chart, and share with partners to discuss the words' meanings.

Use Prefixes and Suffixes

DAY 1 Model the Focus Point

Modeled Writing Sample

I'll admit it. My handwriting is illegible! My teacher Ms. Diecken says it's impossible to read. Sometimes I'm so preoccupied with my handwriting, it's hard to focus on the message. Let's have democracy in the classroom! I vote for word processing.

Note: Reproduce the Word Parts reference (in the Tools file on the Resources CD).

Words are made of different parts. The root is the part of the word that has the basic meaning of the word. We can also add affixes to words. A prefix comes before the root, and a suffix comes after. Understanding those affixes can help you unlock the meanings of words in text. As a writer, understanding affixes can also help you include precise words and focus on spelling. Watch as I begin: *I'll admit... legible!* I want to check word meaning, though. The word *legible* means "able to be read." The Prefixes section in the Word Parts tool shows me that the prefix *il–* means "not." So *illegible* means "not able to be read." That makes sense when we're talking about my handwriting! I'm revising to make the word *illegible*. I can generalize about the spelling when adding *il–*, too. Adding the prefix *il–* does not change the spelling of the root.

Continue discussing the meanings of words with prefixes and suffixes and the ways in which affixes affect spelling, using the words *teacher, impossible, preoccupied,* and *democracy.*

TURN AND TALK **Partners, think together about the prefixes and suffixes in the passage. How do prefixes and suffixes affect meaning? How can writing words with affixes make your writing more meaningful and concise?**

SUM IT UP **Prefixes and suffixes change the meanings of root words. We can generalize spelling rules with some of the affixes.**

DAY 2 Guided Practice

TURN AND TALK **Identify words with suffixes or prefixes in this piece. Look for their meanings on the chart. How do the affixes change meaning? How do they affect spelling?**

SUM IT UP To the class editing chart, add "Use prefixes and suffixes correctly for both spelling and meaning."

Understanding prefixes and suffixes can help you unlock the meanings of words. You can also predict how to spell some words with prefixes and suffixes. Use your spelling consciousness to consider whether the words you spell with affixes "look right."

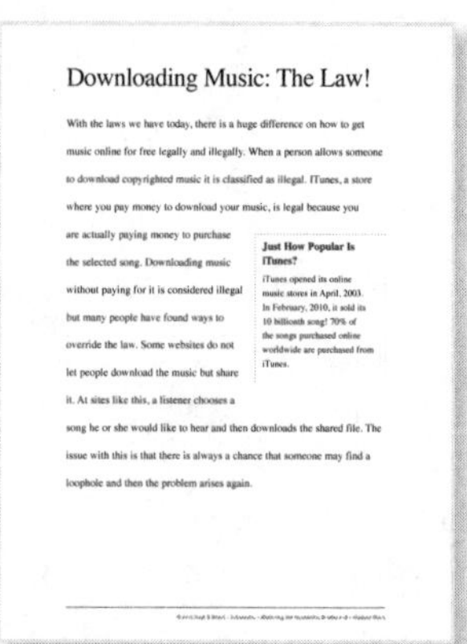

Downloading Music: The Law!

With the laws we have today, there is a huge difference on how to get music online for free legally and illegally. When a person allows someone to download copyrighted music it is classified as illegal. ITunes, a store where you pay money to download your music, is legal because you are actually paying money to purchase the selected song. Downloading music without paying for it is considered illegal but many people have found ways to override the law. Some websites do not let people download the music but share it. At sites like this, a listener chooses a song he or she would like to hear and then downloads the shared file. The issue with this is that there is always a chance that someone may find a loophole and then the problem arises again.

Just How Popular Is ITunes?

iTunes opened its online music stores in April, 2003. In February, 2010, it sold its 10 billionth song! 70% of the songs purchased online worldwide are purchased from iTunes.

Resources CD: Downloading Music: The Law!

DAY 3 Independent Practice

Model how to scan a piece of writing you've selected from a student's writing folder for words with affixes. Use the Word Parts tool to check for spelling and for meaning in context. Then have student editors look through their own writing to check words with affixes for sense and for spelling.

PEER EDIT **Identify words in your writing that include prefixes and suffixes. Did you add any new words with affixes? How did prefixes and suffixes strengthen your writing?**

SUM IT UP **Affixes change the meanings of root words. You can use a word parts reference to determine the meanings of words with affixes and to generalize about the spellings of roots when you add prefixes and suffixes.**

Assess the Learning

- Scan student writing for words with prefixes and suffixes. Assess for correct spelling as well as for correct use of the words in context.
- Ask writers to identify places where they could add words with affixes. Observe to be sure they choose the correct affixes and spell them correctly.

Link the Learning

- Supply groups with index cards that include roots, prefixes, and affixes, one part per card. Have them put the word parts together to create words and use the Word Parts tool to check meaning.
- Students may enjoy writing a list poem to describe a topic in science or social studies. Encourage them to include words with affixes.
- Have students contribute to affix dictionaries. Assign one suffix or prefix each to small groups. The first page of the dictionary should show the affix as well as a definition. Then each group member can create a page with a word that shows the affix, a definition, a sentence with the word used in context, and perhaps an illustration or photo.

Homophones and Easily Confused Words

DAY 1 Model the Focus Point

Note: Pass out copies of the Homophones and Easily Confused Words reference (in the Tools file on the Resources CD).

> **Modeled Writing Sample**
>
> Can you imagine if you're skin color matched the food you ate? That's what happens to the nudibranch (NEW-dih-bronk), a member of the sea slug family. It's name, meaning "naked gills," describes the gills on these animals' backs. Ranging in size from less then an inch to a foot long, colorful and intricate nudibranch live in warm shallow ocean waters.

As writers, it's important for us to focus on meaning. But some words in our writing confuse us. I have trouble sometimes with *a-c-c-e-p-t* and *e-x-c-e-p-t*. If you accept something, you believe it or you agree. The word *except* means "apart from." Using the wrong word could cause real problems for my readers' understanding! This chart shows groups of words that are easily confused and *homophones*, or words that sound alike but have different spellings and meanings. Looking at my writing about sea slugs, I'm wondering if I've used the correct spelling for *its*. It looks like I've made a mistake, because *it's* means "it is." That doesn't make sense in this sentence. Partners, take a look at this text and the reference as we check other homophones and words that we sometimes confuse. Focus on the words *you're* and *then*.

TURN AND TALK Writers, think together as you evaluate this tool. How might you use it to help make your writing clear to your readers?

SUM IT UP Homophones, like *to, two,* and *too,* are words that sound the same but have different spellings and meanings. Some words, like *affect* and *effect,* are often confused. It's important to choose the correct word so that our readers understand our messages.

DAY 2 Guided Practice

TURN AND TALK Partners, talk about the meaning of this writing. Apply what you know about homophones and easily confused words to help this writer. What changes would you suggest?

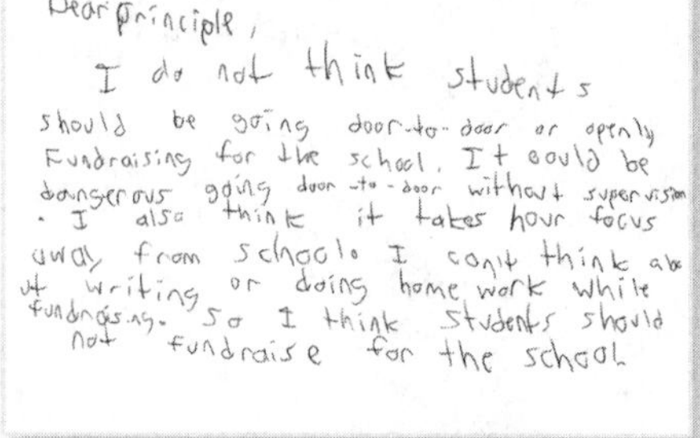

Dear principle,

I do not think students should be going door-to-door or openly Fundraising for the school. It could be dangerous going door-to-door without supervision. I also think it takes hour focus away from school. I can't think about writing or doing home work while fundraising. So I think students should not fundraise for the school

Resources CD: Copyediting Principal

SUM IT UP To a class editing chart, add "Watch for homophones and easily confused words."

To help our readers understand our messages, it's important to select the correct homophone or easily confused word. Consult a reference to be sure you've chosen the right one.

DAY 3 Independent Practice

Model how to scan a piece of writing for homophones or easily confused words, highlighting them in the text. Show how you use the homophone reference to check your work. Have student editors review their own writing for correct use of homophones.

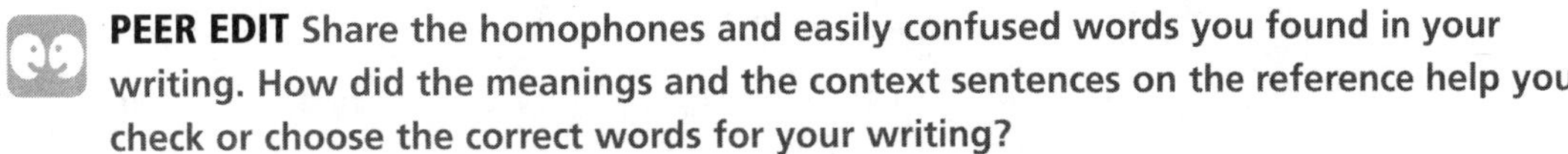

PEER EDIT Share the homophones and easily confused words you found in your writing. How did the meanings and the context sentences on the reference help you check or choose the correct words for your writing?

SUM IT UP Homophones sound the same, but choosing the incorrect homophone can make your writing confusing. Some words are easily confused. It's important to choose the correct one to make writing clear.

Assess the Learning

- Gather student writing samples to scan for homophones. Assess your students' understanding.
- Have students work in their writers' notebooks to create their own context sentences for homophones or easily confused words. Collect notebooks to note which students may need additional support in understanding these word groups.

Link the Learning

- The Homophone and Easily Confused Words tool contains just a sampling of words that are often confusing for middle school students. Provide students with other groups of words that they can add to the reference (or have them research to find more). Students should include both definitions and context sentences.
- Provide cloze sentences with homophones omitted. Partners can work together to choose the correct words for the context. Pairs might enjoy writing sentences for other pairs to "solve." For example: *(write/right) I am learning how to ___ in the style of calligraphy. What is the ____ tool for this job? (through/threw) The quarterback ____ the ball, right ____ the hands of the waiting receiver.*
- Have students create posters to show a pair or group of homophones. Students can include context sentences as well as illustrations to help readers remember which words to use in context.
- Have students examine mentor books for homophones in context. Consider sharing *Miss Alaineus: A Vocabulary Disaster* by Debra Frasier, A Series of Unfortunate Events series by Lemony Snicket, and engaging nonfiction magazines and content area texts.

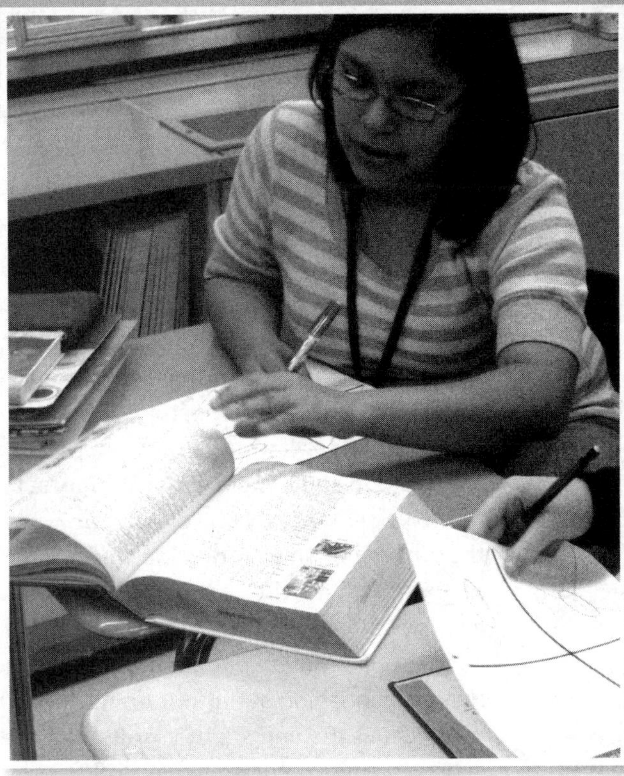

Cycles for Success With Text Features

Authors use text features to present and organize information. We teach students as readers to use text features such as headings and bold print to preview and predict, to scan to prepare for reading. Text features help us identify important messages in text and to understand challenging ideas.

Teaching students to write with text features will allow them to fine-tune their messages, to assist their readers by offering them scaffolds for understanding, and to think hard about what is really important and needs to be emphasized in writing.

Cycles for Success With Text Features

Titles, Headings, and Subheadings

DAY 1 Model the Focus Point

Writers, I've created an explanation about composting—it's a great way to recycle! I'm looking back at my writing, and I'm noticing that, while the information is helpful, it's all crunched together without any organization for my readers. I often write my title when I'm finished writing. Watch as I add a simple title: *Composting: Recycle and Reuse*. Notice that I capitalized all the important words. Now to add some more organization. As I read the first two sentences, *In a forest... at home*, I notice that these are an introduction to composting. As I read on, I notice that the next two sentences are like a "how-to"—how to make a compost bin. Watch as I add a heading, *Making a Compost Bin*. I need to make the heading stand out on its own line. I am capitalizing the important words—not the article *a*.

Modeled Writing Sample

In a forest, leaves fall to the ground, decompose, and create rich soil that makes new things grow. You can do the same thing by making compost at home. Set up a bin in a corner of your yard. Then add the "stuff" that will compost—dried leaves, green ingredients like glass clippings and vegetable scraps, soil that has bugs and worms in it, and water. You can use compost as a mulch. You can also mix compost with sand to make potting soil or place it in a hole before you plant seeds.

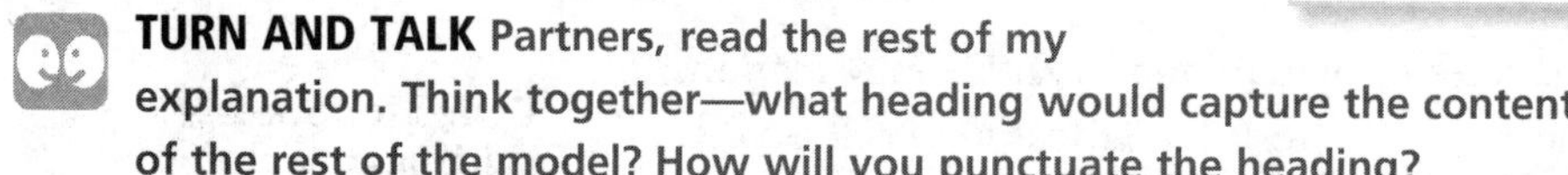

TURN AND TALK **Partners, read the rest of my explanation. Think together—what heading would capture the content of the rest of the model? How will you punctuate the heading?**

Honor students' thinking as you craft a heading:

I heard some great ideas! Watch as I insert another heading—*Using Your Compost*. Notice that I set the heading on its own line, and I capitalize all the words, because they are all important words.

SUM IT UP **A title prepares readers for the purpose and message of the text. Headings keep information organized. They show readers the main ideas of sections of text at a glance.**

DAY 2 Guided Practice

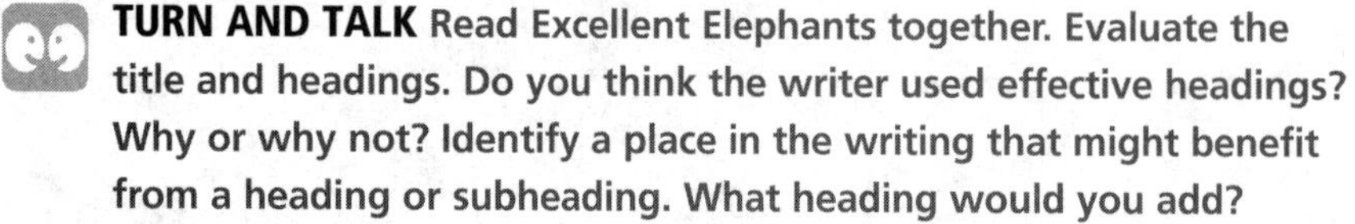

TURN AND TALK **Read Excellent Elephants together. Evaluate the title and headings. Do you think the writer used effective headings? Why or why not? Identify a place in the writing that might benefit from a heading or subheading. What heading would you add?**

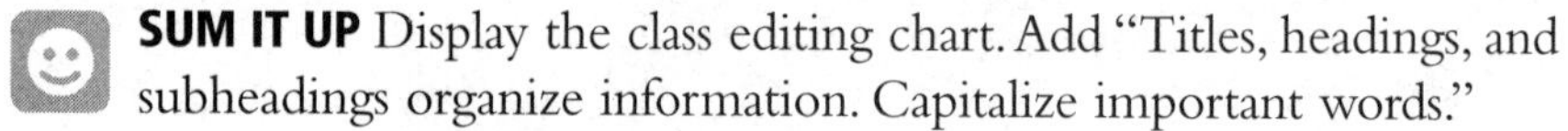

SUM IT UP Display the class editing chart. Add "Titles, headings, and subheadings organize information. Capitalize important words."

Titles key our readers in to the message of the text, and headings and subheadings organize information. Subheadings organize the information under the headings.

Excellent Elephants

What Elephants Can Do

Two Types Of Elephants

Resources CD: Excellent Elephants

DAY 3 Independent Practice

Select a writing sample from a student's writing folder. Think aloud as you check the title and then consider headings and subheadings in the piece. Add a heading or subheading to make organization clear. Then turn responsibility over to student editors to double-check the text features.

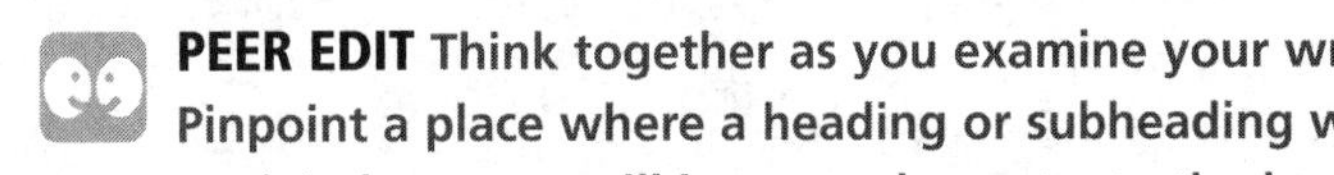

PEER EDIT **Think together as you examine your writing for organizational structures. Pinpoint a place where a heading or subheading would be helpful to your readers. Explain how you will insert and punctuate the heading.**

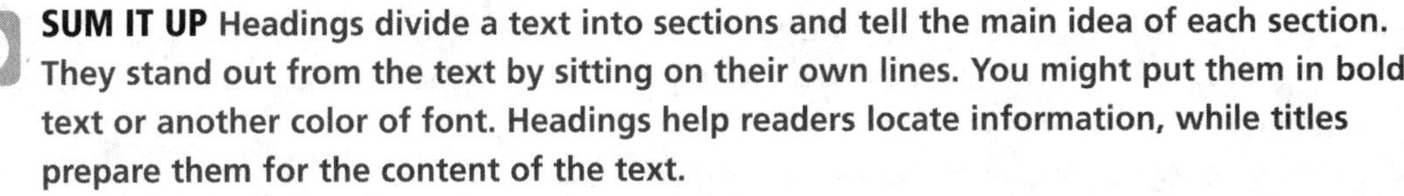

SUM IT UP **Headings divide a text into sections and tell the main idea of each section. They stand out from the text by sitting on their own lines. You might put them in bold text or another color of font. Headings help readers locate information, while titles prepare them for the content of the text.**

Assess the Learning

- Collect students' writing folders to look for their attempts at organizing with headings and subheadings. Note those students who may need assistance to place headings and subheadings in their writing.
- During writing conferences, give students short passages and ask them to create titles for the passages. Check that titles make sense, fitting both purpose and message.

Link the Learning

- This lesson focuses on titles, headings, and subheadings as tools for organization. If students need additional help with capitalization, see the lesson on page 56.
- Take a piece of informational text that includes a title, headings, and subheadings and remove them or cover them with sticky notes. Have students work in teams to write replacements that make sense. Remind students that headings provide previews for readers by capturing main ideas. Students might compare their work with the author's.
- Encourage students to experiment with different types of headings, such as questions, statements, and topics.

Table of Contents

DAY 1 Model the Focus Point

This modeling involves the teacher's using an informational report that was already created. You might also choose a nonfiction mentor text and use it as the basis of the model.

> **Modeled Writing Sample**
>
> **How Does Electricity Work?**
>
> Electricity and Electrons 1
>
> Series Circuits 3
>
> Parallel Circuits 4
>
> Static Electricity........................ 6

I created this great report about electricity—it has information about electronics, different kinds of circuits, and static electricity. I am wondering, though. What if my readers wanted to find information about only one of these topics? How could I help my readers navigate through this text? I am going to create a table of contents, a list of topics at the beginning of the report. First, it's important to organize the information within the report. Watch as I add subheads to each part of the text. I need to make sure to capitalize all words except articles and prepositions of fewer than five letters. Now to create the table of contents: I use a fresh sheet of paper—the table of contents comes before the rest of the text. Notice that I write the title at the top of the table of contents. Now I am looking at my report for the first heading—*Electricity and Electrons*. I write that as my first entry and list the page number. The next section is called *Series Circuits*, so I will add that next, along with the page number. I also notice that a table of contents is different from an index. An index lists topics in alphabetical order, while the table of contents lists them in the order in which they appear.

TURN AND TALK Writers, think together about the table of contents. How does a table of contents help you as you write? How does it help your readers?

SUM IT UP A table of contents lists the major parts of a piece of text along with their page numbers. The entries are in the order in which they appear in the text, not in alphabetical order.

DAY 2 Guided Practice

TURN AND TALK Writers, think together about this table of contents. What information would you expect to find in this book? What feedback would you offer this writer?

SUM IT UP To a class editing chart, add "Put topics and page numbers in text order and match headings to create a table of contents."

A table of contents is an overview for your readers. Be sure to list the topics in the order in which they occur in the text, followed by page numbers. Match page headings to keep your work organized.

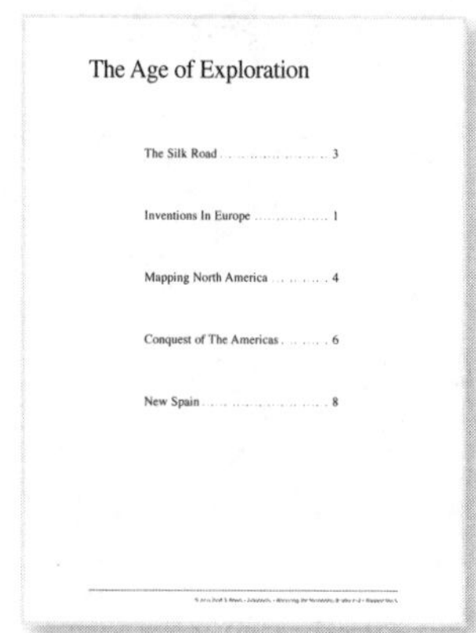

The Age of Exploration

The Silk Road 3

Inventions In Europe 1

Mapping North America 4

Conquest of The Americas 6

New Spain 8

Resources CD: The Age of Exploration

DAY 3 Independent Practice

Locate a piece of writing in a student's folder that includes a table of contents—or would benefit from one. Share your thinking as you proofread or add a table of contents. Then have students locate pieces in their own writing folders to which they might add tables of contents.

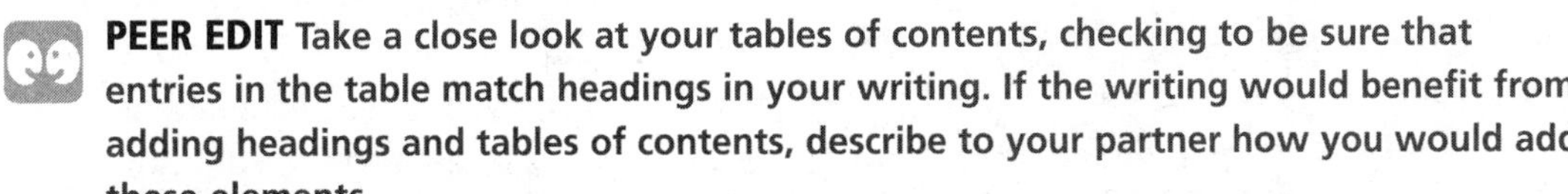

PEER EDIT Take a close look at your tables of contents, checking to be sure that entries in the table match headings in your writing. If the writing would benefit from adding headings and tables of contents, describe to your partner how you would add these elements.

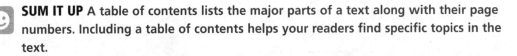

SUM IT UP A table of contents lists the major parts of a text along with their page numbers. Including a table of contents helps your readers find specific topics in the text.

Assess the Learning

- Analyze student pieces for errors, such as topics out of order, topics that don't match headings or content, or entries that are inconsistent.
- Ask students to write a procedural text that explains how to create a table of contents. Assess for understanding.

Link the Learning

- Have students create both headings and tables of contents for mentor texts that do not have those features.
- An index, contained in the back of the text, lists topics in alphabetical order rather than page order. Discuss with students when they would use an index to locate information. Students might create indices for their own or for mentor texts.
- Students who have mastered tables of contents may want to work on glossaries, lists of key terms in alphabetical order. Each glossary entry includes a definition.

Captions

DAY 1 Model the Focus Point

When we create informational text, photographs and illustrations give information in visual ways and help readers understand ideas. I am writing a description of a very unusual animal, the platypus. Watch as I begin to write: *The platypus... saw it.* I think a platypus is so interesting, only a photograph can give my readers a true glimpse into its appearance and its adaptations! I am inserting this photograph. It gives readers a clear picture of a platypus, but I am adding a caption, a sentence that tells my reader what this picture is about: *Webbed toes propel....* Notice that my caption is a complete sentence. This caption gives information that is not included in the main text. The platypus has a unique snout, too. I am including a picture that shows the snout close up. I am sure my readers will want to know more about this! So watch as I write another caption: *A platypus's snout....*

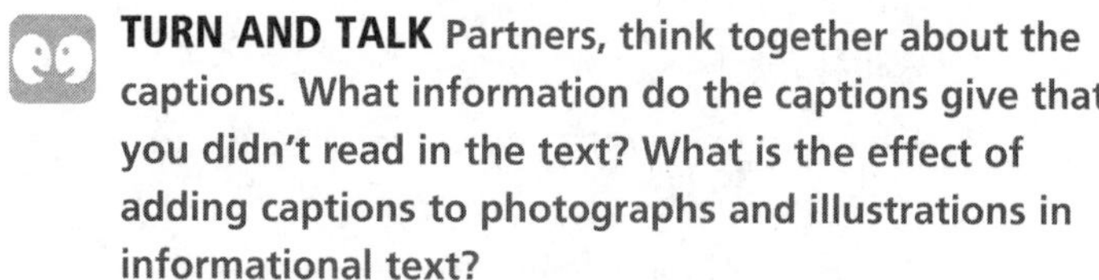

TURN AND TALK Partners, think together about the captions. What information do the captions give that you didn't read in the text? What is the effect of adding captions to photographs and illustrations in informational text?

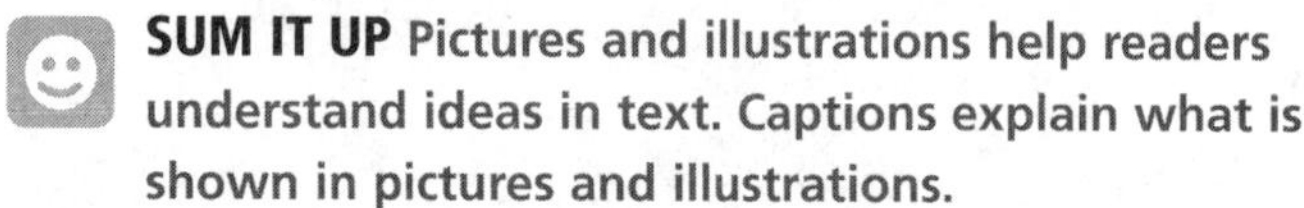

SUM IT UP Pictures and illustrations help readers understand ideas in text. Captions explain what is shown in pictures and illustrations.

Modeled Writing Sample

The platypus, an unusual mammal native to Australia, is one of only a few venomous mammals. Its unusual appearance confused explorers who first saw it.

Webbed toes propel the platypus through the water.

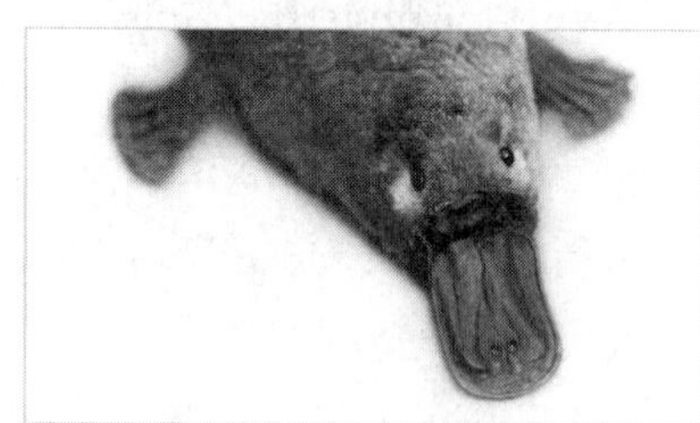

A platypus's snout does not open like a duck's beak—it's a sensory organ.

DAY 2 Guided Practice

TURN AND TALK Writers, take a close look at this piece with an eye on the caption. What information does the caption give you? Is that information in the text, or does the caption give new information? Describe a photograph or illustration that you would add to this piece. What caption would you write to go with it?

SUM IT UP Display the class editing chart. Add "Captions are sentences that tell more about photographs or illustrations."

Informational text often includes photographs and illustrations that tell more about the content. We write captions to explain those photos and illustrations to our readers.

Excellent Elephants

What Elephants Can Do

Elephants are very intelligent and can even sense grief. They like to make music, art, and play with tools. Elephants also have an exceptional sense of hearing and smell. Their trunks are very sensitive and sometimes you can see elephants listening by putting their trunks to the ground and carefully positioning their feet. Elephants do have poor eyesight though.

Elephants can reach up and grab things with their trunks.

Elephants can also make a variety of noises, some being very loud. Elephants are **herbivores**, meaning they only eat plants. They can spend up to 16 hours a day eating plants. Elephants also havea strange social life. Females and Males are very different. The females will spend their entire lives in a tightly knit group of mothers, daughters, sisters, and aunts. Males live mostly **solitary** lives. Most female family groups range from between five to fifteen adults. When a group gets too big, a few of the older daughters will break off and form a new group. A male elephant's life is very different. As he gets older, he will edge away from the group and later on set off on his own. When you see male elephants fighting, you may think it is very fierce and angry, but normally there is no damage or injury at all.

Two Types Of Elephants

There are two types of elephants, the African and the Asian. But in the African elephant genus there are two or three separate species. African elephants can be found in 37 different countries in Africa. You can tell the African elephant from the Asian elephant mainly because of its larger ears. But also the African elephant is much bigger and has a different back then the Asian elephant. African elephants also have tusks in the males and females, where in the Asian only the males do. African elephants are also less hairy then Asian elephants. Asian elephants are also called Indian elephants. The world population is estimated to be 60,000, which is about a tenth of the African elephant population. A lot of Asian elephants are domesticated, while African elephants are normally not domesticated.

Resources CD: Excellent Elephants

DAY 3 Independent Practice

Look through a student's writing folder to find a piece of informational text that would benefit from the addition of a photograph with a caption. Share your thinking as you choose a photo to go with the text and write a caption that offers additional information. Have students look through their own writing folders for informational writing to which they might add photographs or illustrations and captions.

PEER EDIT Apply what you've learned about photographs with captions as you examine these pieces of text. What photographs or illustrations might help readers better understand the content? What captions would you add?

SUM IT UP Photographs and illustrations can add valuable information! But be sure to include captions to help your readers understand what they see. Most captions are complete sentences and tell something new.

Assess the Learning

- Collect student writing samples that include pictures or illustrations with captions. Scan to make sure the text matches the picture and that students used complete sentences in their captions. Note areas that may need further instruction.
- Ask students to use sticky notes to mark photographs with captions in informational text. As they share them with others in small groups, listen in to be sure students understand the kinds of information given in captions and can evaluative their effectiveness.

Link the Learning

- Have students create captions for other kinds of visuals in their writing, such as maps, diagrams, graphs, and so on.
- Have students examine captions in various mentor texts, including textbooks, nonfiction magazines, and newspapers. Encourage them to evaluate the captions as they consider the content that the captions add.
- Provide students with primary source documents, such as photographs of historical events. Work with students to write captions for the photographs. Challenge them to capture the mood of the events in their captions.

Bolded Words and Font Changes

DAY 1 Model the Focus Point

The style and color of text are signals to readers—they draw attention to important information. As I write an explanation about muscles, my goal is to use different fonts and type styles to draw attention to important ideas. After my title, *Your Muscles*, I am starting with a heading that's a question: *What can....* If I were typing, I'd draw attention to the question with italics. Notice that I underline it so that it stands out for my readers. I am writing my first two sentences about the first type of muscles, smooth muscles: *Smooth muscles... digestive system.* Taking a close look at the sentences, I'm thinking that it would help my readers if I bolded the words *smooth muscles*. Why? Because I am going to write about three types of muscles. I'll bold each of the three types of muscles to emphasize them for my readers. Watch as I start my next two sentences with another bold phrase to emphasize a type of muscles: *Cardiac muscles....* I'm noticing that I've included a word my readers may not know, *involuntary*. They might be able to figure it out because of the word *too*—just like smooth muscles, cardiac muscles work without your thinking about them. But I'm going to make that word a different color, blue, and then put that word in a glossary at the end of my report on the human body.

> Modeled Writing Sample
>
> Your Muscles
>
> What can your muscles do?
>
> **Smooth muscles** work without your thinking about it. The muscles in your stomach, for example, squeeze and relax to push food through your digestive system. **Cardiac muscles** are involuntary, too! The cardiac muscles contract and then ease to send blood coursing through your veins. The **skeletal muscles** are voluntary—they only move when you want them to move. They help you stretch, kick a soccer ball, lift things—and smile.

Write the last group of sentences, sharing your thinking as you bold *skeletal muscles.*

TURN AND TALK **Partners, take a look at the bold words, the underlining, and the color. How do they help you understand what you're reading?**

SUM IT UP **The style and color of text can signal readers to pay attention to certain words and concepts. Bold words are often key words that readers need to know.**

DAY 2 Guided Practice

TURN AND TALK **Examine The Grassy Savanna—what advice would you give to this writer about using bold type and other font changes? What ideas would you make stand out by working with bold, underlining and italics, and colored text?**

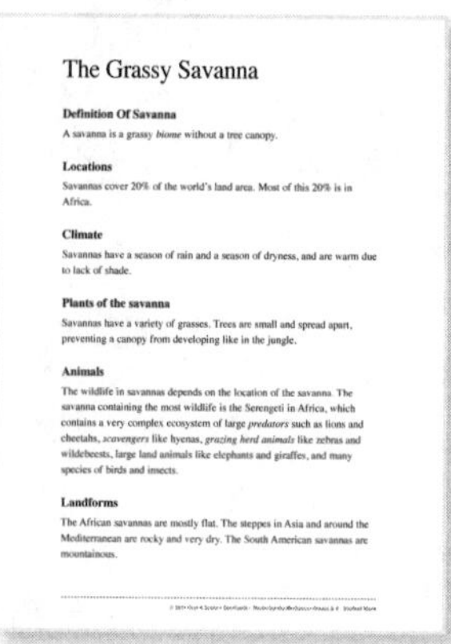
The Grassy Savanna

Definition Of Savanna

A savanna is a grassy *biome* without a tree canopy.

Locations

Savannas cover 20% of the world's land area. Most of this 20% is in Africa.

Climate

Savannas have a season of rain and a season of dryness, and are warm due to lack of shade.

Plants of the savanna

Savannas have a variety of grasses. Trees are small and spread apart, preventing a canopy from developing like in the jungle.

Animals

The wildlife in savannas depends on the location of the savanna. The savanna containing the most wildlife is the Serengeti in Africa, which contains a very complex ecosystem of large *predators* such as lions and cheetahs, *scavengers* like hyenas, *grazing herd animals* like zebras and wildebeests, large land animals like elephants and giraffes, and many species of birds and insects.

Landforms

The African savannas are mostly flat. The steppes in Asia and around the Mediterranean are rocky and very dry. The South American savannas are mountainous.

Resources CD: The Grassy Savanna

SUM IT UP To the class editing chart, add "Bold text and font changes signal important ideas to readers."

When you bold words in the text or use other font changes, you get your readers' attention. Don't bold or specially designate every word! Just the most important ones.

DAY 3 Independent Practice

Select a piece of writing from a student's writing folder. Share your thinking as you scan the text for words with bold and colored type and with other font changes. You might add font changes to some of the words, or remove them if they are overused. Then have student editors take over the tasks.

PEER EDIT Identify a place where bolding a word could make it stand out for your readers. Where might you place italics or underlining to underscore an important idea or question?

SUM IT UP Bold, underlined, and colored text draws readers' attention to important information and helps keep ideas organized.

Assess the Learning

- Ask students to share their writing, pointing out bold or underlined words and explaining the thinking behind their font changes.
- Scan student writing for bold or underlined words. Note areas of difficulty, such as not using bold words at all, overusing bold words, and emphasizing ideas that are not that important.

Link the Learning

- Have students scan mentor texts, such as content area textbooks, magazine articles, and newspapers, for use of bold words and other font changes. They can share examples and discuss their effects.
- Ask students to revisit pieces in their writing folders to determine which might benefit from font changes. Caution them not to overdo, but instead to consider what font changes will be truly helpful for their readers.
- Have students practice creating bold, italic, and color changes with word processing programs. They can write procedural texts to post in the school or class computer center.

Text Boxes

DAY 1 Model the Focus Point

I'm writing today about one of my favorite animals, lemurs! Watch as I write general information about them. I am focusing on the type of animal lemurs are, where they live, and the fact that lemurs are endangered animals: *Lemurs are members. . . are endangered.* This is all great information, but I'm realizing that my readers may want to know more about one particular type of lemur, the ring-tailed lemur. These are the best-known lemurs, and they have interesting habits and bodies. Instead of adding a new paragraph, I want to set the interesting information aside. Watch as I use a text box to highlight these amazing animals! I am drawing a box and starting new text inside the box. Notice I include a title and then just a few interesting sentences. The writing in a text box does not need to be long.

Modeled Writing Sample

Lemurs

Lemurs are members of the primate family. They live only on the island of Madagascar, just east of Africa. The island is home to a number of habitats, such as rainforests and marshlands—and lemurs live in almost all of them. Sadly, both hunting and the destruction of the rainforest have reduced the number of lemurs. All of the more than 30 species of lemur are endangered.

Ring-Tailed Lemurs

These lemurs spend more time on the ground than other lemurs. Ring-tailed lemurs' hind legs are longer than their front legs, so they look interesting when they walk on all fours!

TURN AND TALK Partners, think together about the text box. What new information does the text box give about lemurs? How does setting the information aside in a text box affect your approach to reading the text?

SUM IT UP A text box provides more information about a topic than the text provides. Use a text box to set aside, or emphasize, interesting or important information.

DAY 2 Guided Practice

TURN AND TALK Focus on the text box in Downloading Music. Describe how the writer used a text box to draw your attention to important or interesting information. What text box might this writer add? Explain why it would be helpful.

SUM IT UP Display the class editing chart. Add "Text boxes set aside important or interesting information for the reader."

Text boxes help readers by creating interest or adding important information about a topic.

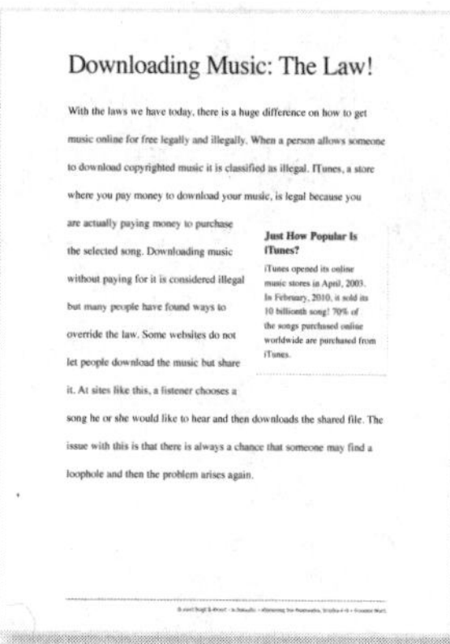

Downloading Music: The Law!

With the laws we have today, there is a huge difference on how to get music online for free legally and illegally. When a person allows someone to download copyrighted music it is classified as illegal. ITunes, a store where you pay money to download your music, is legal because you are actually paying money to purchase the selected song. Downloading music without paying for it is considered illegal but many people have found ways to override the law. Some websites do not let people download the music but share it. At sites like this, a listener chooses a song he or she would like to hear and then downloads the shared file. The issue with this is that there is always a chance that someone may find a loophole and then the problem arises again.

Just How Popular Is iTunes?

iTunes opened its online music stores in April, 2003. In February, 2010, it sold its 10 billionth song! 70% of the songs purchased online worldwide are purchased from iTunes.

Resources CD: Downloading Music: The Law!

DAY 3 Independent Practice

Locate a student's writing sample that has text boxes or would benefit from their addition. Share your thinking as you check that the text box adds interesting or important information. Then have students choose pieces of writing to look over with a new emphasis on text boxes.

PEER EDIT **Verify with your partner that any text boxes you already have in your writing include new or interesting information, are enclosed from the main text, and contain complete sentences. Then identify with your partner a new piece of information that you could place in a text box.**

SUM IT UP **Text boxes are pieces of text that excite your reader or give extra information about a topic. Text boxes are great places for interesting or mysterious facts. Be sure you set them aside from the main text and write complete sentences inside the text boxes.**

Assess the Learning

- Scan student writing for text boxes. Note which students need assistance to place text boxes in their writing and which may need assistance in choosing appropriate information to place in the boxes.
- Confer with individual writers, asking them to show you text boxes in their work, explaining why they used them and how they formed them.

Link the Learning

- Encourage students to return to previous pieces of writing to insert text boxes into their work. Although the emphasis in this lesson is on informational text, ask students how they might use text boxes in narrative, procedural, or persuasive texts.
- Have students scan mentor texts, such as high-quality nonfiction magazines, to examine how writers use text boxes. Encourage students to share great examples of text boxes and talk about what kind of information the text boxes give.
- Share nonfiction books with students. Encourage them to work with partners to craft text boxes on sticky notes and place them in the text.
- Have students experiment with text boxes in their word processing program. They can create procedural texts for adding text boxes and place the procedures near the computers or put them in their writing folders for reference.

Bulleted Lists

DAY 1 Model the Focus Point

Bullets are small dots in writing that help us organize items in a list. I'm writing today about emperor penguins. I find it fascinating that these penguins can survive in such a harsh, cold environment! Watch as I begin my writing: *Emperor penguins... waters.* Now I want to write about the body adaptations and the behaviors that help these penguins survive. I start my sentence just as I would any sentence: *These majestic penguins...* but then end with a colon. I could make a list with commas or semicolons, but bullets make the items stand out. Notice that I put one item after each bullet. Each bullet starts a new line of text. Because each of these items is a noun phrase and not a sentence, I don't include any end punctuation. I'm now listing each of the penguins' adaptations in the bulleted list.

Modeled Writing Sample

Emperor penguins live in one of the harshest environments on Earth, surrounded by frigid air, harsh winds, and icy waters. These majestic penguins have adaptations and behaviors that help them adjust to their surroundings:

- short, densely packed feathers
- a thick layer of fat underneath the skin
- dark-colored skin that absorbs heat
- huddling in large groups

TURN AND TALK **Writers, think together. What is the effect of using bullets instead of placing the items in a series in a sentence?**

SUM IT UP **Bullets organize lists of items. The items in bulleted lists need to be parallel—all nouns or noun phrases or all sentences, for example. If the items in a bulleted list are not sentences, you do not need to put a period after each item in the list.**

DAY 2 Guided Practice

TURN AND TALK **What advice would you give to the writer of this piece about using bulleted lists? Consider how you might better organize the writing by adding a bulleted list. (Students, for example, could organize arguments in favor of zoos with a summarizing bulleted list.)**

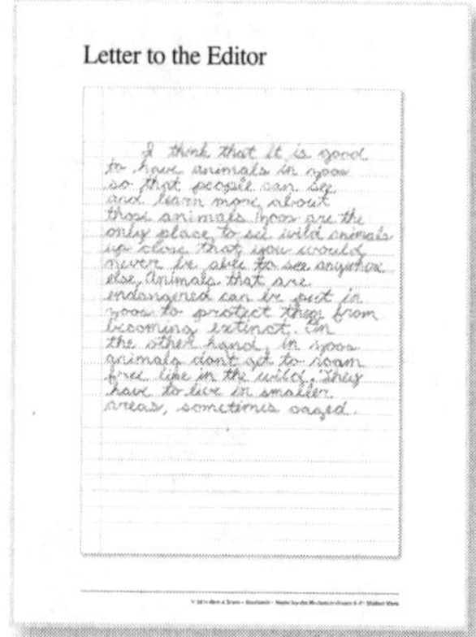
Letter to the Editor

I think that it is good to have animals in zoos so that people can see and learn more about those animals. Zoos are the only place to see wild animals up close that you would never be able to see anywhere else. Animals that are endangered can be put in zoos to protect them from becoming extinct. On the other hand, in zoos animals don't get to roam free like in the wild. They have to live in smaller areas, sometimes caged.

Resources CD: Letter to the Editor

SUM IT UP To a class editing chart, add "Bulleted lists organize ideas in list form to emphasize them for readers."

Items in a bulleted list are easy for readers to scan at a glance. Be sure when you use bullets that the items in the list are parallel—all nouns, all noun phrases, all clauses, and so on. If you introduce the bulleted list with a complete sentence, you don't need to put periods after each item in the list.

DAY 3 Independent Practice

Locate a student's writing sample that includes a bulleted list or that would benefit from adding one. Think aloud as you proofread to check that each item includes a bullet and that each bullet is on its own line. Then turn responsibility over to student editors as they add bulleted lists to their own writing.

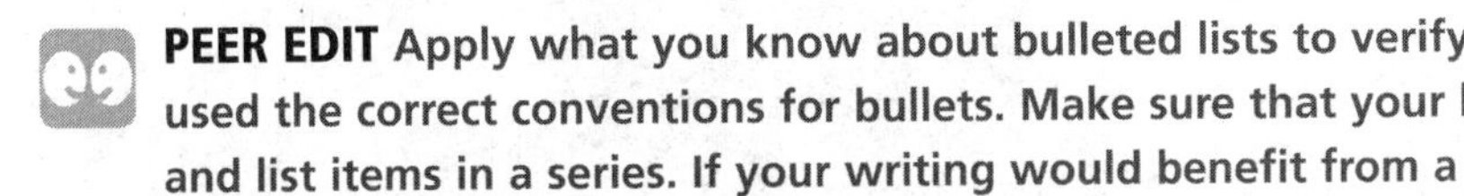

PEER EDIT Apply what you know about bulleted lists to verify that your partner has used the correct conventions for bullets. Make sure that your bulleted lists are parallel and list items in a series. If your writing would benefit from a bulleted list, add the list, thinking about the punctuation.

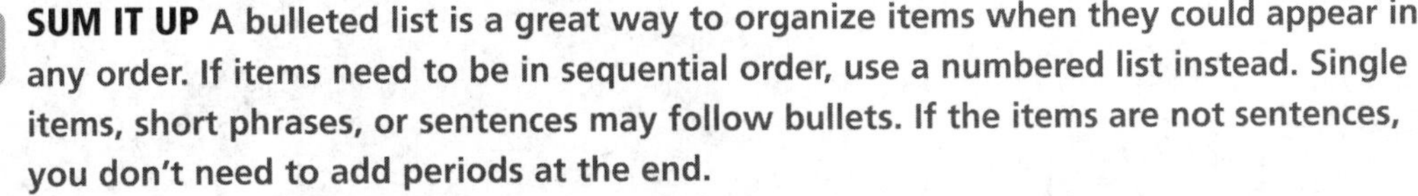

SUM IT UP A bulleted list is a great way to organize items when they could appear in any order. If items need to be in sequential order, use a numbered list instead. Single items, short phrases, or sentences may follow bullets. If the items are not sentences, you don't need to add periods at the end.

Assess the Learning

- Survey students' writing folders for pieces that include bulleted lists. Note error patterns, such as inconsistent list items and punctuation errors, to provide targeted instruction.
- During writing conferences, ask students to point out bulleted lists in their writing. Have them explain why they chose to use a bulleted list rather than a numbered list or items in a series in a sentence.

Link the Learning

- Remind students that they should use numbered items rather than bullets if they are writing a procedural text in which steps need to be done in order. A rule of thumb is that bullets are best for items in which the order of the items could be changed.
- Point out to students that not all style guides agree on how to punctuate bulleted lists. Encourage them to be consistent when they use bulleted lists in their writing. When word processing, using automatic bullets will create a style for punctuating bulleted lists. Most style guides omit ending periods from list items unless those list items are complete sentences.

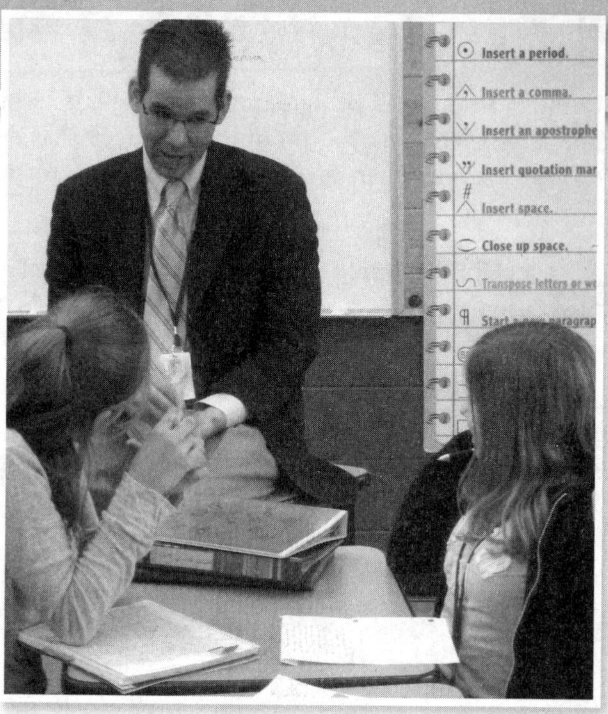

Pulling It All Together Cycles

Pulling It All Together Cycles are fully developed cycles that are linked back to the Yearlong Planner. (See the interior cover of this book.) They are designed to tie together multiple points of learning. These cycles provide intensive review of three weeks' worth of learning within the context of an authentic writing experience intended for a real audience.

Pulling It All Together Cycles

Each cycle features an authentic, rigorous writing activity. You can adapt these cycles to fit content that you are teaching in your classroom or to match subject matter in other content area classes. Note that all the writing activities are nonfiction, designed to stretch students' thinking as they strengthen students' mastery of conventions and mechanics.

Each cycle is tied to skills from the Yearlong Planner. Remember, though, that these are suggestions. The Yearlong Planner is a tool to help you plan your year with your students. Consider your own assessments of students along with your standards to determine which lesson cycles you'll teach. As you create your own yearlong planner, adapt these Pulling It All Together activities by using the features of the writing but changing the strategies to match your lessons.

As in the lesson cycles, share your thinking as you create the model, deliberately using elements of mechanics and conventions. Show students that they can naturally consider multiple elements as they craft text.

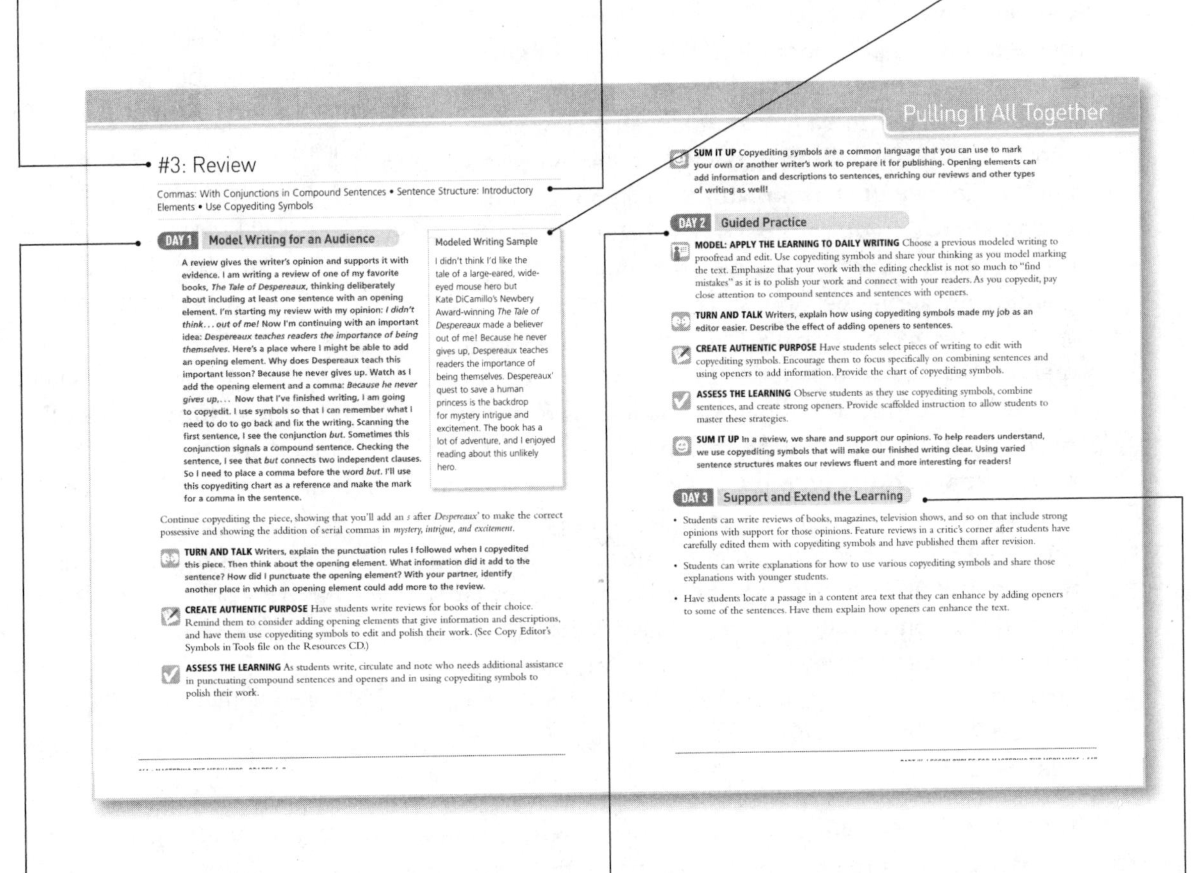

Pulling It All Together

#3: Review

Commas: With Conjunctions in Compound Sentences • Sentence Structure: Introductory Elements • Use Copyediting Symbols

DAY 1 Model Writing for an Audience

A review gives the writer's opinion and supports it with evidence. I am writing a review of one of my favorite books, *The Tale of Despereaux*, thinking deliberately about including at least one sentence with an opening element. I'm starting my review with my opinion: *I didn't think... out of me!* Now I'm continuing with an important idea: *Despereaux teaches readers the importance of being themselves*. Here's a place where I might be able to add an opening element. Why does Despereaux teach this important lesson? Because he never gives up. Watch as I add the opening element and a comma: *Because he never gives up,...* Now that I've finished writing, I am going to copyedit. I use symbols so that I can remember what I need to do to go back and fix the writing. Scanning the first sentence, I see the conjunction *but*. Sometimes this conjunction signals a compound sentence. Checking the sentence, I see that *but* connects two independent clauses. So I need to place a comma before the word *but*. I'll use this copyediting chart as a reference and make the mark for a comma in the sentence.

Modeled Writing Sample

I didn't think I'd like the tale of a large-eared, wide-eyed mouse hero but Kate DiCamillo's Newbery Award-winning *The Tale of Despereaux* made a believer out of me! Because he never gives up, Despereaux teaches readers the importance of being themselves. Despereaux' quest to save a human princess is the backdrop for mystery intrigue and excitement. The book has a lot of adventure, and I enjoyed reading about this unlikely hero.

Continue copyediting the piece, showing that you'll add an *s* after *Despereaux'* to make the correct possessive and showing the addition of serial commas in *mystery, intrigue, and excitement.*

TURN AND TALK **Writers, explain the punctuation rules I followed when I copyedited this piece. Then think about the opening element. What information did it add to the sentence? How did I punctuate the opening element? With your partner, identify another place in which an opening element could add more to the review.**

CREATE AUTHENTIC PURPOSE Have students write reviews for books of their choice. Remind them to consider adding opening elements that give information and descriptions, and have them use copyediting symbols to edit and polish their work. (See Copy Editor's Symbols in Tools file on the Resources CD.)

ASSESS THE LEARNING As students write, circulate and note who needs additional assistance in punctuating compound sentences and openers and in using copyediting symbols to polish their work.

SUM IT UP **Copyediting symbols are a common language that you can use to mark your own or another writer's work to prepare it for publishing. Opening elements can add information and descriptions to sentences, enriching our reviews and other types of writing as well!**

DAY 2 Guided Practice

MODEL: APPLY THE LEARNING TO DAILY WRITING Choose a previous modeled writing to proofread and edit. Use copyediting symbols and share your thinking as you model marking the text. Emphasize that your work with the editing checklist is not so much to "find mistakes" as it is to polish your work and connect with your readers. As you copyedit, pay close attention to compound sentences and sentences with openers.

TURN AND TALK **Writers, explain how using copyediting symbols made my job as an editor easier. Describe the effect of adding openers to sentences.**

CREATE AUTHENTIC PURPOSE Have students select pieces of writing to edit with copyediting symbols. Encourage them to focus specifically on combining sentences and using openers to add information. Provide the chart of copyediting symbols.

ASSESS THE LEARNING Observe students as they use copyediting symbols, combine sentences, and create strong openers. Provide scaffolded instruction to allow students to master these strategies.

SUM IT UP **In a review, we share and support our opinions. To help readers understand, we use copyediting symbols that will make our finished writing clear. Using varied sentence structures makes our reviews fluent and more interesting for readers!**

DAY 3 Support and Extend the Learning

- Students can write reviews of books, magazines, television shows, and so on that include strong opinions with support for those opinions. Feature reviews in a critic's corner after students have carefully edited them with copyediting symbols and have published them after revision.
- Students can write explanations for how to use various copyediting symbols and share those explanations with younger students.
- Have students locate a passage in a content area text that they can enhance by adding openers to some of the sentences. Have them explain how openers can enhance the text.

Day 1

On Day 1, share your thinking as you create a model of authentic nonfiction text. Provide an opportunity for students to examine the model and discuss strategy use. Then have students begin to write using the same form, conventions, and mechanics. Use the assessment suggestions to inform your instruction and track student growth. Sum up the day's learning by explaining—explicitly—how mechanics and conventions lift the form of writing featured in the Pulling It All Together cycle.

Day 2

On Day 2, revisit a piece of writing with an eye toward applying the conventions and mechanics strategies reviewed on Day 1. By selecting a piece of writing you have already done, you are providing a window into the work of a writer—we constantly apply what we've learned to make great connections to our readers! After having students focus on the strategies you modeled, they select pieces of their own writing to which they can apply those focus strategies. Continue to assess which students need additional support with mechanics and conventions.

Day 3

Several suggestions are provided for Day 3. Choose the ideas that best support your learners and their needs. Some ideas focus on the mechanics and conventions, while others focus on the writing form and features. Remember, students need multiple opportunities to apply mechanics and conventions in meaningful contexts. Use the extension ideas to provide those opportunities.

#1: Letter to the Editor

End Punctuation • Spelling Consciousness • Reread to Focus on Purpose and Audience • Bolded Words

DAY 1 Model Writing for an Audience

I am writing a letter to the editor of a local newspaper to share my opinion about an important issue—bicycle helmets. I want my letter to be engaging, so I'm deliberately thinking about including different kinds of sentences. I'm starting with my opinion: *The safety of children in our town is important*. That statement shares my opinion, but to make the beginning catchier, I'm thinking about starting with a question and an exclamation: *Do you consider. . . I do!* Notice that I focused on end punctuation, using a question mark and then marking my strong belief with an exclamation point. I want my words to be spelled correctly, too. As I wrote, I realized I wasn't sure about *inconvenience*. Just to be sure I'd spelled it correctly, I put an *sp* above it as a reminder to check it after writing. After finishing this letter, I reread to be sure that it fits both the audience and purpose. My audience is the editor of a newspaper, so I used more formal language than I would in a note to a friend. And its purpose? To be convincing about bicycle helmet laws. I included a compelling reason—helmets prevent brain injuries. In rereading my work, I'm thinking that I want to emphasize some important words with bold text. Watch as I revise by bolding *safety* and *brain injuries* to get readers' attention.

Modeled Writing Sample

Dear Editor:

Do you consider the **safety** of children in our town important? I do! That's why I'm writing about bicycle helmet laws. Our town needs stronger laws to keep riders safe. I've noticed many cyclists riding without helmets. They must not realize that the inconvenience of purchasing a helmet is worth it. A helmet is the best way to protect the brain in the event of a crash. **Brain injuries** are serious! That's why we need more serious laws to protect our citizens.

Sincerely yours,

Grace O'Brien

TURN AND TALK Writers, talk about the purpose of my writing. What could I have included to be more persuasive? Evaluate whether each punctuation mark fits the sentence. Tell your partner about a strategy you use to check spelling.

CREATE AUTHENTIC PURPOSE Have students write letters to the editor of a local newspaper about an issue important in your school or community. Remind them to use a variety of correctly punctuated sentences, to use their spelling consciousness to guide them in their spelling, to consider whether to bold words, and to reread multiple times with a focus on both audience and purpose.

ASSESS THE LEARNING Monitor which students may need further instruction to use correct end punctuation with a variety of sentences. Look for evidence of spelling consciousness, watching for marking words with *sp* or trying out margin spellings.

SUM IT UP **Our letters are convincing! Paying attention to both the purpose and audience allowed us to craft letters that make a point. Using our spelling consciousness helped us present our best work, and the variety of sentences makes the writing fluent. Bolding some words helped our readings focus on the message!**

DAY 2 Guided Practice

MODEL: APPLY THE LEARNING TO DAILY WRITING Select a piece of modeled writing and check on end punctuation. Share your thinking as you insert a question mark, show strong feeling with exclamation points, and so on. Show students how you mark a word to check on spelling later. Model as you deliberately reread to check for purpose and audience.

TURN AND TALK **Writers, why would I focus on spelling both during and after the writing? Describe the strategies I used to select the correct end punctuation.**

CREATE AUTHENTIC PURPOSE Have students select pieces from their writing folders to reread with a focus on spelling, end punctuation, purpose, and audience. Encourage them to use their spelling consciousness to note words to revisit.

ASSESS THE LEARNING Use your Class Record-Keeping Grid (in the Assessment and Record Keeping file on the Resources CD) to track students who may need additional support in using their spelling consciousness, including correct end punctuation with a variety of sentences, or focusing on purpose and audience.

SUM IT UP **When we use our spelling consciousness as we write, we spot potential errors we can fix. Keeping a close eye on both audience and purpose keeps us focused on our readers and lifts our messages. Sentence variety makes writing interesting and fluent.**

DAY 3 Support and Extend the Learning

- Have students identify strong examples of interrogative, declarative, imperative, and exclamatory sentences in their own writing and in mentor texts and add them to a bulletin board to share. They can highlight end punctuation for reference.
- Invite students to write letters and notes that focus on other purposes and audiences, such as request letters, thank you notes, instructions, and so on.
- Encourage students to compile resources for checking spelling after their spelling consciousness invites them to double-check their words.

#2: Summary

Compound Sentences • Margin Spelling • Use an Editing Checklist • Text Boxes

DAY 1 Model Writing for an Audience

As I write a summary of a simple machine, the wedge, I'm thinking about where I might combine sentences to make my writing more fluent. I'm also focused on spelling. Watch as I write: *What do a tooth... machines*. Now I'm writing about wedges that help us separate things. I find *separate* a tricky word to spell. Is it *s-e-p-e-r-a-t-e or s-e-p-a-r-a-t-e or s-e-p-u-r-a-t-e?* Watch as I try different spellings in the margin. This one—*separate*—looks correct to me. I'll still check it when I edit, though. I'm continuing to write about wedges that hold things together. I'm noticing that these sentences show a contrasting idea—some wedges separate things, other wedges put things together. I'm combining these sentences with a coordinating conjunction, *but*: *Some wedges, like axes, help us split or separate things, but others help us hold things together*. Notice that I put a comma before the conjunction, *but*. Also, I found out during my research that our teeth are wedges! I never thought of my tooth as a simple machine. I am going to add that interesting fact in a text box for my readers. Now that I've finished writing, I am going to edit my work. Using a checklist helps me focus. The first item on my checklist is to check for end punctuation. I'll do that on my first rereading.

Modeled Writing Sample

What do a tooth, a fork, a doorstop, and an axe have in common? They are all wedges. Wedges are triangular-shaped simple machines. Some wedges, like axes, help us split or separate things, but others help us hold things together. Wedges allow us to apply force to make work easier.

Believe It Or Not, It's a Wedge! What wedge do you use every day? Your tooth!

TURN AND TALK **Writers, explain how using an editing checklist and editing for one point at a time helps you focus on your editing. What conjunction might I have chosen if the ideas in the sentences were in a sequence rather than contrasting ideas?**

CREATE AUTHENTIC PURPOSE Encourage students to write summaries that focus on content area learning. Challenge students to choose an important or interesting idea to place into a text box. Be sure that students use editing checklists to guide their editing.

ASSESS THE LEARNING Use a Class Record-Keeping Grid (in the Assessment and Record Keeping file on the Resources CD) to note which students use coordinating conjunctions and commas to create compound sentences. Check on students' work to be sure they are recording correct spellings of words.

SUM IT UP **When you create a summary, try out word spellings in the margins of your drafts. Use compound sentences to create sentence variety. Editing checklists will allow you to focus on one point at a time and produce your best writing!**

DAY 2 Guided Practice

MODEL: APPLY THE LEARNING TO DAILY WRITING Select a piece of modeled writing, rereading it with a close eye on spelling. Look for opportunities to combine independent clauses, sharing your thinking as you choose a coordinating conjunction that reflects the relationship between the sentences. Insert a text box to tell more about a topic. Use an editing checklist to carefully reread for each point.

TURN AND TALK Writers, explain why focusing on one strategy at a time helps your work. What would be most important to include in an editing checklist for summaries?

CREATE AUTHENTIC PURPOSE Invite students to select pieces for focused editing. Encourage them to reread for one editing point at a time, to use the margin to try out spellings, and to combine independent clauses to make writing fluent.

ASSESS THE LEARNING As students reread and edit, use a Class Record-Keeping Grid to note those who need extra help with using margin spellings, combining sentences with coordinating conjunctions and commas, and using an editing checklist for focused rereadings.

SUM IT UP A summary relates important information about a topic. To be sure that our readers understand our summaries, we can use editing checklists to check for each important point. Margin spelling allows us to try out different spelling to make our work clear. Compound sentences connect ideas and text boxes highlight interesting information.

DAY 3 Support and Extend the Learning

- Have students combine independent clauses with each of the coordinating conjunctions. Have them explain how each coordinating conjunction contributes to meaning. Why would they choose one conjunction over another?
- Encourage students to create word banks related to content.
- Use the editing checklists as starting points for students, but encourage them to work with you to create checklists that focus on current cycles as well as on types of writing. Students may also contribute to a rubric for summary writing.

#3: Review

Commas: With Conjunctions in Compound Sentences • Sentence Structure: Introductory Elements • Use Copyediting Symbols

DAY 1 Model Writing for an Audience

A review gives the writer's opinion and supports it with evidence. I am writing a review of one of my favorite books, *The Tale of Despereaux*, thinking deliberately about including at least one sentence with an opening element. I'm starting my review with my opinion: *I didn't think... out of me!* Now I'm continuing with an important idea: *Despereaux teaches readers the importance of being themselves*. Here's a place where I might be able to add an opening element. Why does Despereaux teach this important lesson? Because he never gives up. Watch as I add the opening element and a comma: *Because he never gives up,...* Now that I've finished writing, I am going to copyedit. I use symbols so that I can remember what I need to do to go back and fix the writing. Scanning the first sentence, I see the conjunction *but*. Sometimes this conjunction signals a compound sentence. Checking the sentence, I see that *but* connects two independent clauses. So I need to place a comma before the word *but*. I'll use this copyediting chart as a reference and make the mark for a comma in the sentence.

Modeled Writing Sample

I didn't think I'd like the tale of a large-eared, wide-eyed mouse hero but Kate DiCamillo's Newbery Award-winning *The Tale of Despereaux* made a believer out of me! Because he never gives up, Despereaux teaches readers the importance of being themselves. Despereaux' quest to save a human princess is the backdrop for mystery intrigue and excitement. The book has a lot of adventure, and I enjoyed reading about this unlikely hero.

Continue copyediting the piece, showing that you'll add an *s* after *Despereaux'* to make the correct possessive and showing the addition of serial commas in *mystery, intrigue, and excitement.*

TURN AND TALK Writers, explain the punctuation rules I followed when I copyedited this piece. Then think about the opening element. What information did it add to the sentence? How did I punctuate the opening element? With your partner, identify another place in which an opening element could add more to the review.

CREATE AUTHENTIC PURPOSE Have students write reviews for books of their choice. Remind them to consider adding opening elements that give information and descriptions, and have them use copyediting symbols to edit and polish their work. (See Copy Editor's Symbols in Tools file on the Resources CD.)

ASSESS THE LEARNING As students write, circulate and note who needs additional assistance in punctuating compound sentences and openers and in using copyediting symbols to polish their work.

SUM IT UP **Copyediting symbols are a common language that you can use to mark your own or another writer's work to prepare it for publishing. Opening elements can add information and descriptions to sentences, enriching our reviews and other types of writing as well!**

DAY 2 Guided Practice

MODEL: APPLY THE LEARNING TO DAILY WRITING Choose a previous modeled writing to proofread and edit. Use copyediting symbols and share your thinking as you model marking the text. Emphasize that your work with the editing checklist is not so much to "find mistakes" as it is to polish your work and connect with your readers. As you copyedit, pay close attention to compound sentences and sentences with openers.

TURN AND TALK **Writers, explain how using copyediting symbols made my job as an editor easier. Describe the effect of adding openers to sentences.**

CREATE AUTHENTIC PURPOSE Have students select pieces of writing to edit with copyediting symbols. Encourage them to focus specifically on combining sentences and using openers to add information. Provide the chart of copyediting symbols.

ASSESS THE LEARNING Observe students as they use copyediting symbols, combine sentences, and create strong openers. Provide scaffolded instruction to allow students to master these strategies.

SUM IT UP **In a review, we share and support our opinions. To help readers understand, we use copyediting symbols that will make our finished writing clear. Using varied sentence structures makes our reviews fluent and more interesting for readers!**

DAY 3 Support and Extend the Learning

- Students can write reviews of books, magazines, television shows, and so on that include strong opinions with support for those opinions. Feature reviews in a critic's corner after students have carefully edited them with copyediting symbols and have published them after revision.
- Students can write explanations for how to use various copyediting symbols and share those explanations with younger students.
- Have students locate a passage in a content area text that they can enhance by adding openers to some of the sentences. Have them explain how openers can enhance the text.

#4: Procedure

Sentence Fluency and Variety • Sentence Structure: Interrupters • Singular Subject-Verb Agreement • Titles and Headings

DAY 1 Model Writing for an Audience

Writers, I'm creating a procedural text that will help others make a model for the water cycle. Watch as I begin: *Water cycles. . . .* Notice the verb that I chose. The word *water* is a singular noun, so I used the singular verb *cycles*. I'm continuing: *No other planet contains water in all of its states: liquid, solid, and gas. No other planet* is a singular subject as well, so I chose the singular verb *contains*. I'm thinking about adding an opener to create some sentence variety. Besides, there may be other planets out there with water! So watch as I create the opener: *As far as we know,. . . .* Notice that I placed a comma after the opener. Next, I'm recording the first step of the procedure: *Use a container to make your model*. I'm thinking I need to insert an interrupter to answer the question: What kind of container? I'm revising: *Use a container, such as a shoe box or aquarium, to. . . .* I'm enclosing the interrupter in commas. My writing looks great! But I want to prepare my readers for the content and add some organization. Watch as I add a title and insert a heading to organize the piece. Now it seems crystal clear!

TURN AND TALK Writers, look back at the model and identify different sentence structures. How do those structures make this writing fluent? Explain how that interrupter I added will assist readers.

CREATE AUTHENTIC PURPOSE Have students work with partners to create procedure pieces of their own. Encourage them to vary sentence structures, to use interrupters to clarify ideas, to organize the work with titles and headings, and to check carefully for subject-verb agreement.

ASSESS THE LEARNING While students work with their partners, circulate and observe. Are students deliberately using a variety of sentence structures? Do they use interrupters to give valuable information? Are they making sure that subjects and verbs agree? If not, plan to work with students who need additional support.

SUM IT UP Procedural texts—in fact, *all* kinds of texts—benefit from careful attention to sentence structure. Using a variety of sentence structures makes our writing fluent. Also, subjects and verbs need to agree—check them carefully!

Modeled Writing Sample

The Water Cycle

Water cycles continuously through the atmosphere. As far as we know, no other planet contains water in all of its states: liquid, solid, and gas. Maybe the best way to show this is to build a model.

Make a Model

1. Use a container, such as a shoe box or aquarium, to make your model.
2. Shape a mountain out of clay and place it on one side of the container.
3. Pour water into the container, covering about one quarter of the mountain.
4. Replace the lid, and place a petri dish on top of it.
5. Fill the petri dish with crushed ice. Position a lamp to shine on the "ocean."

DAY 2 Guided Practice

MODEL: APPLY THE LEARNING TO DAILY WRITING Share your thinking as you choose a piece of modeled writing and edit it with an eye toward varying sentence structures, inserting interrupters, and making sure that subjects and verbs agree. Think aloud as you correct any errors in subject-verb agreement.

TURN AND TALK **Writers, explain how I varied sentences. What sentence structures did you see me add? Describe the effect on the writing.**

CREATE AUTHENTIC PURPOSE Have students look through their writing folders to find writing that could benefit from a close examination of sentence structures and another look at subject-verb agreement. Have partners work together to be sure that they've inserted commas for compound sentences, openers, closers, and interrupters.

ASSESS THE LEARNING As partners work together, use the Class Record-Keeping Grid to identify students who need extra support with subject-verb agreement, sentence interrupters, and sentence variety. Gather those who need extra support in small groups for instruction.

SUM IT UP **A procedure shares the steps for making or doing something. It's important that our directions are clear and interesting, so we should check carefully for subject-verb agreement and include a variety of sentences that get our ideas across.**

DAY 3 Support and Extend the Learning

- Provide sentences to which students could add interrupters. Have them work together to identify what kind of information they might want to add and then insert that information.
- Challenge students to locate fluent passages from mentor texts or content area books. Encourage them to identify sentence structures and identify their effect on the reader.
- Have students write additional procedural texts, such as the steps for completing a math problem, the procedure for using a scientific tool, instructions for a game they are playing in physical education, and so on.

#5: Learning Journal or Blog

Capitalization in Titles • Pronouns and Their Antecedents
• Apostrophe: Singular Possessive Nouns

DAY 1 Model Writing for an Audience

A journal is a way to capture our learning. We can keep journals in notebooks, or we can craft journals online as blog entries. I want to write a journal entry from a study of buoyancy, or how well things float. I am starting with the title: *Penny boat Challenge*. I'm thinking about the capitalization rules I know—we capitalize important words in titles. *Boat* is an important word, so I'll change to a capital letter. Now to continue: *I created. . . I was testing my boat's ability to hold pennies without sinking*. Notice that I included an apostrophe and *s* after the word *boat* to show ownership. The ability belongs to the boat, so I need to add the apostrophe and an *s*. Now I'll continue: *I put in 15, one at a time. It held them*. I'm concerned about my pronouns here. In the sentence *It held them*, I know I am writing about my boat. The boat held 15 pennies. But the sentences before this don't give clear antecedents for the pronouns—my readers may not get my message. I should do some revision: *I put in 15 pennies, one at a time. The boat held them*. That's much clearer!

Modeled Writing Sample

Penny boat Challenge

Materials:
Aluminum foil, pennies, large container, water

I created a rectangular boat with short sides. I was testing my boat's ability to hold pennies without sinking. My boat did a great job! I put in 15, one at a time. It held them. Classmates who tried a canoe shape got even better results than I did.

TURN AND TALK Writers, look back at my revision and identify the pronouns and the nouns to which they refer. Evaluate whether the antecedents are clear enough. Then identify the possessive noun. How do you know it's not a contraction? How would the possessive change if I were describing more than one boat?

CREATE AUTHENTIC PURPOSE Students can create learning journals or blogs for any content area—math, science, art, health, social studies, and so on. Encourage them to use clear titles and headings to organize information, being sure that they include correct capitalization. Have them focus on including clear antecedents for any pronouns and checking for correct possessives.

ASSESS THE LEARNING Use your Class Record-Keeping Grid to note those students who have mastered capitalization in titles and headings, clear pronoun referents, and singular possessive nouns with apostrophe and an *s* to show ownership. Provide small-group instruction as needed.

SUM IT UP **Learning journals and blogs capture our discoveries and allow us to share them with others. Titles and headings help us organize our work, so it's important that they are clear, with correct capitalization. Pronouns are helpful in our writing only if they include clear antecedents. Be sure that each pronoun renames a noun in the text.**

DAY 2 Guided Practice

MODEL: APPLY THE LEARNING TO DAILY WRITING Choose a learning journal or another piece of writing that you've previously modeled in class. Highlight the pronouns and share your thinking as you locate their antecedents. Revise for any unclear pronoun referents in the writing. Look also at singular possessive nouns and capitalization, editing for one point at a time.

TURN AND TALK **Writers, identify a pronoun and its antecedent in my writing. Explain how you can tell if the antecedent is clear, and if it's not, how to fix it.**

CREATE AUTHENTIC PURPOSE Have students peruse their writing folders to find pieces to reread with a closer eye on both capitalization and possessive nouns. On a third rereading, have them carefully check for pronouns and antecedents, highlighting both the pronouns and their antecedents.

ASSESS THE LEARNING Collect students' papers to check their mastery of each strategy in this cycle. Provide extra support for those who need it.

SUM IT UP **Professionals in the field use learning journals and blogs to share their findings. Using capitalization in headings, including clear pronoun antecedents, and correctly punctuating possessive nouns go a long way toward making your work accessible for readers.**

DAY 3 Support and Extend the Learning

- Copy a passage from a content area book or other mentor text. Have students work with partners to highlight both the pronouns and their antecedents. Are all the pronouns clear? Students can suggest fixes for any unclear referents.
- Invite students to look through their writing or through mentor texts to find words that include apostrophes. They can classify their findings: singular possessives, plural possessives, and contractions. Have them explain how they can tell the difference.

#6: Lab Report

Regular and Irregular Verbs • Prepositions and Prepositional Phrases • Comma in a Series

DAY 1 Model Writing for an Audience

Watch as I start a lab report with the question I was trying to answer: *How does darkness affect plant growth?* Then I list my hypothesis, or the prediction I had before doing the experiment: *I predict that plants in a dark place will grow more slowly than plants in the light.* Notice the prepositional phrases I am using: *in a dark place* and *in the light.* These phrases show location, and they are so important to my lab report! Without them, my readers wouldn't know where I put the plants. Next comes my procedure, or the steps that I took: *I placed gravel sand and dirt in two cups....* I am noticing a problem here, though. *Gravel, sand, and dirt* are items in a series. That means that I need to separate them with commas to keep the ideas clear for my readers. After I planted, I watered the plants: *I gived each seed an equal amount of water.* I know that doesn't sound right! *Give* is an irregular verb. Instead of forming the past tense with *–ed,* the verb changes spelling. The past tense is *gave,* so I'll place that in the sentence instead.

Continue writing, modeling the deliberate use of prepositional phrases (*of water, in the shade, on a sunny windowsill,* and so on) and the correct form of the irregular verb, *grow.*

TURN AND TALK **Writers, talk about the strategies I used as I wrote. How did I know which verbs were irregular? How could I have double-checked that I was using the correct form? What other items in a series might you add in a summary of this experiment?**

CREATE AUTHENTIC PURPOSE Ask the science teacher to work with you to create an authentic experience for a lab report. As students write, have them pay special attention to irregular verbs, prepositions, and items in a series.

ASSESS THE LEARNING Confer with writers to have them classify regular and irregular verbs in their writing. Ask them to identify prepositions. If they have placed items in a series, have them point out the items and the commas. Determine which students may need additional support.

Modeled Writing Sample

Plant Growth

QUESTION:

How does darkness affect plant growth?

HYPOTHESIS:

I predict that plants in a dark place will grow more slowly than plants in the light.

PROCEDURE:

I placed gravel, sand, and dirt in two cups. I planted bean seeds approximately ½ " below the surface.

I gave each seed an equal amount of water.

I placed one plant in the shade and one on a sunny windowsill.

For two weeks, I watered each plant equally.

RESULT:

The plant on the windowsill grew 2 more inches than the plant in the shade.

SUM IT UP **Prepositions are important in science writing, because they help us describe position and time—those are so important in experimental results! Using commas to highlight items in a series and paying close attention to irregular verbs allows us to clarify ideas.**

DAY 2 Guided Practice

MODEL: APPLY THE LEARNING TO DAILY WRITING Select a piece of modeled writing that you can revisit, paying close attention to irregular verbs, items in a series, and prepositions. Share your thinking as you deliberately check verb forms and use a reference to make sure that you've chosen the correct form of irregular verbs. Read for prepositions and items in a series.

TURN AND TALK **Writers, identify a regular verb and an irregular verb in my writing. How can you tell the difference? Where might you place an additional prepositional phrase to give readers more precise information?**

CREATE AUTHENTIC PURPOSE Have partners peruse their writing folders to find content area pieces for rereading and revising. They can classify verbs as regular and irregular and talk about how they form the past tense of each. Invite them to highlight prepositions as well as items in a series and check to be sure that they have included correct punctuation.

ASSESS THE LEARNING As partners work together to reread their writing, identify any students who may need assistance with prepositions, regular and irregular verbs, and commas in a series. Provide extra support.

SUM IT UP **Many science reports include items in a series—it's important to punctuate them correctly. Consider how to make your content clear by including prepositional phrases.**

DAY 3 Support and Extend the Learning

- Ask students to list procedures for an experiment using commas to separate items in a series. Check for parallelism, as students may list all gerunds, all infinitives, all independent clauses, and so on.
- Have students scavenge mentor texts for regular and irregular verbs. They can record sentences in T-charts, highlighting the verbs in the sentences.
- Ask students to write directions, either for doing a procedure or for reaching a location. Have them highlight the prepositions in their writing.

#7: Explanation: Cause and Effect

Linking and Auxiliary Verbs • Commas with Closers • Homophones and Easily Confused Words • Captions

DAY 1 Model Writing for an Audience

As I am writing an explanation of what causes an avalanche, I am paying attention to verbs and looking for a place to insert a descriptive closer. Watch as I write: *An avalanche is....* Notice the linking verb, *is*. A linking verb is perfect here—it links the subject of the sentence, *avalanche*, to its definition. As I continue, I'm including an auxiliary verb, *has*, because this sentence starts with the word *suppose*. Now I'm continuing: *The packed snow cannot support its own immense wait*. This sentence sounds right, but checking my easily confused words reference and the context of the passage, I realize that I should use *weight* instead of *wait*. The sentence makes a lot more sense now! In wrapping up, I write: *Consequently, an avalanche could occur*. This might be a great sentence to which to add a closer to include more details about what an avalanche looks like. Watch as I replace the period with a comma and add the closer: *sending snow hurtling down the mounting*. I have created text that will help my readers visualize, yet it makes sense to add a photo to show the awesomeness of an avalanche! Watch as I add a photo and caption: *An avalanche....*

TURN AND TALK Writers, take a close look at my verbs. Classify them as action verbs, linking verbs, or auxiliary verbs. Identify another place where I might add a closer. Explain how to add it.

CREATE AUTHENTIC PURPOSE Have students craft cause-and-effect paragraphs. Remind them to pay attention to linking and auxiliary verbs, add information with at least one closer, and to reread to be sure they've used correct homophones and have checked for easily confused words. If appropriate, students can add stock photos and craft captions to accompany them.

Modeled Writing Sample

An avalanche is any amount of snow sliding down a mountain. Suppose that a huge layer of snow has accumulated on a mountainside. The packed snow cannot support its own immense weight. As a result, the snow layer is vulnerable to an avalanche. If a person stepped on the shaky layer of snow, the snow would become loose. Consequently, an avalanche could occur, sending snow hurtling down the mountain.

An avalanche sends snow racing down the mountainside.

ASSESS THE LEARNING Circulate with your Class Record-Keeping Grid to note which students have mastered using linking and auxiliary verbs, have used context to choose a correct homophone, and have created closers set off with commas. Provide support for those students who need it.

SUM IT UP **Choosing verbs for impact makes our writing clearer to readers. When we take care to choose careful closers and use context to choose the correct homophone, we free our readers to focus on causes and effects.**

DAY 2 Guided Practice

MODEL: APPLY THE LEARNING TO DAILY WRITING Choose a piece of modeled writing that you can reread to focus on linking and auxiliary verbs. Deliberately insert a closer to add description. Reread to check that you have chosen the correct homophones or easily confused words.

TURN AND TALK **Describe how I figured out which homophones to use in my writing. What was the effect of adding closers to a few of the sentences?**

CREATE AUTHENTIC PURPOSE Have partners select pieces of writing to insert closers. Have them check both sides of a sentence with a linking verb to make sure that information on each "side" of the verb is linked.

ASSESS THE LEARNING Note students who need additional help using the correct forms of linking and auxiliary verbs. When you spot a homophone in student writing, ask the student how he or she chose the correct word.

SUM IT UP **When you carefully consider context and use a reference, choosing the correct homophone is simple! You've used a great mix of action, linking, and auxiliary verbs to show action, relationships, and tense.**

DAY 3 Support and Extend the Learning

- *Appear, feel, grow, look, prove, remain, smell, sound, taste,* and *turn* are all words that can function as action or linking verbs. Have students write pairs of sentences that use the verbs—one as an action verb and one as a linking verb.
- Ask students to return to informational text that they have written to insert a photograph with a caption.

#8: Brochure

Plural Possessive Nouns • Gerunds • Subjective and Objective Case Nouns and Pronouns

DAY 1 Model Writing for an Audience

Brochures are great tools for delivering information—they describe tourist spots, sell products, promote services, give health advice, and so on. I'm creating a brochure for a new store. In my first sentence, I'm writing about shirts that belong to many people! So I use the plural possessive, adding an *s* to make the word plural and then an apostrophe to show possession. I'm creating some catchy copy for my brochure: *Do your clothes need to be cleaned? Bring them to us!* I can make this writing a little leaner by replacing the infinitive with a gerund—*cleaning.* Notice that I chose the word *us* for the second sentence. I used the preposition *to*, so I needed to include a pronoun that works as the object of a preposition.

Model the rest of the brochure, sharing your thinking as you form the plural possessives *members'* and *clothes'*, include the gerund *pricing*, and correctly use the subjective case pronoun *you*.

> **Modeled Writing Sample**
>
> Extend your shirts' lives!
> Buy new jeans for less!
>
> Come to Cathy's Closet—where gently used clothes find new closets.
>
> Do your clothes need cleaning? Bring them to us!
>
> Not sure how much to charge for your treasures? Let us do the pricing.
>
> Our staff members' can-do attitudes will let you know that when you've come to us, you've come to the right place.
>
> Cathy's Closet. Where clothes' dreams come true.

TURN AND TALK Writers, talk about pronouns in the writing. Explain how I chose *us* instead of *we*. What generalizations can you make about pronoun choice? Describe together how gerunds function in the sentences in my text.

CREATE AUTHENTIC PURPOSE Have students create brochures of their own. To narrow purpose, have them create brochures promoting school programs. Remind them to pay close attention to plural possessive nouns, to use the correct forms of pronouns, and to consider how gerunds are used in their writing.

ASSESS THE LEARNING Confer with writers, asking them to point out their pronouns and explain how they decided which pronouns to use. Have them show you possessive nouns and tell how they formed the possessives. Finally, ask them to point out a gerund so you can be sure they haven't confused gerunds with *–ing* verbs. Note which students may need additional support.

SUM IT UP A brochure is designed to give information and capture attention, so we want to be sure that we've written as clearly as we can. It's important to pay attention to pronouns and possessives to be sure our writing makes sense. Words with *–ing* may be verbs, but gerunds can function as nouns or adjectives. Watch to be sure you're using them correctly.

DAY 2 Guided Practice

MODEL: APPLY THE LEARNING TO DAILY WRITING Choose a piece of writing you've previously modeled to proofread for pronouns, possessives, and gerunds. Share your thinking as you choose between subject and object pronouns and as you decide how to form possessives based on whether the nouns are singular or plural. Insert a gerund that functions as a noun or as an adjective.

TURN AND TALK **Writers, why is it important to use correct pronouns and possessive nouns? Explain how you know which ones to choose in sentences.**

CREATE AUTHENTIC PURPOSE Have partners look through their writing folders to find writing that might need a second look. Have partners work together to locate possessive nouns and check that they are formed correctly. Have them be sure they have correctly used pronouns as subjects and objects. If students have not used gerunds as nouns or adjectives, encourage them to insert at least one into their writing.

ASSESS THE LEARNING Use your Class Record-Keeping Grid to note which students have difficulty using the strategies. Consider reteaching cycles with small groups.

SUM IT UP **You are using sophisticated constructions like gerunds in a variety of ways and deliberately choosing subjective and objective nouns and pronouns as well as creating possessives—you have mastered so many strategies!**

DAY 3 Support and Extend the Learning

- Ask students to create brochures to support content area learning. A health unit, for example, could include brochures about nutrition or exercise. A unit on social studies might include travel brochures to far-off places—and far-off times. Students might create persuasive brochures about topics that are important in the school or community.
- Provide groups of sentences in which words that end with *–ing* function as both verbs and as gerunds. Have students identify gerunds and classify them according to parts of speech.
- Have students locate possessive nouns in mentor texts, classify the possessives as singular or plural, and rewrite them, changing singular to plural and plural to singular.

#9: Explanation: Sequence

Sentence Fluency and Variety • Colons and Semicolons • Reread to Focus on Organization

DAY 1 Model Writing for an Audience

As I write an explanation of the sequence involved in a heartbeat, I am looking closely at my sentences, varying their structures to keep them engaging. Because this is about the heart, I am capturing my readers' attention with fragments that sound like heartbeats: *Lub dub. Lub dub.* I know we don't usually write fragments, but I think this is a great way to start a sequence about heartbeats! Now I'm describing that sound: *The heartbeat makes a distinctive sound.* This is true—and descriptive—but I want to revise by adding a closer that will give even more information. Watch as I add a comma and then the closer: *most noticeable when. . . .* In my next sentence, I am writing a list of movements in the body that make hearts beat. Notice that as I write, I use a colon to introduce the list. Now, to tell more about the heart: *The heart has two atria. Each atrium is paired with a ventricle.* I'm noticing that these sentences are very closely related. Since I have a goal to vary sentence structures, I'm revising to make this a compound sentence. I'll join them with a semicolon: *The heart has. . . .*

> **Modeled Writing Sample**
>
> Lub dub. Lub dub. The heartbeat makes a distinctive sound, most noticeable when you're afraid, excited, nervous, or panting from exercise. Your heartbeat is caused by movements: electrical impulses, contractions, opening, shutting. The heart has two atria; each atrium is paired with a ventricle. On each side of the heart, blood first enters the upper atrium. Then the blood flows through a valve into the ventricle and exits through another valve, coursing from the heart back into your body.

Continue modeling, sharing your thinking as you add an opener to one sentence and a closer to another. After you have finished, model rereading to look at organization, pointing out the words *first* and *then* as keys to understanding the sequence of a heartbeat.

TURN AND TALK Writers, fluent writing sounds smooth when read aloud. Reread the model together and talk about fluency. Is this writing fluent? In what ways could it be improved?

CREATE AUTHENTIC PURPOSE Ask students to write a sequence of events. Challenge them to strive for fluency and variety in sentence structures, to use a colon to introduce an idea, and to connect two independent clauses with a semicolon. After writing, students should reread to check for sequence.

ASSESS THE LEARNING As students write, check their work to see which may need assistance to craft a variety of sentences and combine them to make fluent writing.

SUM IT UP A sequence presents ideas in order, so it's important for us to check the organizational pattern. It's important, too, to vary the sentences to keep our readers engaged.

DAY 2 Guided Practice

MODEL: APPLY THE LEARNING TO DAILY WRITING Select a piece of text from a writing folder that you can revisit to revise. Share your thinking as you check for appropriate use of colons and semicolons. Intentionally vary sentence structures for fluency. Reread to focus on organization.

TURN AND TALK Writers, identify the organization that I used for this piece of text. Evaluate how well my writing matches its purpose. Describe something I did to make the passage more fluent. What suggestion would you make for including a compound sentence or a sentence with an opener, closer, or interrupter?

CREATE AUTHENTIC PURPOSE Have partners each choose a piece to read aloud to each other to focus on fluency. Partners can suggest changes to sentence structures to make the writing flow more smoothly. Have students also proofread for colons and semicolons and reread for organization.

ASSESS THE LEARNING Observe to see which writers make changes that increase fluency. Collect writing to check on punctuation and organization. Plan to assist those who have not yet mastered the skills.

SUM IT UP A sequential piece needs solid organization, and you reread to check. You also are crafting fluent passages and making sure to use colons and semicolons correctly.

DAY 3 Support and Extend the Learning

- Have students write sequential pieces to focus on content such as life cycles, important events in history, the formation of rock or weather, the steps in solving a math problem or solving a dispute between friends, and so on.
- Encourage students to add sequence word and transitions to a word bank that they can keep for reference. Students might include *at first, first of all, to begin with, in the first place, at the same time, for now, for the time being, the next step, in time, in turn, later on, meanwhile, next, then, soon, in the meantime, later, while, earlier, simultaneously*, and *afterward*.

#10: Personal Narrative

Complete Sentences and Fragments • Plural Subject-Verb Agreement • Commas With Nonessential Elements

DAY 1 Model Writing for an Audience

A personal narrative captures just a small time in the life of the writer. I want to include some dialogue in my narrative to capture the moment. Watch as I begin: *"C'mon, Dad. . . it."* Notice that my first piece of dialogue is a sentence fragment. As writers, it's our goal to write complete sentences. But this fragment sounds like natural speech, so I am going to leave it in. The next part of the dialogue is a sentence. Who or what does something? The cars. What do they do? They drive. I used the verb *drive* instead of *drives* because my subject, *cars*, is plural. Because of that, I needed a plural verb. Further down, I write, *The road led right to the creek—and through it*. But, I want to explain a bit more about the road and why it was made to go right through the creek. I'm inserting a descriptive phrase, *built long ago*, to give some more information about the road. Notice that, because this phrase is not essential to the sentence, I'm enclosing it in commas.

Finish the writing, explaining that you are choosing a plural verb to go with the subject *drivers* and deliberately using fragments to add drama and emphasis.

Modeled Writing Sample

"C'mon, Dad. All the other cars drive through it."

"No, we're taking the bridge," Dad insisted.

What did we want to drive through? The creek! The road, built long ago, led right to the creek—and through it. Drivers maneuver through water all the time, right? But not our dad!

One day, Dad surprised us by taking the road instead of the bridge. Sputter. Spit. Click. The car choked and stopped, right in the middle of the bubbling, babbling water.

TURN AND TALK **Writers, evaluate whether the fragments are effective in this piece. Then focus on the nonessential elements in the sentences. Describe how we can tell whether an addition to a sentence is an essential element or a nonessential one.**

CREATE AUTHENTIC PURPOSE Have students write personal narratives to capture moments in their own lives. Encourage them to focus on a pivotal moment or episode rather than an entire vacation or school year! Have them consider whether or not they want to use a fragment for emphasis or to quote dialogue. Have them check carefully for subject-verb agreement.

ASSESS THE LEARNING As students write, confer with individuals and gauge which may need further assistance with subject-verb agreement, commas with nonessential elements, and deliberate and careful use of fragments.

SUM IT UP **Writers, we check to be sure that we've included complete sentences in our work, but sometimes fragments can be used for effect! Nonessential elements can add enticing descriptions or extra information to sentences. Be sure to enclose them in commas.**

DAY 2 Guided Practice

MODEL: APPLY THE LEARNING TO DAILY WRITING Select a modeled writing that you have done, preferably a narrative. Model your thinking as you check for complete sentences and deliberate over whether a fragment is an appropriate addition. Proofread for correct use of commas and for subject-verb agreement.

TURN AND TALK **Evaluate my fragments in the narrative. Do you think including a fragment in this position is a wise choice? Explain why or why not. Then identify plural subjects in the writing. Describe how I chose the correct verbs to agree with the subjects.**

CREATE AUTHENTIC PURPOSE Have students select personal narratives or other writing from their own folders or notebooks to reread with an eye toward subject-verb agreement. Once they have proofread for that editing point, have them locate a place where an intentional fragment could add drama or emphasis. Encourage them to insert a nonessential element to inform or describe.

ASSESS THE LEARNING Collect student writing and assess for appropriate sentences, subject-verb agreement, and comma usage with nonessential elements. Note those who may need to return to the lesson cycles to revisit the strategies.

SUM IT UP **Writers, your personal narratives capture slices of time rich with feelings and descriptions. By deliberately considering the use of fragments, you emphasized exciting moments. Checking subject-verb agreement and commas lifted your writing even more!**

DAY 3 Support and Extend the Learning

- Give students passages from content area texts. Ask them to work together to consider where they might insert an intentional fragment to add a description or a moment of excitement to the piece.
- Share high-quality personal narratives with students to help them understand the genre. Work with them to identify nonessential elements and fragments in these texts that enhance the writing.
- Have students check sentences with plural nouns for subject-verb agreement. Challenge them to change the nouns to singular nouns and make appropriate changes in verbs.

#11: Thesis and Support

Reread to Focus on Precise Words • Spelling Consciousness • Use an Editing Checklist

DAY 1 Model Writing for an Audience

A thesis statement is something that the writer believes and wants to prove. I want to prove the thesis that schools should put healthy drinks in drink machines. As I add support for this thesis, I'm focus on my spelling and on using precise words. Let me start with my thesis and one sentence of support: *Schools need to replace the sugary, caffeinated things in machines with healthier stuff. Experts agree that over half of the children in America eat way more than 90% of the sugar they should.* As I reread, I'm focusing on precision. What things should schools replace? I'm focusing on drinks, not food. Is there a better way to say *agree* when it comes to experts? I like the word *concur*, because it sounds a bit more formal, like what scientists do. The word *consume* is a bit more precise than *eat*. I'm not sure how to spell *consume*, though. But I don't want to leave a word out just because I don't know how to spell it! So I'll mark it with an *sp* to note that I should check it later. I've finished my support for the thesis, but I want to make sure that this work is flawless, because this thesis is so important to me! Watch as I edit with an editing checklist. I am reading my text one time for each point. That keeps me focused.

Modeled Writing Sample

Schools should be required to replace the sugary, caffeinated beverages in machines with healthier alternatives. Experts concur that over half of the children in America consume more than 90% of their daily allowance of sugar through these drinks. For Americans of all ages, sugary drinks like soda and juice make up the majority of their calories. The average teen gets as much sugar a day from sweetened drinks as he or she should receive from all foods.

TURN AND TALK **Writers, think together. How did the editing checklist guide my work as an editor? What revision points did it allow me to find? Explain what spelling consciousness is. Identify how I used it in my work.**

CREATE AUTHENTIC PURPOSE Have students work together to craft support for a thesis statement. You might give them a thesis statement about an issue in your school or a character or theme from literature. Encourage them to use precise words and to exercise their spelling consciousness. Provide an editing checklist.

ASSESS THE LEARNING Observe students, looking for evidence of spelling consciousness and attention to precise words. Watch as students use their editing checklists to edit for one point at a time. Gather those who need additional support based on your assessments.

SUM IT UP **Writers, supporting a thesis takes a lot of precision! Your precise words will help your readers understand your message. You employed your spelling consciousness, and you used a checklist to polish your writing.**

DAY 2 Guided Practice

MODEL: APPLY THE LEARNING TO DAILY WRITING Model how to select a piece of writing and reread it with a fresh eye toward precise words and a close focus on spelling. Share your thinking as you edit, one editing point at a time, and correct mistakes.

TURN AND TALK **Writers, identify a place where a precise word might make the message clearer. What strategies did you see me use to ensure that my spelling makes sense?**

CREATE AUTHENTIC PURPOSE Have students look through their writing folders to find pieces to reread with an eye toward creating precision in word choice, spelling words correctly, and editing with a checklist.

ASSESS THE LEARNING Observe as students edit to ensure that they reread for each editing point. Collect their papers to look for evidence of spelling consciousness and precise words.

SUM IT UP **The strategies that you've learned strengthen support for a thesis. When your sentences are carefully crafted with precise words and correct spelling, your writers can't help but be convinced! You used an editing checklist, not to ferret out "mistakes," but to polish your writing until it was your very best.**

DAY 3 Support and Extend the Learning

- Share various ways to support a thesis: examples, classification, comparison and contrast, persuasive arguments, and so on. Talk about the importance of including researched facts and/or textural support to prove a thesis statement, and provide models and practice as students are ready.
- Share mentor text with precise words, such as Walter Wick's *A Drop of Water* or any science books by Seymour Simon. Discuss the effect of the precise words on the message and on the learning of the content.

#12: Feature Article

Commas With Opening Elements • Verb Tenses: Present, Past, and Future • Pronouns and Their Antecedents

DAY 1 Model Writing for an Audience

I'm writing a feature article to capture our band's victories at a festival! I'm starting with my lead: *Members of the Patriots Band returned from their appearance at the Cherry Festival.* I'm thinking that this isn't very precise. When did they return? A month ago? Yesterday? I'm inserting an opener to make that clear: *Just last week, members....* Notice that I place a comma after the opener. I am also checking my verb tense. Since this event happened last week, the verb should be in the past tense. Now I'm continuing: *They were exhausted after it, but....* I'm pausing a second to check this pronoun. I'm realizing that I understand the pronoun, but the antecedent isn't clear for my readers. It's not clear if they were exhausted from their appearance or from the festival. So I'm revising: *They were exhausted after their busy schedule....* I eliminated the pronoun because its antecedent was too unclear.

Modeled Writing Sample

Just last week, members of the Patriots Band returned from their appearance at the Cherry Festival. They were exhausted after it, but they were excited to have won two trophies—best band and best color guard. Next week, the Patriots will travel to the Midwest Band Festival. They hope to bring home more kudos—and great memories!

Continue your modeling. Focus on the opener, *next week*; the use of the present and future tense; and the clear antecedent for the pronoun *they*.

TURN AND TALK Reread with your partner. On your first reading, check that commas are placed after opening elements. On a second reading, look for appropriate use of verb tenses. Finally, reread to be sure that all pronouns have clear antecedents. Share what you notice.

CREATE AUTHENTIC PURPOSE Let students know that they will work with partners to write feature articles about classroom or school events to share with the community in a print or online newsletter. Encourage them to include descriptive opening elements and to check for verb tenses and antecedents for pronouns.

ASSESS THE LEARNING As partners write their articles, check their work to identify students who may need extra assistance with verb tenses or with pronoun-antecedent agreement.

SUM IT UP Writers, writing for an audience requires careful attention to what we produce. Your focus on specific strategies made your work polished and ready for publication!

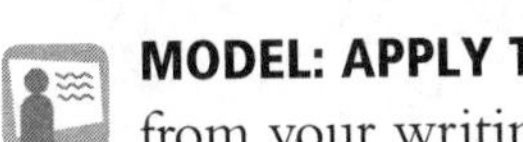

DAY 2 Guided Practice

MODEL: APPLY THE LEARNING TO DAILY WRITING Model how to select a piece of writing from your writing folder and reread to check for verb tense and pronouns and their antecedents. Share your thinking as you identify a place where an opener will add interest and set the scene. Share your ideas as you make any adjustments to your piece.

TURN AND TALK Writers, describe what you saw me do as I checked my writing. How did I know that verb tenses were correct—or that they needed to change? What clues in the writing guided me? How can we remember to check that each pronoun has a clear antecedent?

CREATE AUTHENTIC PURPOSE Have students look through their writing folders to find a piece of writing that might need a second look at opening elements, verb tenses, and pronoun referents. Have partners work together to check on antecedents and to be sure that verbs tell when the action took place (or will take place in the future).

ASSESS THE LEARNING As partners work together to reread their writing, identify students who may need extra support with verb tenses and with pronouns and antecedents. Consider revisiting the lesson cycles to provide them with extra support.

SUM IT UP You've done a masterful job of using verb tense to show action that already happened, that is occurring on a daily or habitual basis, and that will happen in the future. Your attention to antecedents makes all your pronouns clear. And you thought hard about where to add opening elements so that they add valuable or interesting information.

DAY 3 Support and Extend the Learning

- Encourage students to create feature articles about content area learning experiences that they can publish in classroom or school newsletters.
- Provide copies of passages from content area texts or other mentor texts. Have students highlight pronouns and then underline their antecedents. Are any unclear? Have students work together to fix them!
- Move beyond past, present, and future tenses to talk about how to form and use verbs in additional tenses: present perfect (*I have walked*), past perfect (*I had walked*), and future perfect (*I will have walked*).

#13: Critical Analysis of Literature

Gerunds • Capitalizing Titles • Dashes

DAY 1 Model Writing for an Audience

A critical analysis is an opportunity to explore the meaning of a text. I'll start with an opening sentence: *In her novel The Outsiders, S. E. Hinton quotes Robert Frost's "Nothing gold can stay."* I've included a few titles, so I want to check on my capital letters. I know that only important words in a title are capitalized, so I didn't capitalize *the*. But *the* is the first word of the title, so I should revise it. I'll need to add capital letters to the poem's title, too. I'm continuing: *What is the poem's meaning?* Did you notice that I have a gerund in the sentence? The gerund functions as a noun. That's easy to figure out, because it comes after a possessive. Only nouns and pronouns can "own" things! Watch as I continue: *The first line could mean different things.* Rereading, I'm thinking it might make sense to insert that first line in my writing to jog my readers' memories. I'm using a set of dashes to make that insertion.

Modeled Writing Sample

In her novel *The Outsiders*, S. E. Hinton quotes Robert Frost's "Nothing Gold Can Stay." What is the poem's meaning? The first line—"Nature's first green is gold"—could mean different things. It might mean that the green of spring has turned to gold—autumn. It could also mean that nature's first green is valuable because it is fleeting. Either way, the poem shows that things that are precious don't always last.

Continue modeling, pointing out the use of the word *fleeting* as an adjective and using a dash to emphasize the idea of autumn.

TURN AND TALK Writers, take a closer look at my critical analysis. Evaluate my use of dashes. Do you think they were the best punctuation to use for the purpose? Identify gerunds in the writing and explain whether they function as nouns or adjectives. How can you tell?

CREATE AUTHENTIC PURPOSE Give students a piece of text to use as the basis for a critical analysis. After you discuss the meaning of the text, have students work with partners to craft their analyses. Encourage them to check for capitalization of titles as well as for correct use of dashes and gerunds.

ASSESS THE LEARNING As students create their analyses, observe to check for capitalization of titles, and proper use of dashes and gerunds. Note those students who need additional assistance and provide instruction.

SUM IT UP Because we're writing about a piece of literature, it's important for us to remember to properly capitalize words in titles. Also, gerunds can brighten a piece of writing, and dashes can help us insert explanations or excerpts directly into our sentences.

DAY 2 Guided Practice

MODEL: APPLY THE LEARNING TO DAILY WRITING Select a piece of writing from a writing folder or a previous model you created and reread to focus on capitalization, gerunds, and dashes. Share your thinking as you use a set of dashes to insert a parenthetical element. If the writing does not include a gerund, model placing a gerund into the piece.

TURN AND TALK **Partners, work together to locate a gerund in the writing. How does the gerund work in the sentence? Identify the information enclosed in the dashes and explain why the dashes are located in that position in the sentence.**

CREATE AUTHENTIC PURPOSE Have partners search through their folders for pieces of writing that include titles. Have them read to check for capitalization. Encourage them to insert an interrupter with dashes that creates drama or emphasis or that adds new information.

ASSESS THE LEARNING As partners work together, ask them to point out any gerunds in their writing. Then collect finished papers to assess for correct capitalization of titles and for appropriate use of dashes. Note any students who may need additional instructions.

SUM IT UP **Writers, our analyses of literature need to include correct capitalization to represent literary works, which you did. Your use of dashes added variety along with great information! You've included gerunds as both nouns and adjectives, adding sophistication to your writing as you've captured ideas.**

DAY 3 Support and Extend the Learning

- Make sure that students interpret texts fully before writing analyses. An analysis includes opinions, but it also includes support for those opinions in the text.
- Ask students to create a guide to capitalization by writing titles of works they have read and highlighting capital letters. Display as a reference tool.
- Give students sentences with gerund substitutions. Example: *Daniel likes to swim. /Daniel likes swimming. My cat enjoys naps. /My cat enjoys sleeping.* Encourage students to find other artful uses of gerunds in mentor texts to share with classmates.

#14: Poem

Plural Possessive Nouns • Indefinite Pronouns • Use Root Words

DAY 1 Model Writing for an Audience

I want to capture some facts about the different branches of science in a poem. A poem like this will help me remember the science—and share it with others in a descriptive way! My first line is a branch of science: *geology*. To be sure I understand both spelling and meaning, I'm using my word parts chart to remind me that *logy* means "the study of," and *geo* has to do with Earth. Geology has to do with the origin of rocks, so that's my second line. Notice that I am writing about many rocks, not just one. So I form the plural, *rocks*, and then put an apostrophe after the word to show plural possession. I'm starting my last line with an indefinite pronoun, *each*. I remember that *each* is an indefinite pronoun that takes the singular form of the verb, so I'm continuing: *Each forms because of processes on Earth.*

Continue modeling with the next stanza, using word parts, sharing thinking about plural possessives, and writing a line with an indefinite pronoun.

Modeled Writing Sample

Branches of Science

Geology,

Rocks' origins,

Each forms because of processes on Earth.

Biology,

Animals' and plants' adaptations,

All live in environments especially suited to them.

Astronomy,

Stars' and planets' characteristics and locations,

Some remain unknown to us.

TURN AND TALK Work with your partner to identify the indefinite pronouns in the poem. Which are singular and which are plural? Explain how you know. Locate a plural possessive noun, and change it into a singular possessive noun. Describe how to make that change.

CREATE AUTHENTIC PURPOSE Invite students to write poems about content area topics. Encourage them to use the Word Parts reference (in the Tools file on the Resources CD) to think carefully about both spelling and meaning as they write. Challenge writers to include at least one plural possessive noun and one indefinite pronoun in their poems.

ASSESS THE LEARNING Confer with individuals as they write. Have them point out any words that have parts that are clues to both meanings and spellings. Then ask them to explain how to form plural possessives and to point out an indefinite pronoun in the writing. Provide additional instruction as necessary.

SUM IT UP Poems can be both artistic and informational! Paying attention to mechanics and conventions helps our readers focus on content and appreciate our descriptions.

DAY 2 Guided Practice

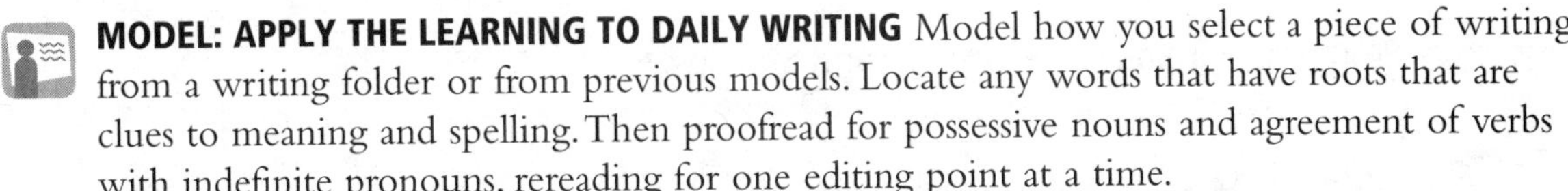

MODEL: APPLY THE LEARNING TO DAILY WRITING Model how you select a piece of writing from a writing folder or from previous models. Locate any words that have roots that are clues to meaning and spelling. Then proofread for possessive nouns and agreement of verbs with indefinite pronouns, rereading for one editing point at a time.

TURN AND TALK **Choose a word from your writing that has a root with a meaning clue: Partners, take a close look at this word. Using your Word Parts reference, talk about the meaning. Explain how the word parts might help you spell the word if you didn't know how to spell it.**

CREATE AUTHENTIC PURPOSE Have students choose pieces of writing to edit with an eye toward plural possessive nouns and indefinite pronouns. Students should make sure they've correctly punctuated plural possessive nouns and made indefinite pronouns agree with their verbs.

ASSESS THE LEARNING Scan students' work for plural possessives and indefinite pronouns. Take note of those who need additional instruction to use them with confidence in their writing.

SUM IT UP **Writers, a word parts reference can help you understand words you encounter in text as well as help you create writing with sophisticated terms to instruct your readers.**

DAY 3 Support and Extend the Learning

- Create index cards with root words, suffixes, and prefixes. Have students combine them to form words. They should explain what the words mean and write them in context sentences.
- Remind students that the indefinite pronouns are *all, another, any, anybody, anyone, anything, each, everybody, everyone, everything, few, many, nobody, none, one, several, some, somebody,* and *someone.* Have students look through mentor texts to find examples of indefinite pronouns that they can share with classmates. Cartoons and newspaper articles are great sources of indefinite pronouns!
- Invite students to write poems that center on one content area topic. Gather poems to display in content area classrooms.
- Have students create "word families," lists or graphic organizers that contain words that are all derived from the same root.

#15: Written Argument

Possessive Pronouns • Infinitives • Prefixes and Suffixes

DAY 1 Model Writing for an Audience

I'm crafting the written argument I sent to my mom when I wanted to decorate my own bedroom. I thought hard about my mom's arguments—and what I could write to counter them. *Our living spaces reflect who we are. It's important to express ourselves. That's why I want to redecorate my room.* Notice I started with the possessive pronoun *our.* I used the plural possessive to show that living spaces are important for many people, not just me! My third sentence shows precision, too. I added a prefix, *re–*, to the word *decorate.* Notice that the base word did not change spelling when I added the prefix, and that I used the prefix to show that my room is already decorated—I just want to change it! This sentence also includes an infinitive phrase, *to redecorate my room.* This infinitive functions as a direct object. What do I want? I want to redecorate my room. I pay special attention to infinitives to be sure I'm using them correctly in my sentences. Share your thinking as you deliberately consider the meanings of words with prefixes and suffixes (*impossible, motivation, questionable*), focus on the function of an infinitive (*to be tidy*), and consider which possessive pronouns to use (*my, your*).

Modeled Writing Sample

Our living spaces reflect who we are. It's important to express ourselves. That's why I want to redecorate my room. You think it's impossible for me to keep my room clean, but new decorations will be motivation to be tidy. You think my taste is questionable. But I'll clear all my decisions with you first and listen to your advice.

TURN AND TALK Writers, identify the infinitive phrases in the poem. How do you know the phrase is an infinitive and not a prepositional phrase? Now find a word with a prefix or suffix. Explain how the affix changes meaning.

CREATE AUTHENTIC PURPOSE Ask students to write letters to parents that contain written arguments. Encourage them to consider their parents' arguments and counter their points of view. Challenge them to include possessive pronoun, infinitive phrases, and words with affixes.

ASSESS THE LEARNING Ask writers to point out a possessive pronoun in their work and explain how it shows ownership. Is the pronoun singular or plural? How can they tell? As time allows, discuss infinitive phrases and prefixes and suffixes.

SUM IT UP A written argument is a polite way to convince someone to adopt our point of view. When we craft arguments, paying attention to mechanics and conventions shows seriousness and sincerity about the topic. Think carefully as you use words with prefixes and suffixes. Do they convey the meaning you are hoping to convey?

DAY 2 Guided Practice

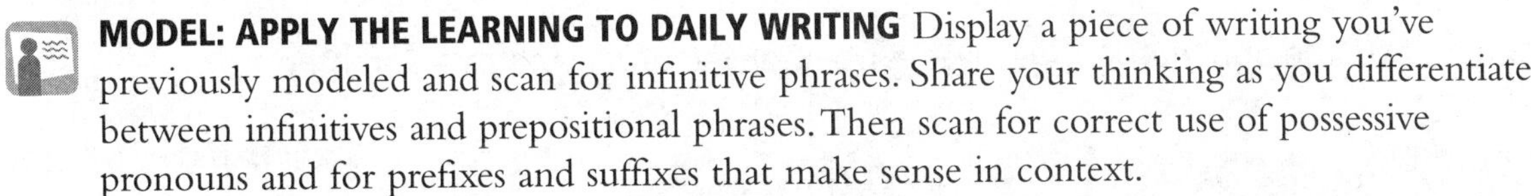

MODEL: APPLY THE LEARNING TO DAILY WRITING Display a piece of writing you've previously modeled and scan for infinitive phrases. Share your thinking as you differentiate between infinitives and prepositional phrases. Then scan for correct use of possessive pronouns and for prefixes and suffixes that make sense in context.

TURN AND TALK Explain how I knew which possessive pronoun to use in my writing. Then scan for words with prefixes or suffixes. How do they change the meaning of the base word? Are they correct in the context of the sentence? Explain why or why not.

CREATE AUTHENTIC PURPOSE Ask pairs to work together to scan pieces of writing with an eye toward possessive pronouns, correct uses of prefixes and suffixes, and correctly used infinitive phrases. Have students explain their thinking as they revise.

ASSESS THE LEARNING Scan students' writing to examine possessive pronouns, infinitive phrases, and prefixes and suffixes. Do students consider both meaning and spelling of word parts? Note students who may need additional instruction.

SUM IT UP To be compelling, written arguments need our close attention to mechanics and conventions. By checking possessive pronouns, you make sure to attribute ownership in a way that makes sense. You've thought carefully about prefixes and suffixes for tools to both meaning and spelling. And you've done a great job of differentiating between infinitive phrases and prepositional phrases with *to*.

DAY 3 Support and Extend the Learning

- Share persuasive techniques, such as bandwagon ("Everyone else is doing it!"), testimonial (famous people endorse a product), and emotional appeal (using language that makes appeals to readers' emotions). Encourage students to experiment with these techniques in advertisements.
- Have students mine mentor texts for examples of words with prefixes and suffixes. Students can copy the words on sentence strips, write the meanings of the affixes and roots, and display the words on a bulletin board.

#16: Explanation: Classification

Comparative and Superlative Adjectives • Use Copyediting Symbols • Parentheses

DAY 1 Model Writing for an Audience

I'm starting a classification about different types of animals: *Classifying animals allows us to better understand their traits. The main classifications are vertebrates and invertebrates.* I'm thinking that my readers need more information than this, though. Will they know what these words mean? I'm adding a definition for each word. I enclose those definitions in parentheses, because I'm including the information to clarify. Now I'm continuing: *Invertebrates are plentifuller then invertebrates.* That doesn't sound right at all! *Plentiful* is an adjective to which I've added *–er* to create the comparative form. Instead, I need to add the word *more* before the adjective: *Invertebrates are more plentiful then invertebrates.*

Modeled Writing Sample

Classifying animals allows us to better understand their traits. The main classifications are vertebrates (animals with backbones) and invertebrates (animals without backbones). Invertebrates are more plentiful then invertebrates. Within each group we can further classify animals. Birds, reptiles, Amphibians, fish, and Mammals are all vertebrates.

Finish the modeling. Then share your thinking as you use copyediting symbols to mark a missing comma after the opening element *within each group*, to change *then* to *than*, and to mark lowercase letters for *amphibians* and *mammals*.

TURN AND TALK Identify a comparative adjective. Explain how the adjective would be different if it were comparing three classes of animals instead of two. What if the adjective were a word like *big*?

CREATE AUTHENTIC PURPOSE Have students write to classify items, such as hot and cool colors, foods in the food pyramid, types of music, types of rocks, and so on. Encourage them to use a comparative or superlative adjective in their writing and to include parentheses for a definition or explanation.

ASSESS THE LEARNING Support writers who may need assistance with comparative and superlative adjectives or parentheses. Observe as students copyedit to see which need additional instruction to use copyediting symbols.

SUM IT UP Classifications often include definitions. Consider using parentheses to enclose definitions so that the flow of the writing is uninterrupted. Pay attention to comparative adjectives. While some take *–er* and *–est* to compare, others require the addition of *more* and *most*.

DAY 2 Guided Practice

MODEL: APPLY THE LEARNING TO DAILY WRITING Choose a piece of modeled writing from a previous session. Read with a close eye on adjectives, paying attention to where you used them to compare. Scan for parentheses as well before you take a last look at the piece, using copyediting symbols to mark the work for a final revision.

TURN AND TALK **Writers, talk about the use of parentheses in my model. What kind of information is included in the parentheses? Explain the effect of placing that information within parentheses. Also, do my comparatives look right?**

CREATE AUTHENTIC PURPOSE Have students look for pieces to revise in their own writing folders. They might start by looking for parentheses or thinking about where they might insert parenthetical elements. Then have them look again at adjective use before editing for one point at a time and using copyediting symbols to mark text for further "fixing."

ASSESS THE LEARNING As students reread their pieces as editors, watch for those who may need extra support with adjectives and with punctuation marks such as parentheses. Observe, also, for ease in using copyediting symbols. Offer assistance to those who need it.

SUM IT UP **Writers, your repertoire of skills has grown! You use copyediting symbols confidently to make work ready for publishing. You make comparisons that deepen your readers' understanding, and you use sophisticated punctuation such as parentheses to add information (or asides) to your writing.**

DAY 3 Support and Extend the Learning

- Delve more deeply into classification. You might share a formula for classifying—sort things into useful categories, be sure that all the categories are parallel, and give examples that fit each category. Remind students that, in a classification essay, each category needs support. A typical organization might be an introductory paragraph with a thesis and then a paragraph telling about each category.
- Have students classify adjectives that they find in their reading of mentor texts or content area texts: those that form the comparative and superlative with *–er* and *–est* and those that require *more* and *most.* Have students generalize a rule for understanding when to use each strategy. (In general, longer words require *more* and *most.*)
- Help students understand that copyediting symbols are used to fix mechanical errors. They should take care when they copyedit others' work that they are not changing meaning but instead focusing on presentation.

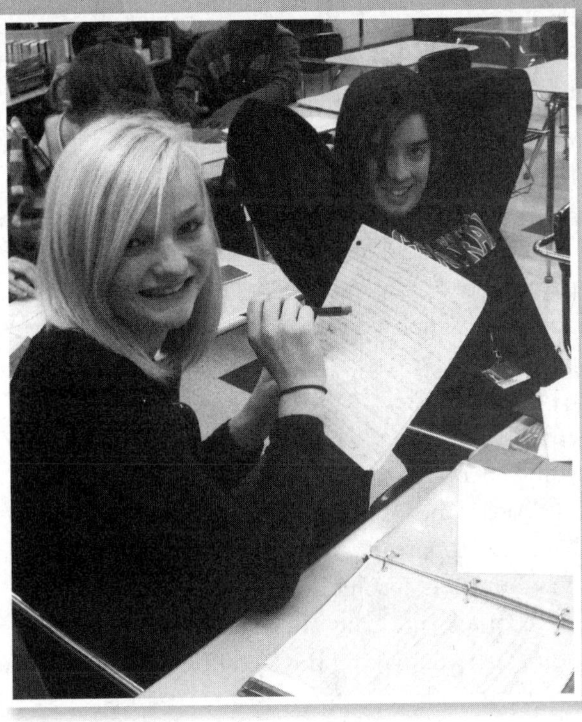

Power Burst Lessons

For learning to be long lasting, learners need opportunities to explore their understandings in more than one context. They need experiences that are not designed to teach new content but instead are opportunities to review and support the transfer of learning to other contexts.

The Power Burst Lessons are learning experiences that fit nicely into small windows of time. When you have 5 to 10 minutes, slip in one of these interactive experiences to review recently addressed conventions and mechanics. Many of these lessons have modeling. Our hope is that after a time or two of your explicit modeling, students can do these activities independently. Many of them can be repeated as students gain new knowledge through completion of lesson cycles.

Power Burst Lessons

Express Lane Edits

In his book *Mechanically Inclined*, Jeff Anderson describes a method for editing called an "express lane edit." The idea behind an express lane edit is to make the editing process move quickly—just like the express lane in a grocery store. A quick edit, narrowed to just a few editing points, one point at a time, focuses students on the rereading of a piece of writing with only a few strategies in mind.

Each student starts with a piece of first-draft writing, such as a passage from a writing folder or notebook. Create a model to share your thinking. After writing, think aloud about an editing point on which you have recently focused, such as using apostrophes for contractions and possessives. Create a "check-out" list with the items for your express lane edit, such as apostrophes and capital letters. Model as you read the piece twice, once editing for apostrophes and once editing for capital letters. In a "receipt" box, note any changes that you made to your piece. If your piece required no changes, note that as well.

If students do not find any errors on a first reading, ask them to read a second time. You might have students read word-for-word backwards if they still have not found errors. They can then write in their receipt box: *I found no errors.*

Express lane edits are quick! They are designed to allow students to focus on just an editing point or two, making this activity perfect for small pockets of time to follow up on cycles that you've introduced.

Secret Sentences

To create "secret sentences," write parts of sentences on individual pieces of paper, one word or punctuation mark per piece of paper. Distribute the pieces of paper randomly to team members. Members should move themselves around to arrange their words and punctuation into a sentence, checking for a beginning capital letter, punctuation marks, word order, and so on. Once students have arranged themselves, discuss with them the strategies they used to create sentences. How did recent cycles for patterns of grammar use or punctuation help them unlock the secret sentence?

You might begin with sentences culled from texts, including content area texts and selections from read-alouds. As students gain experience with secret sentences, branch out to less familiar sentences that provide a review of grammatical structures, recently learned mechanics, spelling rules, and conventions. Include a variety of sentence structures—complex sentences with openers and closers, embedded nonrestrictive elements, and so on. Sentences should be rich with varied punctuation and interesting language structures.

Consider sentences from mentor texts, such as:

> "I slumped in my seat, feet up on the glove compartment, wearing an A&S baseball hat with the brim yanked low over my forehead."
>
> —*Pictures of Hollis Woods*, Patricia Reilly Giff

> "Flames race through the treetops, sometimes faster than a person can run, burning at temperatures hot enough to melt steel."
>
> —*Wildfires*, Seymour Simon

> "Everything of any value had been stripped away and only the rusting carcasses remained, heaped one on top of the other, waiting to be fed into the crusher."
>
> —*Stormbreaker*, Anthony Horowitz

Extending Secret Sentences

Students will enjoy working in teams to write secret sentences for other teams to "solve." Meet with teams to check drafts of their sentences before they write the words and punctuation marks on individual pieces of paper.

Prepare additional sheets of paper with words that could be substituted or inserted into the sentence. For example, you might create sheets of paper with additional verbs. Have students substitute their verbs into the sentence and discuss how the meaning of the sentence changes with the changing of the verb. After students complete a sentence, you might give other students adverbs or adjectives. As students determine where to fit themselves into the sentences, you can discuss placement of modifying elements.

Scavenger Hunt

Use a piece of text reproduced on a transparency, document camera, or interactive whiteboard to demonstrate how to survey a selection for an element of conventions or mechanics on which you focused during a recent cycle. Highlight that convention with a highlighter pen. As time allows, discuss the convention you highlighted. If you are scavenging for apostrophes, for example, have students sort apostrophes used for possessives and contractions. If you scavenged for subjects and verbs, you might discuss agreement or verb tense. Give scavenger hunts purpose and punch, having students search for Fascinating Commas, Powerful Verb Choices, Engaging Lead Sentences, and so on.

Once students are familiar with the Scavenger Hunt idea, have individuals, partners, or teams survey reading selections, weekly magazines, newspapers, and so on, keeping a tally of their findings and collecting terrific sentences to display in the room.

Students will enjoy looking for commas and thinking about how they are used in diverse selections such as Kate DiCamillo's *The Tale of Despereaux* and Martin Luther King Jr.'s "I Have a Dream" speech. They might scavenge for powerful phrases that serve as adverbs in such selections as Jim Murphy's *An American Plague* or Walter Wick's *A Drop of Water.* As students continue to gain more skill in conducting Scavenger Hunts with different purposes, encourage them to work with partners to conduct Scavenger Hunts through pieces in their own writing folders.

Combining Sentences

Although short, simple sentences have their place in fluent writing; students need to strive for variety in their sentence structures. The *Writing Next* report (Graham & Perin, 2007) indicates that teaching adolescents how to write increasingly complex sentences enhances the overall quality of students' writing.

Provide practice—and targeted "hunts"—so that students learn to combine sentences in ways that create richer, more interesting statements.

Examine Mentor Texts

Have students look through mentor texts for examples of compound and complex sentences after you have identified examples. Students can indicate both the sentences as well as conjunctions that were used to combine independent and dependent clauses. Mentor texts for compound sentences might include Nancy Farmer's *The House of the Scorpion,* Wendelin Van Draanen's *Flipped,* content area textbooks, articles in quality nonfiction magazines, and so on.

Model

Show students several short, simple sentences, such as:

> Seismic waves move through the earth. The strong waves shake the earth. The waves move toward the earth's surface. They shake the ground and anything else there.

Model how to combine the ideas in the short sentences in different ways to create compound and complex sentences, such as:

> Strong, seismic waves move through the earth, and they shake the ground and anything else on the surface.
>
> Shaking the ground and anything on it, strong seismic waves move through the earth and toward the surface.
>
> Seismic waves shake the earth as they move through it, and they shake the ground and anything on it when they reach the surface.

Point out that you are not simply putting together sentences with *and.* Instead, you are choosing important ideas from each sentence and combining them to make parallel sentences that make sense! Discuss other coordinating conjunctions as well: *for, nor, but, or,* and *yet.* Have students experiment using these conjunctions and discuss the effect of using them on the meanings of sentences.

Guide Practice

Provide partners with short sentences on sentence strips. Start with two sentences. As students gain proficiency, you can give them three or more sentences to combine. Have them add more words to create new sentences that are longer and more interesting. Point out that adding commas and connecting words will help them as they combine sentences. Have them share their sentences with other pairs and in larger groups.

Extensions

As students gain proficiency combining ideas in compound sentences, you can provide sentences, phrases, and clauses to combine so that students have practice making compound sentences, complex sentences with introductory elements followed by commas, complex sentences with appositives, and complex sentences with closing elements set aside by commas.

Provide students with compound sentences (and complex sentences, as they gain more mastery). Have them rewrite the longer sentences into two or more shorter ones.

Have students create and use a rubric for evaluating their combined sentences. They might focus on meaning, length, rhythm, and so on.

	Yes	No
Meaning: Does the combined sentence have the same meaning as the short sentences?		
Length: Is the new sentence too wordy?		
Fluency: Does the combined sentence flow naturally?		
Fluency: Does this combined sentence fit well with the sentences around it?		
Fluency: Is sentence fluency for the overall passage supported by this sentence revision?		

Marvelous Mentors

Designate bulletin board space with engaging headings that invite students to add examples from texts they have read, including short stories, novels, essays, poems, biographies, articles, and so on. Headings might include Powerful Verbs, Precise Nouns, Fabulous Prepositional Phrases, Engaging Openers, Realistic Dialogue, and so on. Consider starting with a heading that corresponds to a cycle you are studying and then adding headings as you introduce additional cycles.

Model

As you read aloud from a text, pause to notice a sentence that uses an opening that captures your attention, a powerful verb that helps you picture the action, dialogue that sounds like "real people" talking—perhaps a focus from a current or previous cycle. Place a sticky note on the page to "save" it for after your reading, and then add the sentence to the bulletin board.

Practice

Pause to share a sentence from a text you are reading. As you focus on the sentence, discuss its elements with students. Under which heading would students place it? Why? Would they create another heading for the sentence? Add the sentence—and the heading—to the bulletin board.

Independent Practice

As students read independently, encourage them to be on the lookout for examples of your current bulletin board topics. They can mark the examples in their texts with sticky notes, share them with partners, and add their most powerful examples to the board. If you see students only one or two periods a day, encourage them to bring examples from their content area reading to add to the display. You might also look for strong examples in student papers to add to the bulletin board.

Stretch and Shorten

As a lead-in to this activity, read aloud from and celebrate a text such as Gary Paulsen's *Dogsong,* in which the author expertly crafts short sentences for maximum impact and emotion. A two-word sentence popped in between two compound sentences can add amazing punch to writing!

Help students think about stretching two-word sentences as well. You might focus on content with sentences such as the following about the flooding of the Nile:

Waters rose.

Rivers flooded.

Seedlings emerged.

Crops matured.

Civilization thrived.

Ask students if these groups of words are sentences. You might model with one sentence:

> Is this group of words, *waters rose*, a sentence? Let's take a close look. What is the sentence about? *Waters*. What did the waters do? *They rose*. So this group of words is a sentence. It has a subject and a verb.

Model stretching the sentence:

> What could I add to make this sentence even stronger? I could write when the waters rose. I could explain the speed with which the waters rose. I could describe the water. Let me try to make this sentence richer and more engaging: *Every spring, the swirling waters of the Nile quickly rose past their banks.*

Have students work in pairs or small groups to stretch the other sentences by adding words or phrases. You might focus the stretching by asking students to add certain elements, such as an adjective, an opener with a comma, an appositive, a closer, an adverb, a prepositional phrase, and so on. Remind students to use correct punctuation as they stretch their sentences.

Students can also shorten long sentences. Provide groups with pieces of text that consist of three or four long sentences. Ask students to think about the impact of shortening one of the sentences to just two words. How can sentence shortening make their writing more powerful? After groups have each shortened one sentence, have them share their results and discuss how shortening particular sentences added fluency and variety to their writing.

Extensions

Challenge students to write two-word sentences about content in social studies, science, and math.

Encourage students to find two-word (or very short) sentences in mentor texts, such as poems, short stories, picture books, articles, content area texts, and so on. Have them add the two-word sentences to a chart. During "power burst time," students could choose two-word sentences from the chart to expand.

Have students use two-word sentences as they write headlines for classroom studies and school events. They can further stretch their thinking by using alliteration in their work.

Punctuation Power (and More!)

Write sentences that reflect your current and past lesson cycles—and do not include punctuation! Place the sentences in a folder or large envelope that students can access. Students can rewrite sentences, inserting appropriate punctuation. Consider using concepts such as the following.

Apostrophes

- Include sentences with plural and singular possessives that need apostrophes, such as *The teams equipment was loaded on the bus* and *The players helmets were left behind!*
- Add sentences with irregular plurals, such as *The childrens parents were waiting to take them home.*
- Incorporate sentences with possessive pronouns and contractions, such as *I dont like its flavor.*
- Include sentences with easily confused words that contain apostrophes, such as *Theyre hoping to see their cousins at the reunion.*

Commas

- Add sentences that require commas in a series, such as *The eruption was sudden fiery and intense* and *At the beach, we saw crashing waves ball-chasing dogs and frolicking children.*
- Include sentences with appositives that students need to set off with commas—or encourage them to add appositives into the sentences you include.
- Incorporate both compound and complex sentences, such as *You may think of pyramids as prisms but earlier pyramids were rectangular* and *Before the Egyptians buried their dead the bodies went through a complicated purification process.*

Dialogue

- Include sentences that have tag lines *(she exclaimed, he snorted, they inquired)* at the beginning, in the middle, and at the end.
- Include examples that need quotation marks within a quotation.

Grammar

- Include sentences with grammar challenges such as unclear pronoun antecedents, incorrect verb tense or pronoun case, dangling modifiers, nonparallel structures, and so on.

Spelling

- Include sentences with misspelled words and encourage students to use their spelling consciousness to identify misspellings and then to apply spelling strategies to correct the words they identify.

Word Degrees

Work with students on choosing precise words as you discuss "word degrees."

Start with a cloze sentence, such as: *"I am hungry,"* ____ *the giant.* Ask students to list five words that fit the sentence and rank them in order of intensity. Model with a set of words in rank order, such as *whispered, whined, grunted, exclaimed,* and *roared.* Once you have modeled, ask students to follow your lead.

You might also give students a pair of words that are opposite, such as *timid* and *brazen.* Have them list words that come between these opposites. After they have listed the "between words," they can work in teams to rank the words in order from least to most intense.

Create a folder with possible word pairs for students to use to create "word degree" continuums. You might include *dejected/elated, dull/glistening, whisper/shout, sad/giddy, modest/ arrogant,* and so on. Post finished continuums on your wall so that students have "wall thesauruses." They can add new words they learn to the continuums as well.

List Them!

Students need to have at the ready lists of words to help them with spelling, organization, and so on. The Word Bank (in the Tools file on the Resources CD) is a great tool for students to capture words that they have difficulty spelling. The word wall then becomes a reference. Students can also use the word wall to capture words related to content or words related to writing organization, such as transitions, persuasive words, words that signal cause and effect, words that signal comparisons, and so on.

When students begin a new content unit, encourage them to begin lists of content words, including vivid verbs and adjectives and precise nouns, which they can include in their content writing. When students work with new writing forms or organizational patterns, have them list essential words. Teams can work on lists to post on the wall, or pairs can work on lists to place in writing folders. Encourage students to use these lists as references throughout the year, adding to them when they learn new words or phrases.

PART V

Tools: References and Resources for Your Classroom

The tools presented in this section are designed to be both references and resources for your students that empower their work as writers. We are providing thumbnails of each tool here for your reference. Full-sized, easily reproducible versions of these sheets are available on the Resources CD for this book.

The first resource, the Word Bank, can be used for a variety of purposes. Middle school writers need visual access to the academic vocabulary associated with social studies, science, math, art, and so on. Students might use the Word Bank form to collect these groups of words related to specific units of study.

Encourage students to create and add to word banks related to writing purposes. While one word bank, for example, could focus on transitional words and phrases, others might focus on persuasive words, words that signal comparisons, words that differentiate between causes and effects, and so on. A word bank can also serve as a spelling reference. When students have difficulty spelling particular words, they can use resources to find the correct spellings and then add them to the word banks. This assures

Contents

that word banks are not stagnant! Students' recording of correct spellings serves as reinforcement as they create personalized references.

The Create Your Own Resource pages are also references that students can personalize. With sample sentences from mentor books and exemplars they create themselves, learners will have tools that support and lift the writing they produce. We encourage you to have your students keep their resources in their writing folders and add to them throughout the year.

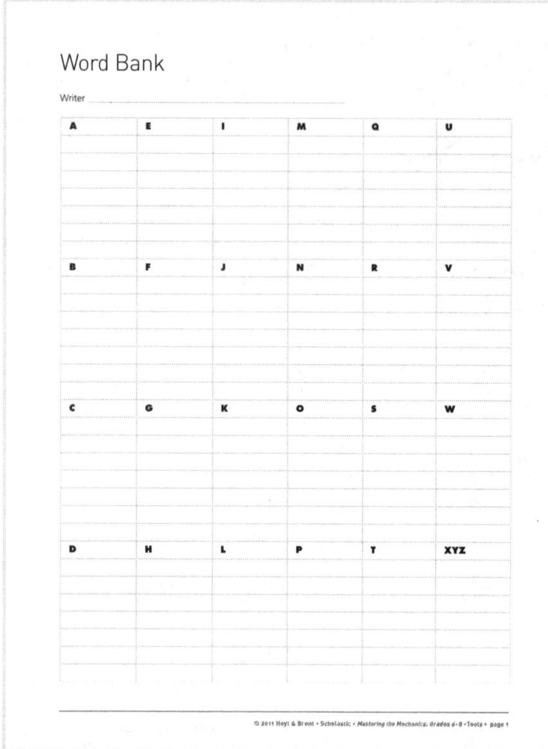

Word Bank

Writer ______

A	E	I	M	Q	U
B	F	J	N	R	V
C	G	K	O	S	W
D	H	L	P	T	XYZ

Word Bank

Students can use this word bank in a variety of ways, including the following:

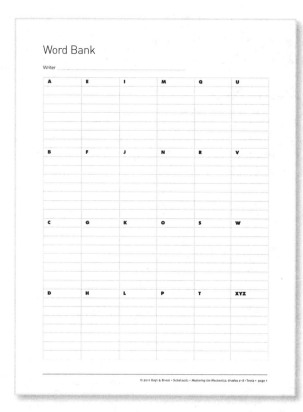

- **As a personal spelling list, students can note words that are difficult for them, use resources to be sure they are spelling them correctly, and add the correct spellings to a word bank for references.**
- **As a content area word bank, students can gather words on a variety of topics, such as heredity, ancient cultures, algebra, and famous artists and their techniques. They can use the word bank as a reference for their writing.**
- **As a writing purposes word bank, students can use one word bank for transition words, another for prepositions, another for conjunctions, and so on.**

Reference: Commonly Misspelled Words

Reference: Commonly Misspelled Words

Use this reference to be sure you've spelled words correctly! If misspelled words turn up in your writing again and again, consider adding them to your personal spelling word bank.

a lot	conscience	immediately	remember
a while	conscious	importance	resistance
absence	curiosity	independent	responsible
accidentally	dangerous	interrupt	restaurant
achieve	definitely	its	safety
across	develop	judgment	science
actually	different	knowledge	sense
all right	disappoint	miscellaneous	separate
apparently	embarrass	muscle	sincerely
appearance	environment	necessary	successful
argument	especially	noticeable	surprise
basically	exercise	occasion	temperature
beautiful	existence	occurred/occurrence	therefore
because	experience	occurring	thorough
beginning	familiar	opportunity	together
believe	finally	permanent	tomorrow
breathe	fortunately	persistent	truly
built	forty	piece	unfortunately
business	forward	possession	until
calendar	friend	preferred, preferring	vegetable
certainly	further	probably	Wednesday
character	government	publicly	weight
coming	guard	pursue	weird
committee	happened	realize	wherever
completely	heard	really	which
	humorous	receive	yield
		recommend	
		referred	

Reference: Homophones and Easily Confused Words

Reference: Homophones and Easily Confused Words

Create sample sentences in your writer's notebook for easy reference.

Homophones are words that are pronounced the same but have different meanings. They may be spelled the same, as in *rose* (a flower) and *rose* (the past tense of the verb *rise*). They may have different spellings, as in *to, two*, and *too*. As you write, consider the context to choose the correct homophone or word that may be confused with another. Create mentor sentences in your writer's notebook for easy reference.

Words	Function/Purpose	Example Sentences
accept	*Accept* is a verb that means "to believe, to agree, or to say *yes*."	I hope the traveling baseball team will accept me as a new member!
except	*Except* means "excluding" or "apart from."	All my friends except Dionis are able to attend my party.
affect	*Affect* is usually a verb that means "to have an influence on."	Bad weather might affect our planned picnic.
effect	*Effect* is usually a noun that means "a result."	Lightning is the effect of electricity in clouds.
all ready	If you are *all ready*, you are completely prepared.	I am all ready to see the movie!
already	*Already* is an adverb that describes something that happened before a certain time.	Wait, we've already seen that film.
are	*Are* is a linking verb.	We are excited for our trip to the beach.
hour	*Hour* is a unit of time.	We'll leave in an hour.
our	*Our* is a possessive adjective.	Mom packed our lunch, towels, and sunscreen.
beside	*Beside* is a preposition that means "next to."	I sat beside my best friend.
besides	*Besides* is an adverb that means "as well" or a preposition that means "in addition to."	What games will we play besides baseball and soccer?
buy	*Buy* is a verb that means "to purchase." *Buy* can also be a noun. (That was a great buy!)	Let's buy healthy food for our picnic by the lake.
by bye	*By* is a preposition, while *bye* is the short form of "good-bye."	After the picnic, we all said, "Bye!" and went home.
farther	*Farther* is an adjective or an adverb. It means "to or at a more distant point."	Today, we ran five miles. We'll run farther tomorrow.
further	*Further* is an adjective or adverb that means "to or at a greater extent or degree."	We'll have no further discussion about the proposal until we do some more research.
few	*Few* is an adjective that means "small in number." Use *few* with objects you can count.	Few foods I like are as healthy as carrots!
less	*Less* is an adjective used to compare small amounts.	I am trying to eat less unhealthy food.
its	*Its* is a possessive pronoun.	The dog carried its puppy in its mouth.
it's	*It's* is a contraction that means "it is."	It's fun to play with the little puppies.

know	*Know* is a verb that refers to realizing or understanding something.	Do you know how to solve this problem?
no	*No* is an adjective meaning "none" or "not" or an interjection that is the opposite of *yes*.	No, I don't. But let's try to figure it out!
lay	*Lay* means "to place something down." *Lay* is also the past-tense verb of *lie*.	Lay the book on the table.
lie	*Lie* means "to recline."	Lie down on the couch!
lose	*Lose* is a verb that means "to misplace" or "to be defeated."	My little brother is going to lose his tooth.
loose	The adjective *loose* is the opposite of *tight*.	The tooth has been loose for weeks!
passed	*Passed* is the past-tense form of the verb *pass*.	We passed the park on our way to school.
past	*Past* is a noun referring to a time before the present. It can also be an adjective, an adverb, or a preposition.	I played at that park often in the past.
principal	A *principal* is a person who plays an important role. *Principal* can also mean "chief or most important."	The principal led the school assembly.
principle	A *principle* is a rule or standard.	Our coach's most important principle is respect for teammates.
right	*Right* can function as the opposite of *left* or as a synonym for "correct."	Please turn right on Garfield Street.
write	*Write* functions as a verb.	I am going to write the directions to make them easier to follow.
stationary	*Stationary* is an adjective that means "not moving."	The deer in the clearing was stationary.
stationery	*Stationery* is paper used for writing.	Celia used her stationery to write a note about seeing the deer.
than	Use the word *than* for comparisons.	I think Helen is braver than I am.
then	*Then* indicates a certain time.	She dove off the high-dive first, and then I gave it a try.
they're	*They're* is a contraction that means *they are*.	They're joining us at the play.
their there	While *their* is a possessive pronoun, *there* indicates direction.	Our seats are close to the front, but their seats are back there.
through	*Through* is a preposition that means "passing across" or an adjective that means "finished."	The ball zipped through the air when the pitcher wound up and threw it.
threw	*Threw* is the past tense of the verb *throw*.	
to too	While the word *to* indicates direction, the word *too* means "also."	The Huskies are going to the football tournament. The Eagles are going, too.
two	*Two* is a number.	Each team will play two games.
who's	*Who's* is a contraction that means "who is."	Who's visiting our classroom?
whose	*Whose* is a possessive pronoun.	I think that's the author whose book we are reading!
your	*Your* is a possessive pronoun.	You shared your lunch when I forgot mine.
you're	*You're* is a contraction that means "you are."	You're a great friend.

Action Research: Word Parts

Action Research: Word Parts

Writer ....

Knowing word parts can help you understand the meanings of words you encounter in your reading. Word parts can also help you as you write. When you know the meanings of root words, prefixes, and suffixes, you can choose words that make sense in your writing. If your spelling consciousness is telling you that a word doesn't "look right," you can use this word part resource to check that you've correctly spelled roots, prefixes, and suffixes. As you research, note words from mentor texts that include these word parts. Each table includes rows for you to record other roots, prefixes, and suffixes you find as you research, too!

Root Words

Root	Meaning	Example	Mentor Text/Word in Context
alter	other	alternate	
amphi	both ends; all sides	amphibious	
ann, enni	year	annual	
aqua	water	aquarium	
aud	sound	auditorium	
bio	life	biography	
chron	time	chronological	
demo	people	democracy	
dic	speak, say	dictate	
equ	equal	equality	
fac	make, do	manufacture	
geo	earth	geography	
graph	writing, printing	telegraph	
hydro, hydr	water	dehydrate	
log	word	dialogue	
metri, meter	measure	thermometer	
min	small	minute	
phon, phono	sound, voice	telephone	
scrib, script	write	scribe	
therm	heat	thermal	

Prefixes

Prefix	Meaning	Example	Mentor Text/Word in Context
a–, an–	not, without	*asocial*	
ab–	away from	*abnormal*	
ad–	movement to, change into	*adjoin*	
ambi–	both	*ambivalent*	
ante–	before, preceding	*anteroom*	
anti–	against	*antiwar*	
auto–	self	*autobiography*	
be–	all over, completely, covered with, caused to be	*beset, bemuse, bejeweled, becalm*	
bi–	two	*bicentennial*	
circum–	around	*circumference*	
com–, con–	with, together	*community, connect*	
de–	down, away, removal	*descend, device*	
dia–, di–	through, across	*diameter*	
dis–	removal, opposite of	*disadvantage*	
en–	put into, bring into the condition of	*engulf, enlighten*	
ex–	out of, from	*exhale, exit*	
ex–	former	*ex-player*	
extra–	outside, beyond	*extracurricular*	
hemi–	half	*hemisphere*	
hyper–	over, more than	*hypertension*	
hypo–	under	*hypodermic*	
il–	not	*illegal*	
im–	not	*impossible*	
in–	not, without	*invisible, inappropriate*	
in–	into	*incorporate*	
inter–	between, among	*interstate*	
intra–	within, beside	*intramural*	
ir–	not	*irregular*	

micro–	small	*microscope*	
mono–	one	*monarchy*	
non–	absence of, opposite	*nontoxic*	
out–	surpassing, exceeding, outside of	*outperform, outbuilding*	
over–	excessively, completely, upper, outer, above	*overconfident, overcoat*	
poly–	many, several	*polygon*	
post–	after	*postgraduate*	
pre–	before	*preschool*	
pro–	in favor of, forwards or away, before in time	*project, propulsion, prologue*	
re–	back, again	*rerun*	
semi–	half, partly	*semicircle*	
sub–	under	*submarine*	
sur–, super–	over, above	*surcharge, superhuman*	
syn–, sym–	with, together	*synonym, symbiosis*	
tele–	distant, far off	*telephone*	
trans–	across	*transatlantic*	
ultra–	beyond, extreme	*ultraviolet*	
un–	not, reversal	*unacceptable, unplug*	
under–	beneath, lower in rank, not enough	*underarm, underdeveloped*	

Suffixes

Suffix	Meaning	Example	Mentor Text/Word in Context
–ia, –y	act, state	*mania, democracy*	
–ic, –tic, –ical, –ac	having to do with	*dramatic, cardiac*	
–ics	having to do with	*optics*	
–ism	belief in	*pacifism*	
–ist	person who believes	*pacifist*	
–logy	study of	*biology*	
–or, –er	person who takes part in	*actor, teacher*	

Suffixes That Make Words Nouns
–ation (explore, exploration), *–sion* (persuade, persuasion), *–er* (lead, leader), *–cian* (music, musician), *–ness* (happy, happiness), *–al* (arrive, arrival), *–ary* (diction, dictionary), *–ment* (treat, treatment), *–y* (jealous, jealousy)

Suffixes That Make Words Adjectives
–al (accident, accidental), *–ary* (imagine, imaginary), *–able* (tax, taxable), *–ly* (sister, sisterly), *–y* (ease, easy), *–ful* (forget, forgetful)

Suffixes That Make Words Adverbs and Verbs
Adverb: *–ly* (sad, sadly)

Verb: *–ize* (terror, terrorize), *–ate* (hyphen, hyphenate)

Create Your Own Resource: Complex Sentences With Participial Phrases

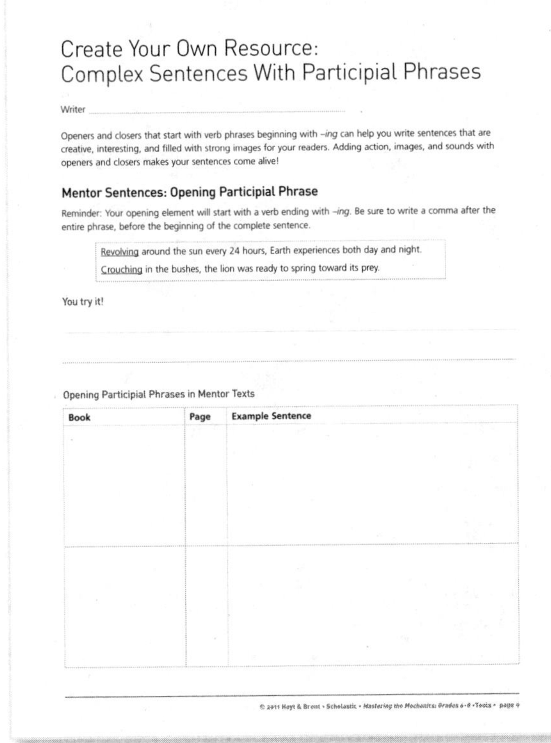

Create Your Own Resource: Complex Sentences With Participial Phrases

Writer ______________________

Openers and closers that start with verb phrases beginning with *-ing* can help you write sentences that are creative, interesting, and filled with strong images for your readers. Adding action, images, and sounds with openers and closers makes your sentences come alive!

Mentor Sentences: Opening Participial Phrase

Reminder: Your opening element will start with a verb ending with *-ing*. Be sure to write a comma after the entire phrase, before the beginning of the complete sentence.

> Revolving around the sun every 24 hours, Earth experiences both day and night.
> Crouching in the bushes, the lion was ready to spring toward its prey.

You try it!

____

____

Opening Participial Phrases in Mentor Texts

Book	Page	Example Sentence

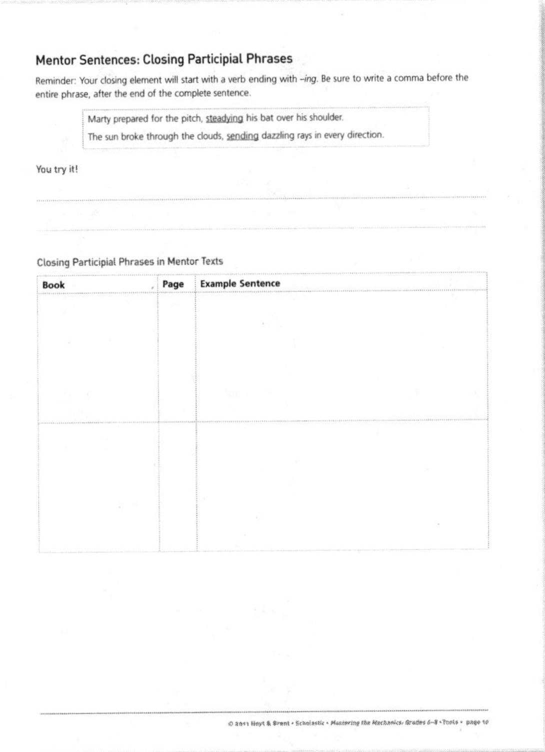

Mentor Sentences: Closing Participial Phrases

Reminder: Your closing element will start with a verb ending with *-ing*. Be sure to write a comma before the entire phrase, after the end of the complete sentence.

> Marty prepared for the pitch, steadying his bat over his shoulder.
> The sun broke through the clouds, sending dazzling rays in every direction.

You try it!

____

____

Closing Participial Phrases in Mentor Texts

Book	Page	Example Sentence

Create Your Own Resource: Compound Sentences

Writer ______________________

Commas and coordinating conjunctions can help us combine short, choppy sentences into more interesting structures. These tools can help us create sentences that flow smoothly and sound more natural. Remember to include a comma before the coordinating conjunction.

Coordinating Conjunctions: *for, and, nor, but, or, yet, so*

Separate Sentences	Compound Sentence
Some students like to study after school. I prefer to study in the morning.	Some students like to study after school, but I prefer to study in the morning.
Igneous rocks are created with heat. Sedimentary rocks are created with pressure.	Igneous rocks are created with heat, and sedimentary rocks are created with pressure.

You try it!

Search mentor books for compound sentences. Look for coordinating conjunctions and commas as you search. Underline the coordinating conjunctions in your sentences. Collect additional examples in your writer's notebook for reference.

Book	Page	Compound Sentence	Simple Sentences Combined to Make Compound Sentence

What have you learned about creating longer, more natural sentences out of short sentences?

____

____

Create Your Own Resource: Compound Sentences

Create Your Own Resource: Transition Words

Writer ....

Transition words create connections between ideas and cue readers about important information.

Purpose	Example of Transition Words
Time/sequence (the order in which something happens)	first, second, third, before, during, after, today, tomorrow, yesterday, until, next, then, as soon as, finally, afterward, earlier, meanwhile, now, since, soon
To show place/location	above, across, against, along, adjacent to, beyond, by, down, on the opposite side, nearby, to the left of
Compare/contrast (show differences)	however, but, although, on the other hand, similarly, even though, still, though, yet, also, likewise
Conclude, summarize, or emphasize a point (the end of the writing is coming)	finally, in conclusion, therefore, in other words, in summary, last
Add information	first, also, and, besides, in addition, for example, next, finally, for instance, specifically, in fact, of course, to illustrate, for instance
Example or illustration	specifically, for example, in fact, of course, to illustrate, for instance

Locate sentences in mentor texts that include transitions. Underline the transitions.

Book	Page	Sentence	The author's purpose for using the transition is . . .

Create Your Own Resource: Transition Words

Create Your Own Resource: Verb Types

Writer ....

A verb shows action or links the subject to another word in the sentence.

Action Verbs

An **action verb** tells what the subject is doing. Some experts believe that the verb is the most important part of speech. Precise verbs make writing specific and clear.

EXAMPLES: Rainwater *trickled* down the windowpane. The snake *slithered* through the sand.

Linking Verbs

A **linking verb** links a subject to a noun or to an adjective that comes after the verb.

Linking verbs: Forms of *be: is, are, was, were, am, been*
EXAMPLE: My brother *is* talented.

Action verbs that can function as linking verbs: *feel, look, remain, seem, smell, sound, taste*
EXAMPLES: That sauce *tastes* spicy. Sandpaper *feels* rough.

Helping Verbs

Helping verbs come before the main verbs in sentences. They help state the action or show when the action is taking place.

A verb that is made of a helping verb and a main verb is a **verb phrase**.

Helping verbs: *is, are, was, were, am, been, have, had, has, do, did, can, will, could, would, should, must, may, shall*
EXAMPLE: We *will study* in the library after school. (The verb phrase *will study* tells about an action happening in the future.)

EXAMPLE: The impatient sled dogs *had been waiting* for the start of the race. (The verb phrase *had been waiting* shows action that started and ended in the past.)

As you review mentor texts, list sentences that include vivid action verbs, linking verbs (forms of *be* and action verbs that function as linking verbs), and verb phrases with helping verbs. Underline the verbs and verb phrases in the sentences you record.

Action Verbs	Linking Verbs	Verb Phrases (use helping verbs)

Create Your Own Resource: Verb Types

Reference: Regular and Irregular Verbs

To form the past tense of most verbs, you add *–ed*. Verbs to which you add *–ed* to create the past and the past participle are called *regular verbs*.

EXAMPLE
Present Tense: To get plenty of exercise, we walk to school.
Past Tense: Yesterday, we walked even though it was raining!
Past Participle: By the end of last week, I had walked 10 miles.

Irregular verbs do not follow this pattern. Instead, they change spelling to form the past tense and the participle form.

Use this list of common irregular verbs for reference:

Present	Past	Past Participle
be	was, were	been
become	became	become
begin	began	begun
blow	blew	blown
break	broke	broken
bring	brought	brought
build	built	built
buy	bought	bought
catch	caught	caught
choose	chose	chosen
do	did	done
drink	drank	drunk
drive	drove	driven
eat	ate	eaten
fall	fell	fallen
feel	felt	felt
find	found	found
fly	flew	flown
forget	forgot	forgotten
freeze	froze	frozen
get	got	gotten
give	gave	given
go	went	gone
grow	grew	grown
have	had	had
hear	heard	heard
hide	hid	hidden
keep	kept	kept
know	knew	known
lay	laid	laid
leave	left	left

Present	Past	Past Participle
lie	lay	lain
make	made	made
pay	paid	paid
quit	quit	quit
read	read	read
ride	rode	ridden
run	ran	run
say	said	said
see	saw	seen
sell	sold	sold
send	sent	sent
shake	shook	shaken
shine	shone	shone
sing	sang	sung
sit	sat	sat
speak	spoke	spoken
spring	sprang	sprung
stand	stood	stood
steal	stole	stolen
swim	swam	swum
take	took	taken
teach	taught	taught
tear	tore	torn
tell	told	told
think	thought	thought
throw	threw	thrown
wake	woke	woken
wear	wore	worn
win	won	won
write	wrote	written

Reference: Regular and Irregular Verbs

Create Your Own Resource: Understanding Adverbs and Prepositional Phrases

Create Your Own Resource: Understanding Adverbs and Prepositional Phrases

Writer ....

An **adverb** tells where, when, how, and to what degree. An adverb often ends in *–ly.*

EXAMPLES:	**Where**	*here, there*	**When**	*now, soon*
	How	*joyfully, quickly*	**To What Degree**	*very, slightly*

A **preposition** relates a noun or pronoun to another word in the sentence.

COMMON PREPOSITIONS: *about, above, across, after, against, along, among, around, at, before, behind, below, beneath, beside, between, by, down, during, except, for, from, in, in front of, inside, instead of, into, like, near, of, on, on top of, out of, outside, over, since, through, to, toward, under, underneath, until, up, upon, with, within, without*

A **prepositional phrase** is a group of words that includes a preposition, its object, and any adjectives or articles that come between the preposition and object.

EXAMPLE: Look for your book on the top shelf.

As you look through mentor texts or your content area books, write sentences from these books that contain adverbs and prepositional phrases. Underline the adverbs and the prepositions.

Book	Sentence With Adverbs or Prepositional Phrases

What did you notice about adverbs and prepositions in the books you reviewed? How did they lift the writing?

Create Your Own Resource: Pronouns

Create Your Own Resource: Pronouns

Writer ....

Pronouns take the place of nouns or noun phrases in your writing. To be sure that you have correct subject-verb agreement, it's important to know which indefinite and demonstrative pronouns are singular and which are plural. For reflexive pronouns, it's important to know which are singular and which are plural so that you can make sure pronouns and their antecedents agree.

Indefinite Pronouns

Indefinite pronouns don't have an exact number.

Singular: *another, anybody, anyone, anything, each, either, everybody, everyone, everything, little, much, either, nobody, no one, nothing, one, other, somebody, someone, something*

EXAMPLES: Anybody is welcome to come to our show!

Do you prefer strawberries or blueberries? Actually, either is great!

Plural: *both, few, many, others, several*

EXAMPLES: Did you hear all the storms last night? Several were spotted nearby!

We expected just a few actors for try-outs, but others were there, too.

Singular or Plural: *all, any, more, most, none, some*

EXAMPLE: Is the entire team on the bus? Yes, all are here!

Demonstrative Pronouns

Demonstrative pronouns point to nouns or stand in for them.

Singular: *this, that*

Plural: *these, those*

EXAMPLES: This is the narrative piece of which I'm most proud!

Those are the seeds that are ready to plant.

Reflexive Pronouns

Reflexive pronouns rename the subjects of action verbs.

Singular: *myself, yourself, himself, herself, itself*

Plural: *ourselves, yourselves, themselves*

EXAMPLES: I hurt myself on the slide.

The band members called themselves "Serious Business."

Relative Pronouns

Relative pronouns join clauses to make complex sentences.

that, who, whom, whose, which, where, why

EXAMPLES: This is the bridge that my group built.

My teacher, whose book was published this year, writes great poems!

As you read through mentor texts, watch for these various types of pronouns. Write the sentences you find and highlight the pronouns. Identify the type of pronoun it is and whether it is singular or plural.

Book	Sentence	Pronoun—Type/S or P?

Create Your Own Resource: Understanding the Parts of Speech

Create Your Own Resource: Understanding the Parts of Speech

Writer ____________________

The English language has thousands of words, but they can all be divided into eight groups called the *parts of speech*. For each part of speech, write a sparkling sentence from a mentor text or your own writing. Highlight the word that functions as that part of speech.

Nouns name a person, place, or thing EXAMPLES: *boy, Charlie, city, happiness*	**Pronouns** take the place of a noun EXAMPLES: *I, me, you, she, he, we, you, they, us*
Verbs express an action or state of being EXAMPLES: *drop, write, am, was running*	**Adjectives** describe a noun or pronoun EXAMPLES: *delighted, hungry, anxious*
Interjections express strong emotion or surprise EXAMPLES: *Ouch! Wow!*	**Conjunctions** connect words, phrases, clauses, and sentences EXAMPLES: *and, or, but, so, because, although*
Adverbs and Adverb Phrases tell when, how, and to what degree (describe a verb, an adjective, or another adverb) EXAMPLES: *quickly, happily, very, quite, to the movies, as seldom as possible*	**Prepositions** relate nouns or pronouns to another word in a sentence EXAMPLES: *in the book, at home, with my younger brother, along the busy highway*

Reference: Copy Editor's Symbols

Reference: Copy Editor's Symbols

Symbol	Meaning	Example
∨’	Insert an apostrophe	The cat’s toy is under the couch.
≡ (CAP)	Capitalize	We visited Green Bay, wisconsin
⊂⊃	Close up	We'll visit tomor row
^,	Insert comma	We had cereal milk and toast for breakfast.
℘	Delete	Our test was yesterday ~~Wednesday.~~
℘ (closed)	Delete and close up	The beggining is the place to start!
^	Insert	Our show is Wedesday.
#	Insert space	You need alot of vegetables in a healthy diet.
¶	Paragraph	"Please?" I asked. "Well, finish your homework first," said Mom.
⊙	Add period	Elephants are mammals
(set/?)	Add question mark	Did you see the full moon last night. (set/?)
∨“ ∨”	Add quotation marks	I read an article, The Fossa Madagascar.
^:	Insert colon	The list includes these items pencils, pens, and paper.
^;	Insert semicolon	I laughed she cried.
(sp)	Spelling	Molly quickly became my freind.
∽ (tr)	Transpose	My birthday is in Febuary. (tr)
(stet)	Stet (keep it the same)	(sp) stet "I can't believe it!" shouted the inventor.
lc	Lowercase	My Grandma agreed.

Guide to Works Cited

Guide to Works Cited

When you include the work of other writers in your research, it is important to credit them for their work. Use this guide as a reference for one way to make correct citations for a bibliography.

Print Sources

Book with one author:
Author. *Title of Book*. City of publication: publisher, date of publication.
Hinton, S. E. *The Outsiders*. New York: Speak, 1997.

Book with two authors:
Authors (in the order they are given in the book). *Title of Book*. City of publication: Publisher, date of publication.
Smith, Elizabeth, and David Wright. *Rocks and Minerals*. Chicago: Macmillan, 1995.

Article in an encyclopedia and other familiar reference books:
Author of article (if available). "Title of Article." *Title of Book*. Date of edition.
"France." *World Book Encyclopedia*. 1998.

Article in a periodical:
Author (if available). "Title of Article." *Periodical Title*. Date: page.
McDowell, Jonathan. "Space Junk." *National Geographic Explorer.* May, 2010: 8.

Interview Conducted by the Researcher

Name or person interviewed. Type of interview. Date of interview.
Sherwin, Jade. Personal Interview. 20 Feb. 2009.
Cavanaugh, Laura. Telephone Interview. 14 Mar. 2010.

Electronic Sources

Publications on CD-ROM:
Author (if available). "Title of Article." *Title of Product*. Edition or version (if relevant) CD-ROM. City of publication: Publisher, date of publication.
Cashman, Katharine V. "Volcano." *World Book Multimedia Encyclopedia*. 1999 ed. CD-ROM. Chicago: World Book Inc., 1999.

Online Sources

Encyclopedia article:
Author (if shown). "Title of Article." *Name of Encyclopedia*. Publisher, date of publication (if available). Date of online visit.
"Animal Rights." *Compton's Living Encyclopedia*. Compton's Learning Company, 1996. 22 Aug. 1999.

World Wide Web:
Author (if known). "Title of Article." *Title of Complete Work*. Date of online visit. <full http address>.
Yamashita, Michael. "Mosaic of Marco Polo." *National Geographic*. 15 June, 2001. <http://travel.nationalgeographic.com/travel/countries/marco-polo-photos>

Yearlong Planner

Consider: Are there any lessons that should appear multiple times?

	September	October	November	December	January	February	March	April	May	June
WEEK 1										
WEEK 2										
WEEK 3										
WEEK 4										

Yearlong Planner

PART VI

Assessment and Record Keeping

The assessment resources and record-keeping sheets in this section are designed as suggestions. You may find that some perfectly match the needs of your students or your personal preferences in record keeping, while others may require modification. We encourage you to make these resources your own or use them as springboards for the creation of tools that will work for you and your learners.

We have deliberately highlighted several kinds of assessments for your consideration. You will notice opportunities for students to chart their own growth with editing checklists and self-reflections. (For more on editing with checklists, see Express Lane Edits, page 196.) The cloze activities we've included will allow you to assess proficiency with pronouns and verbs. We encourage you to use the cloze activities as models in creating your own cloze experiences focused on any number of conventions and mechanics. There are also classroom planning and assessment grids designed to support your observations of learners, to assist in your creating small groups with similar needs, and to allow you to coach writers during one-on-one conferences.

Most of all, select the tools that will empower you to watch your students closely. Observations and ongoing daily assessments give power to instruction and enable you to respond to the needs of individuals and gather small groups with similar needs. You are the driving force in instruction. You are the only one who truly sees your students as individuals and can select supports that will lift their learning.

You can access the reproducibles on the following pages on the Resources CD.

Contents

Editing Checklists

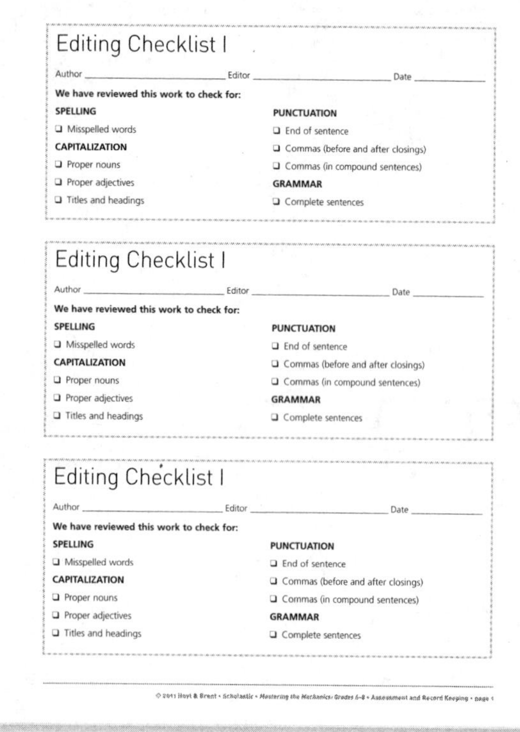

Editing Checklist I

Author ________________ Editor ________________ Date ________

We have reviewed this work to check for:

SPELLING
- ❑ Misspelled words

CAPITALIZATION
- ❑ Proper nouns
- ❑ Proper adjectives
- ❑ Titles and headings

PUNCTUATION
- ❑ End of sentence
- ❑ Commas (before and after closings)
- ❑ Commas (in compound sentences)

GRAMMAR
- ❑ Complete sentences

Editing Checklist I

Author ________________ Editor ________________ Date ________

We have reviewed this work to check for:

SPELLING
- ❑ Misspelled words

CAPITALIZATION
- ❑ Proper nouns
- ❑ Proper adjectives
- ❑ Titles and headings

PUNCTUATION
- ❑ End of sentence
- ❑ Commas (before and after closings)
- ❑ Commas (in compound sentences)

GRAMMAR
- ❑ Complete sentences

Editing Checklist I

Author ________________ Editor ________________ Date ________

We have reviewed this work to check for:

SPELLING
- ❑ Misspelled words

CAPITALIZATION
- ❑ Proper nouns
- ❑ Proper adjectives
- ❑ Titles and headings

PUNCTUATION
- ❑ End of sentence
- ❑ Commas (before and after closings)
- ❑ Commas (in compound sentences)

GRAMMAR
- ❑ Complete sentences

Editing Checklist II

Author ________________

Editor ________________

Date ________________

We have reviewed this work to check for:

SPELLING
- ❑ We corrected spelling on:

____

____

____

- ❑ Resources that helped us check spelling include:

____

____

____

CAPITALIZATION
- ❑ Proper nouns
- ❑ Proper adjectives
- ❑ Titles and headings

PUNCTUATION
- ❑ Commas before and after closings
- ❑ Commas in compound sentences
- ❑ Punctuation in dialogue

GRAMMAR
- ❑ Complete sentences
- ❑ Subject-verb agreement
- ❑ Pronouns agree with antecedents

REVISING POINTS
- ❑ The writing matches the purpose.
- ❑ The organization makes sense.

Editing Checklist II

Author ________________

Editor ________________

Date ________________

We have reviewed this work to check for:

SPELLING
- ❑ We corrected spelling on:

____

____

____

- ❑ Resources that helped us check spelling include:

____

____

____

CAPITALIZATION
- ❑ Proper nouns
- ❑ Proper adjectives
- ❑ Titles and headings

PUNCTUATION
- ❑ Commas before and after closings
- ❑ Commas in compound sentences
- ❑ Punctuation in dialogue

GRAMMAR
- ❑ Complete sentences
- ❑ Subject-verb agreement
- ❑ Pronouns agree with antecedents

REVISING POINTS
- ❑ The writing matches the purpose.
- ❑ The organization makes sense.

Editing Checklist III

Author ________________

Editor ________________

Date ________________

We have reviewed this work to check for:

SPELLING

We used these resources to check spelling:

____

____

____

- ❑ Words we corrected:

____

____

____

- ❑ We thought about context to choose the correct homophone.
- ❑ We checked the word parts list for meanings and spellings.

PUNCTUATION
- ❑ End punctuation
- ❑ Punctuation in dialogue
- ❑ Apostrophes in contractions
- ❑ Apostrophes for possession
- ❑ Commas in a series
- ❑ Commas in complex sentences
- ❑ Commas in compound sentences
- ❑ Commas with nonrestrictive elements

GRAMMAR
- ❑ Sentences are complete.
- ❑ This piece has no run-on sentences.
- ❑ Each verb agrees with its subject.
- ❑ Verb tense is correct.
- ❑ Transition words and phrases link ideas.
- ❑ Pronoun case is correct.
- ❑ Comparative forms of adjectives are correct.
- ❑ Verbs are carefully selected to serve as engines of sentences.

EDITING POINTS
- ❑ The writing of the text matches the purpose.
- ❑ Verbs are active, and nouns are precise.

Editing Checklist III

Author ________________

Editor ________________

Date ________________

We have reviewed this work to check for:

SPELLING

We used these resources to check spelling:

____

____

____

- ❑ Words we corrected:

____

____

____

- ❑ We thought about context to choose the correct homophone.
- ❑ We checked the word parts list for meanings and spellings.

PUNCTUATION
- ❑ End punctuation
- ❑ Punctuation in dialogue
- ❑ Apostrophes in contractions
- ❑ Apostrophes for possession
- ❑ Commas in a series
- ❑ Commas in complex sentences
- ❑ Commas in compound sentences
- ❑ Commas with nonrestrictive elements

GRAMMAR
- ❑ Sentences are complete.
- ❑ This piece has no run-on sentences.
- ❑ Each verb agrees with its subject.
- ❑ Verb tense is correct.
- ❑ Transition words and phrases link ideas.
- ❑ Pronoun case is correct.
- ❑ Comparative forms of adjectives are correct.
- ❑ Verbs are carefully selected to serve as engines of sentences.

EDITING POINTS
- ❑ The writing of the text matches the purpose.
- ❑ Verbs are active, and nouns are precise.

Editing Checklist IV

Author ________________ Editor ________________ Date ________

We have reviewed this work to check for:

VERBS
- ❑ Verb tense is consistent.
- ❑ Verbs agree with subjects in number.
- ❑ Sentences include the correct forms of linking verbs.

PRONOUNS
- ❑ Pronouns agree with antecedents.
- ❑ Pronouns show gender and number.
- ❑ Possessive pronouns are used correctly.

SENTENCES
- ❑ Sentences are complete. Any fragments are intentional.
- ❑ Subjects and verbs agree.
- ❑ Sentence openers vary.

Editing Checklist IV

Author ________________ Editor ________________ Date ________

We have reviewed this work to check for:

VERBS
- ❑ Verb tense is consistent.
- ❑ Verbs agree with subjects in number.
- ❑ Sentences include the correct forms of linking verbs.

PRONOUNS
- ❑ Pronouns agree with antecedents.
- ❑ Pronouns show gender and number.
- ❑ Possessive pronouns are used correctly.

SENTENCES
- ❑ Sentences are complete. Any fragments are intentional.
- ❑ Subjects and verbs agree.
- ❑ Sentence openers vary.

Editing Checklist IV

Author ________________ Editor ________________ Date ________

We have reviewed this work to check for:

VERBS
- ❑ Verb tense is consistent.
- ❑ Verbs agree with subjects in number.
- ❑ Sentences include the correct forms of linking verbs.

PRONOUNS
- ❑ Pronouns agree with antecedents.
- ❑ Pronouns show gender and number.
- ❑ Possessive pronouns are used correctly.

SENTENCES
- ❑ Sentences are complete. Any fragments are intentional.
- ❑ Subjects and verbs agree.
- ❑ Sentence openers vary.

Interactive Writing Assessment

Interactive Writing Assessment

Focus on capitalization, punctuation, grammar, or editing.

Date ____________ Title of Writing ____________________ Writer ____________________

Writer

As I look at this writing, I am proud of ________________________________

I would still like to improve on ________________________________

Peer Editor

As I look at this writing, what I notice that is done exceptionally well is ________________________________

My advice to this writer would be to continue to work on ________________________________

Teacher

As I look at this writing, I notice that you've done a great job of incorporating ________________________________

One area that we could study further to add to your writing is ________________________________

Skills I Can Use

Writer ____________________

Skill I have mastered	Date

Skills I Can Use

Yearlong Rubric

Yearlong Rubric

Writer ....

Check the sentences that describe your writing to chart your growth as a writer.

Teacher: Use the *Teacher* column to assess the learner's strategy use. Use the empty rows to add skills and strategies that you are developing with your learners. Use the rubric to plan for both small group and individualized instruction.

Strategy	September		December		April	
REVISING AND EDITING	Student	Teacher	Student	Teacher	Student	Teacher
I revise with purpose and audience in mind.						
I focus on the organization of the piece when I revise.						
I revise with a focus on precise words.						
I know how to use an editing checklist to edit for each editing point.						
I use copyediting symbols as tools in my editing.						

Strategy	September		December		April	
CAPITALIZATION	Student	Teacher	Student	Teacher	Student	Teacher
I capitalize the beginnings of sentences.						
I capitalize proper nouns and proper adjectives.						
I correctly use capital letters in titles, headings, and abbreviations.						

Strategy	September		December		April	
PUNCTUATION	Student	Teacher	Student	Teacher	Student	Teacher
I use correct end punctuation.						
I correctly punctuate dialogue.						
I correctly use apostrophes in contractions.						
I correctly use apostrophes in singular and plural possessive nouns.						
I use commas for items in a series.						
I correctly use commas and coordinating conjunctions in compound sentences.						
I correctly use commas with opening and closing elements.						
I use commas to set off appositives in sentences.						
I correctly use dashes, parentheses, brackets, and ellipses in my writing.						
I correctly use colons and semicolons in my writing.						

Strategy	September		December		April	
SENTENCE STRUCTURE	Student	Teacher	Student	Teacher	Student	Teacher
I write complete sentences.						
I only include fragments sparingly and deliberately.						
I combine sentences with coordinating conjunctions and commas.						
I insert appositives to add more information to sentences.						
I use openers and closers to add more information to sentences.						

Strategy	September		December		April	
GRAMMAR	Student	Teacher	Student	Teacher	Student	Teacher
I write sentences with parallel structures.						
I use powerful adjectives as descriptors.						
I use the correct verb tense and keep tense consistent.						
I use appropriate action verbs, linking verbs, and helping verbs.						
My subjects and verbs agree.						
Pronouns in my writing have clear antecedents and agree with them in number and gender.						
I use the correct forms of possessive pronouns.						
I use the correct cases of nouns and pronouns at various places in sentences.						

Strategy	September		December		April	
SPELLING	Student	Teacher	Student	Teacher	Student	Teacher
I use my spelling consciousness to determine when words are misspelled.						
I use word banks and margin spelling as strategies to spell words correctly.						
I use words I already know and consider word parts to spell words correctly.						
I consider the meanings and spellings of prefixes and suffixes as I write.						
I use context to figure out which homophone or easily confused word to use in a sentence.						

Strategy	September		December		April	
TEXT FEATURES	Student	Teacher	Student	Teacher	Student	Teacher
I organize my writing with titles, headings, and subheadings.						
I include a table of contents when appropriate in my work.						
I add explanatory captions to visuals in my writing.						
I consider how bolded words and font changes emphasize important ideas in my writing.						
I use text boxes to set aside important or interesting information.						
I use bulleted lists to organize ideas. My lists are parallel.						

Text Features Record Sheet

Text Features Record Sheet

Researcher ....

Text features make ideas clearer for our readers by organizing information and emphasizing interesting or important facts. Hunt for text features in mentor texts—and keep track of the text features you use in your own work!

Mentor Text

Title	Headings and Subheadings	Table of Contents	Captions	Bold Words	Font Changes	Text Boxes	Bulleted Lists

Your Own Writing

Title	Headings and Subheadings	Table of Contents	Captions	Bold Words	Font Changes	Text Boxes	Bulleted Lists

Writer's Self-Reflection

Name ....

Take a close look at your writing. Think about your work as a writer and what you hope to accomplish with future pieces.

1. What new mechanics or conventions skills did you use in your writing? Explain how they helped your work.

2. As you reread your work, what do you think are the strengths of your writing?

3. Describe your editing. What process did you use? What changes did you make?

4. What kind of feedback did you receive from peer editors? How did you include the feedback?

5. What mechanics and conventions skills do you want to try to use in your next piece of writing? What would you like to learn more about?

Writer's Self-Reflection

Class Record-Keeping Grid

Reproduce this grid to give you a snapshot of your writers' abilities. Record the date and students' names as well as the skills you are assessing. As you examine student work, listen in on peer editing sessions, and meet with your learners in writing conferences, noting which students have mastered the skill and which may need further instruction. Use your results to inform your instruction and choose the lesson cycles for your class.

Class Record-Keeping Grid

Assessment Tool: Cloze for Verb Tense and Agreement

The very first Ferris wheel ________________ in 1893. It ________________ a huge structure! Standing as tall as a twenty-five-story building, the super-sized ride could ________________ over two thousand people at once.

was builded / was built	were / was	carried / carry

The Ferris wheel was part of a big fair—the Columbian Exposition. Fair organizers ________________ the Exposition for the city of Chicago, Illinois. Only twenty years before, much of Chicago ________________ down in a massive fire. By 1890, though, Chicago ________________ from the devastation.

plan / planned	had burnt / had burned	had nearly recovered / having nearly recovered

The fair was so huge, it opened a year later than expected. But the planners ________________ an amazing fair! It was the first in history to be lit with electricity. Fair goers ________________ at the exhibits and the gleaming exhibition buildings. Above the entire Exposition, the Ferris wheel ________________.

creates / had created	marveled / marvels	looms / loomed

A mechanical engineer from Galesburg, Illinois, ________________ the ride. George Washington Gale Ferris wanted something big for the Exposition. His first Ferris wheel ________________ two 500-horsepower engines to work. It had 36 cars, and each car ________________ 60 people! Most people in 1893 ________________ more than a few stories off the ground. But over one and a half million people ________________ up, up, up—264 feet above Earth. No Ferris wheel since then has matched the first in size.

designs / designed	required / requiring	holded / held
have not been / had not been	traveled / travel	

Note to teacher: Place the selections on the overhead or provide copies for partners. Partners think together to identify the correct verb to complete each sentence. Students will find verb choices after each paragraph.

Assessment Tool: Cloze for Verb Tense and Agreement

Assessment Tool: Commas

A unique fish gets its name from its odd shape. With no muscles a shapeless body and a density just less than the density of water it floats along above the sea floor. It looks like a mass of jelly yet its face seems almost human. This odd fish the blobfish is rarely seen by humans.

Blobfish are not known for their hunting skills. They stay put floating just above the sea floor waiting for food to drift by. Sea urchins and mollusks make a tasty meal for a blobfish! The blobfish simply waits for an animal to come by and eats it.

Called "miserable-looking" and described as among the world's ugliest animals blobfish live in deep coastal waters near Australia and Tanzania. Sadly blobfish are becoming endangered. Fishermen drop nets in deep water to catch crab and lobster but they may accidentally scoop blobfish in their nets. People do not eat blobfish. Once they are exposed to air blobfish die.

Note to teacher: Review with students the uses of commas: with descriptors or items in series, in compound sentences, in complex sentences, and with appositives. Have students work together to identify where in the passage commas belong.

Assessment Tool: Commas

Assessment Tool: Cloze for Pronouns and Antecedents

In August 1909, paleontologist Earl Douglass spied eight *Brontosaurus* tailbones at the top of a sandy ledge. The *Brontosaurus* bones were not the only fossils Douglass unearthed. In the same remote corner of Utah, Douglass and his team found the remains of *Stegosaurus, Allosaurus,* and others—ten kinds of dinosaurs in all. Douglass had made a huge discovery. He soon found out that that one single cliff in Utah had more fossilized remains than any other one place in the world!

But how did all the dinosaur bones end up in such a dry place? Douglass and other scientists figured out that a river ran through the area millions of years ago. It often overflowed its banks, drowning many dinosaurs. Their fleshy parts rotted, but their bones stayed in the water, where they were buried under gravel and sand.

The river dried up millions of years later, but then new rivers flowed through the area. Minerals in the water entered into the bones. They turned the bones hard, into fossils. When the Rocky Mountains formed, pushing the earth upward, they exposed the fossilized bones. Douglass and other scientists found them centuries later!

Note to teacher: Place this passage on the overhead and show students how to:

- Underline pronouns in the first paragraph
- Identify the antecedent for each pronoun and draw a line from each pronoun to its antecedent
- Work together to identify pronouns and antecedents in the second and third paragraphs

Assessment Tool: Cloze for Pronouns and Antecedents

Bibliography

Anderson, J. (2005). *Mechanically inclined: Building grammar, usage, and style into writer's workshop.* Portland, ME: Stenhouse.

Anderson, J. (2007). *Everyday editing: Inviting students to develop skill and craft in writer's workshop.* Portland, ME: Stenhouse.

Angelillo, J. (2002). *A fresh approach to teaching punctuation: Helping young writers use conventions with precision and purpose.* New York: Scholastic.

Calkins, L., & Louis, N. (2003). *Writing for readers: Teaching skills and strategies.* Portsmouth, NH: Heinemann.

Department of Education, Edith Cowan University. (2006). *First Steps: Writing map of development.* Perth, Western Australia: Edith Cowan University.

Fletcher, R., & Portalupi, J. (2001). *Writing workshop: The essential guide.* Portsmouth, NH: Heinemann.

Graham, S., & Perin, D. (2007). *Writing next: Effective strategies to improve writing of adolescents in middle and high schools.* New York: Carnegie Corporation.

Graves, D. (1994). *A fresh look at writing.* Portsmouth, NH: Heinemann.

Harwayne, S. (1992). *Lasting impressions: Weaving literature into the writing workshop.* Portsmouth, NH: Heinemann.

Harwayne, S. (2001). *Writing through childhood: Rethinking process and product.* Portsmouth, NH: Heinemann.

Ray, K. W. (1999). *Wondrous words.* Portsmouth, NH: Heinemann.

Routman, R. (2005). *Writing essentials: Raising expectations and results while simplifying teaching.* Portsmouth, NH: Heinemann.

Sitton, R. (2006). *Rebecca Sitton's sourcebook series for teaching spelling and word skills.* Scottsdale, AZ: Egger Publishing.

Taylor, B. M., Pearson, P. D., Peterson, D., & Rodriguez, M. C. (2002). Looking inside classrooms: Reflecting on the "how" as well as the "what" in effective reading instruction. *The Reading Teacher, 56*(3), 270–279.

Topping, D. H., & Hoffman, J. S. (2006). *Getting grammar: 150 new ways to teach an old subject.* Portsmouth, NH: Heinemann.

Index

S

T

U

V

W

Y